Lucien Biart

My Rambles in the New World

Lucien Biart

My Rambles in the New World

ISBN/EAN: 9783744713535

Printed in Europe, USA, Canada, Australia, Japan

Cover: Foto ©ninafisch / pixelio.de

More available books at **www.hansebooks.com**

Frontispiece.

MY RAMBLES
IN THE NEW WORLD.

By LUCIEN BIART,

AUTHOR OF "THE ADVENTURES OF A YOUNG NATURALIST."

TRANSLATED BY
MARY DE HAUTEVILLE.

LONDON:
SAMPSON LOW, MARSTON, SEARLE & RIVINGTON,
CROWN BUILDINGS, 188, FLEET STREET.
1877.

(All rights reserved.)

TO MY BROTHER

EDWARD,

WHO IS NOW RAMBLING IN THE TROPICAL REGION OF QUEENSLAND,

I DEDICATE MY TRANSLATION OF

MONSIEUR BIART'S RAMBLES ON THE AMERICAN CONTINENT.

MARY DE HAUTEVILLE.

TRANSLATOR'S NOTE.

THE only liberty which I have ventured to take with this work of M. Biart's has been in giving it a new title. The title of the original work is *À Travers L'Amérique*, a literal translation of which would have approached too nearly the title of an English work already existing; besides which, I venture to think it scarcely conveys to the reader so clear an idea of the character of the work as that which I have chosen. In all other respects I have adhered as closely to the original as has been consistent with rendering it into what I trust may be considered readable English.

CONTENTS.

LABRADOR

CHAPTER		PAGE
I.	The *Siren*—Floating ice-blocks—Master Simeon—Greenland—Cortereál—A salvage—Ouanga	1
II.	The little Esquimaux—The toilet of an uncivilized beauty—An ill-bred child—Civilizing effects of an accordion—Mr. and Mrs. Stewart—A house under the snow—Mrs. Oblouk-Kanick ...	11
III.	The sledge drive—A rustic supper—The Oblouk-Kanick household—A snow village—Origin of the Esquimaux—A new use for buttons—Return to Canada	21

A CANADIAN FAMILY.

I.	The Canadian cross-bill—On a hunting excursion—A chance meeting—What a few acres of snow were worth—Montcalm and Wolfe—The St. Lawrence—Quebec—The forests—The storm—An American hat—A wrong direction—Another meeting	30
II.	Miss Louise—Arrival at the Secret Valley—Grandfather Martin—A patriarchal evening—What is Mr. Peter?—A mistake—An *enfant terrible*—Another search for the *Loxia*	41
III.	A panorama—An unexpected meeting—Luncheon in the woods—Pleading in Miss Louise's favour—Return to the farm—Pleading in Peter's favour—" All's well that ends well "—The *Loxia*	51

NIAGARA IN WINTER.

| I. | The coasts of Canada—Sir John Burton—Miss Mary's cloak—Halifax—A sledge drive—A restaurant in a cellar—An oyster-fight—American liberty—Sir John again ... ... | 61 |
| II. | The palisades of the Hudson—A stolen repast—Is it he?—The Falls—The suspension bridge—Blondin's rope—Under the Niagara—Cincinnati—An introduction ... ... | 69 |

SAN FRANCISCO.

The Chinese theatre—A fellow-countryman—The El Dorado of Cortez—The village of San Francisco—A rich proprietor—A gaming-room—A Yankee, Yankee, and a half—" A bird in the hand is worth two in the bush " 80

TORTOISE ISLAND.

CHAPTER   **PAGE**

I. Departure from Havre—Deerfoot—Señor Baudoin—Count Monistrol and Baron Martin—The trade winds—Equatorial calm—The Phaeton—An arrest 87

II. Scarcity of fresh water—The calm — Flying-fish — Dorado—Tropical grass—St. Domingo—Tortoise Island—Freebooters and pirates—An unexpected meeting 96

III. Return to ship—The captain and Doña Clara—A man-of-war—The pursuit—Prisoners!—Baudoin's departure—The spermaceti whales—Campeachy—Lambert again—André-Marie ... 105

A WATERSPOUT AT SEA.

St. Thomas—The Reverend Mr. Smith—The waterspout at sea—A wish realized—Fears calmed 116

CHRISTMAS DAY AT HAVANNAH.

I. Havannah—Preliminary formulas—A good dinner—In search of a lodging—A restless night 121

II. Fraternity—Sons and daughters of kings—Abuse of saffron—A negro ball 129

FROM HAVANNAH TO NEW ORLEANS.

I. Departure from Havannah—The slavery question—The Gulf Stream—The Mississippi—A kidnapping business 138

II. Departure for Méssangère—The unfortunate Thomas—The danger of letting a dress get wet—A New Yorkist, and a native of Louisiana—A curious way of getting a husband 146

III. Molière and the education of women—New Orleans—Scarcity of filtered water—The *Cincinnati* and the *Jackson*—Ball on board—A guest without knowing it—Conclusion 155

THE HORSE-TAMER.

The mouse-coloured horse—Yankees and Texians—An accident—Alone!—Don José—The wild horse—A terrible night ... 167

TENOCHTITLAN.

Arrival of the Spaniards at Mexico—The palaces of Montézuma—The modern town—The National Palace—The theatres—Itinerant merchants—Society 179

THE PEARL FOREST.

CHAPTER   PAGE

I. Isidro—Don Anastasio Véga—The Pearl Forest—The Hermit's Cave—The ambush 186

II. The flight—A deliverer—A walk in the forest—Old José—An unexpected meeting—The bandits' retreat 194

III. The nocturnal walk—Indian and half-breed—Méthal—The Hermit's Ravine 206

IV. The venture—An unfortunate meeting—Salvador Rendon—The right of the strongest—Pray for him 214

THE TUXPANGO CASCADE.

The sick child—The Escamela river—The fox—The cascade—A tiger 225

THE SERPENT-CHARMER.

The *curado*—Chépé Solana—The huaco plant—The trial—Fears calmed 234

THE DEAD CITY.

I. Bishop's River—Indian cooking—Eulalio and Célestin—The king of vultures—A newly married couple—Wedding-feasts—The cotton plants—Wild turkeys—An escort of alligators ... 240

II. A virgin forest—Alligators—A rough alarm—Wild bulls—A victim—Paroquets and cardinals—An Indian family—Flies—The lake 248

III. Lake Vignon—A serious misadventure—The bird of the sun—Discouragement—*La terre tempérée*—The cascade—Excursion on foot—The black tiger—The Dead City 256

IV. The mist—Aërial gardens—An armadillo—The temple—Sculptures and hieroglyphics—The coral snake—The ibis—*Belzebuth* monkeys—The tapirs—A nest of rattlesnakes—Monteuczoma 265

THE UNICORN.

Nor Rosalino—The *antéburro*—Lying in ambush—An anxious moment—The unicorn—The tapir 275

THE GROTTO OF THE TOLTECS.

I. Guatemala—The Toltecs—The grotto—Necessary precautions—A general panic 283

II. Discouragement—Useless entreaties—New excursions—An unexpected meeting—Discoveries—Departure 289

AZTEC EDUCATION.

True Aztecs—A father to his son—A mother to her daughter   295

LIST OF ILLUSTRATIONS.

Portrait of the author	...	*Frontispiece*
"With the oars he formed a kind of bridge"	...	To face page 12
"Ouanga had just fallen on the frozen ground"	...	" 24
Quebec	...	" 33
"She took the hunter's arm"	...	" 40
"'Uncle!' cried he, with emotion"	...	" 58
New York	...	" 67
"The water covered me with frozen foam"	...	" 76
"I entered the room"	...	" 85
"Seize that wretch...."	...	" 95
"Rolling the barrels...."	...	" 102
"The column seemed to have two funnels"	...	" 118
Keeping Christmas in Havannah	...	" 130
"Hold!"	...	" 149
New Orleans	...	" 159
Negroes clad in the traditional costume of Figaro		" 163
"'Let go!' cried Manuel"	...	" 176
"I thought I heard the cracking of branches"	...	" 177
Mexico	...	" 180
"Pretty Lola laughed at all obstacles"		" 194
"The bandits surrounded an immense fire"	...	" 201
"The tiger seemed to be contemplating the fall"		" 229
"I am killed"	...	" 238
"The married couple arm in arm"	...	" 246
"The bulls filed past us by hundreds"	...	" 251
"Before us spread a valley...."	...	" 263
"I fired"	...	" 281
"This room—full of stalactites...."	...	" 292

MY RAMBLES IN THE NEW WORLD.

LABRADOR.

CHAPTER I.

The *Siren*—Floating ice-blocks—Master Simeon—Greenland—Corteréal—A salvage—Ouanga.

"Port the helm!" cried the captain.

The sailor at the wheel rapidly executed this command; then, gently as a well-bred horse, the *Siren* turned towards the left, dipped her bows in the waves and glided alongside a mountain of ice, with which she had barely escaped a collision.

This was the third time since break of day, that is to say, since about two o'clock, that the little schooner, bearing the musical name of *Siren*, had grazed those enormous blocks of ice, which, especially towards the approach of summer, are borne by the currents from Baffin's Bay, as far south as Newfoundland, often even farther than that. We had left Quebec a month ago, and at this moment, 20th of May, 1851, were alongside the bare, desolate coast of Labrador. The lowering sky was the colour of lead; the north wind whistled furiously through the rigging; on our left rose gigantic cliffs, covered with a thick mantle of ice.

"A fine temperature, sir," said the captain to me in a cheerful tone, as he came towards the poop, where I was standing. "A fine temperature!"

The thermometer, I had just informed myself, showed fifteen degrees below zero; therefore the captain's remark, "A fine temperature," seemed somewhat ironical. I had hardly been a quarter of an hour on deck, and notwithstanding the thick fur cloak in which I was enveloped, I was beginning to shiver and to have serious doubts as to the presence of my nose in the middle of my face. The eight sailors composing our crew, muffled up to their eyes in furs, like myself, were walking to and fro, heaving the ropes, which were so stiffened by the frost as to be like bars of iron. From the time we left the St. Lawrence, I could not sufficiently admire those men who, day and night alike—and our days then consisted of barely four hours—paced the frozen deck of the *Siren*, ever ready to execute the difficult and perilous orders of the captain or the first mate.

I was preparing to return to the cabin of the schooner, a narrow room where a cast-iron stove at white heat kept up an incessant roar, when my host and fellow-traveller, Master Simeon (he was so called by all on board), appeared on deck.

"A fine temperature," cried he, in his turn, rubbing his fur gloves one against the other.

Then, after having carefully examined the horizon, he came and stood by me.

Master Simeon, a Canadian of French origin, was partly the cause of my presence on the coast of Labrador this 20th of May, 1851: we had made the passage from Liverpool to Boston together, and during this trip I had more than once spoken to my companion of the vague desire I had to visit the polar regions. Master Simeon listened to me, smiling to himself whilst he smoked his everlasting briar-root pipe, and one fine day he suddenly offered to realize my dream. He had dealt in furs for ten years, and possessed a trading-station on the coast of Labrador. Directly we reached Boston he intended to pay his friends at Quebec a short visit, and then re-embark on board the *Siren*, bound for his northern trading-stations, where she would get her cargo of bear, fox, and hare skins, barrels of oil, fish, and walrus tusks which his *employés*, living in the snow in latitude 50°, were to collect for him from the

Esquimaux during the winter. Master Simeon generously offered me a berth on board his schooner, promising to take me to witness the mode of taking seal, white bear, and walrus. I accepted his offer, and at the moment my companion joined me on deck, I was not regretting my imprudence for the first time.

"I see with pleasure that you are beginning to get accustomed to our breezes," said the merchant, whose good-humour was invariable. "Here you have been on deck more than twenty minutes; allow me to compliment you on your powers of endurance."

"I shall never become accustomed," I replied, "to the feeling of being perpetually transformed into an icicle, and still less to seeing myself adorned with a blue nose every time I dare look in the glass."

"But you, such a lover of the picturesque, do you not admire those immense white cliffs, that grey sky, those waves covered with floating icebergs?"

"I am dreaming regretfully, Master Simeon, of the sunny south down yonder between San Domingo and the Havanahs, where the sky is blue, the sea vermilion, and where, instead of a bare, white, uniform coast, the eye rests on hills crowned with palm trees."

"I only promised you seals, white bears, and walrus," said my companion with his hearty laugh, "and, God willing, I will keep my word. Before forty-eight hours are over, unless the wind changes, we shall be at the station, and you will then be able to refresh yourself after your long captivity."

"Where are we, then?" I asked.

"If my eyes were as good as that cider-duck's which you see flying over us, I should perceive, looking to the right, a country which I shall visit next year, for I have a trading-station there also. If you would like to accompany me . . ."

"No, thank you," cried I this time. "If I return from this voyage I will certainly not try it again, and I shall be off at once to thaw under the tropics. But what country are you speaking about?"

"Greenland."

"The true Esquimaux country?"

"Yes, and the country of the red fox and white hare. It is a curious land, rather cold, but quite worth the trouble of a visit. And however disinclined you may feel at present, still . . ."

"I will answer you in six months' time from the Gulf of Mexico; meanwhile, Greenland interests me. Where is your trading-station?"

"At Julianeshaab, a pretty little town, where some of your countrymen live."

"Good Heavens! what do they trade in there?"

"There is hardly any other trade in these regions except that for furs, oil, and dried fish. I have often heard it stated," continued Master Simeon, "that Greenland is an island, and I am very much inclined to believe it. This land, as you doubtless know, was first discovered by the Irishman, Eric Randa, who settled here in 982. The colony founded by this predecessor of Columbus in the discovery of America, existed until the year 1436. Since then the Danes, the possessors of Greenland, have founded two settlements there: one through the influence of the missionary Egède; the other, in 1733, through the Moravian Brothers. But you are shivering; let us go back to the stove."

"Not just yet," said I; "if Greenland is to our right, we have before us Baffin's Bay."

"Precisely so. We have been for several days on the route which explorers take in search of the North Pole, on the Ross and Franklin track. Baffin's Bay, from whence come the icebergs against which we have to defend ourselves, was discovered, in 1616, by the English pilot, William Baffin, then in search of a passage into the open sea. Baffin's Bay is about four hundred leagues in length and twenty-five in width; it communicates with the Atlantic Ocean by Davis's Straits."

"And the land along which we have been coasting for the last three days is Labrador?"

"Yes and no; we are in sight of the numerous islands which border the coasts of that curious country. But if no contrary wind delays us we shall see the true coast of Labrador tomorrow, and the end of our voyage northwards."

My companion again insisted on taking me back to the stove, and this time I yielded. The grey clouds gradually cleared off the horizon, and here and there strips of blue appeared in the sky. Numerous birds were flying about, but they kept themselves at such a distance from the schooner, that I could not distinguish to what species they belonged.

When once cosily settled near the stove, Master Simeon lit his pipe, stretched himself in an armchair, and I again questioned him on Labrador. He told me that this vast country, which is, in short, nothing but the continuation of Canada, was discovered, in 1501, by the Portuguese Corteréal. Struck, they say, with the fertility of the lands which he saw—which appears to me rather paradoxical—Corteréal gave his discovery the name of *Labrador,* that is to say, *land of labour.* Now, although the southern part of Labrador affords the agriculturist some miserable chances of harvest, there is not even that much in the north, which, almost perpetually buried under snow, has scarcely two months of summer. Thus, certain geographers affirm that it is the industry of the natives which has given the land the name of Labrador, taking this word in the sense of work-shop. This is a question which, at the present day, has scarcely any interest, and, like Master Simeon, I leave the solution of it to others. In Labrador, as in Greenland, the society of the Moravian Brothers has founded settlements for the civilization of the native Indians and Esquimaux.

The interior of Labrador, which the French traveller d'Anville had a glimpse of, is in reality unexplored. It is only known that a chain of mountains traverse it from north to south, and that vast sheets of water—inland seas, in fact—continue in some way the line of Canadian lakes. Towards the Pacific Ocean, Labrador has for frontier Hudson's Bay, then a stretch of country partly unknown as far as Russian America, recently acquired by the Americans, and known under the name of Alaska.

About three o'clock in the afternoon, when the sun was

disappearing below the horizon, I put on my fur coat and
climbed up on to the poop. Before us was the continual black
line of water mingling with the horizon, and to our left
mountains of ice. I ventured as far as the bows of the *Siren*,
where a man on watch, relieved from hour to hour, stood night
and day, with attentive observation, to guard against the floating
banks of ice so formidable on these coasts. Twenty times since
our departure we had escaped striking against these moving
rocks, a collision with which we avoided through the protection
of Providence, for our captain's skilful tactics alone would not
have sufficed to save us. The long northern nights are generally
clear; but the negligence of a sailor might cause the loss of a
ship in a moment. To say the truth, and I repeat it intention-
ally, I never knew men more devoted, more resolute, more
inured to hardships, in a word, men gifted with a greater amount
of courage, than the bold fishermen of the northern seas. There
is no occupation under a temperate climate, however laborious it
may be, which can be compared with that of the seaman whose
means of livelihood consist in braving snow, rain, and icebergs,
and living almost always in darkness, ever between life and death.

Instead of turning round on my approach, the sailor on
watch, stationed near one of the cat-heads of the *Siren*, continued to examine the horizon carefully.

"Anything new, Montbars?" I asked of him.

"I hardly know, sir; I have been trying for the last ten
minutes to make out what it is I can see, or rather, what I
could see only a minute ago."

"And what did you see?"

"A human being stretching out imploring arms towards us,
from the peak of that islet yonder."

I drew near the sailor, and, following the directions he gave
me, examined in my turn the spot indicated. Before long, I
thought I saw a human form moving about.

"Ring the bell, sir," cried Montbars to me, just as I was
about to communicate my impression to him. "By Heaven!
there is some one shipwrecked there."

Obeying the sailor, I vigorously rang the bell; Master

Simeon, the captain, and all the sailors, with the exception of the man at the helm, ran at once towards the prow.

"What have you discovered?" asked Master Simeon; "a rock, a walrus, or a seal?"

"Nothing of that kind, sir," replied Montbars, "unless the Labrador seals have arms, which is hardly probable. Look at the peak of that last islet to leeward: there is a human being there, or I am short-sighted."

The telescopes were rapidly pointed and directed towards the spot which I described with the sailor.

"Good Heavens! can it be some one shipwrecked there?" cried Master Simeon.

"It is more likely an Esquimaux, or some Indian, whose boat has been damaged," said the captain; "but, we have just entered Hudson's Strait, and this coast is uninhabited."

"A human creature must not call to us in vain," replied the shipowner.

"Hallo there, lads," added he, turning towards the sailors; "lower a boat quickly."

"Stay, Master Simeon," said the captain, putting up his hand to stop the sailors already at work; "we will get a little nearer the coast first; we can do so without danger."

"Be it so, but look sharp about it."

Each sailor, forgetting the terrible cold, redoubled his efforts; in a moment our course was changed, and the *Siren*, lashing the water, left a white wake on the black surface of the sea. The sun had disappeared, and twilight was gradually growing fainter. The high cliffs assumed a more formidable aspect in proportion as we drew near the coast; but at the same time their lines became more confused, especially towards their base.

"It will be dangerous to go nearer," said the captain, suddenly.

He gave orders and the ship gradually hove to.

"Confound this darkness!" cried Master Simeon. "Who knows if in an hour's time we shall be able to find the island?"

"Let us lie to; in this way we shall not risk losing twenty-four hours," said the captain.

" And the currents—where will they take us to?" resumed Master Simeon. By Heaven!" added he, after a moment's silence, "here we are hesitating whilst a human creature is perhaps in want of our immediate help. God protects those who do their duty, my friends. Lower the boat quickly, and let two of you be ready to go with me."

"Remain on board, Master Simeon," said the boatswain; "this is our business."

"It is my business as well. I was a sailor before being ship-owner, and I have not forgotten my noble calling."

I hastened to offer my services.

"As to you, Mister Parisian," continued Master Simeon unceremoniously, "I do not doubt either your good-will or your courage, but on this occasion you may be in our way instead of being useful. Stay where you are, and do not let the fire go out; we shall want to unfreeze our moustaches soon. Have a lantern hung on the port-side, captain, and send up a few rockets now and then to light us on our way. Gently, lads! Are we ready?"

"Yes, sir," answered the three sailors who had taken their places in the boat.

"Pull away, then."

The oars struck the water and the little boat set off. For a quarter of an hour we saw her dancing on the waves. Suddenly she disappeared; she had just entered the shadow thrown by the cliffs.

Almost an hour—one of the longest in my life, I believe—passed in cruel suspense. We were enveloped in darkness, and the surf of the waves against the sides of the *Siren* was the only sound to be heard. We were all crowding on the port-side, and trying to pierce the darkness, whilst the wind whistled plaintively through our stiffened rigging.

"They are calling," said a sailor.

We listened anxiously, but there was no other sound save that of the wind and sea.

"Ring the bell, lads, and run a lantern up to the masthead," said the captain.

Soon the bell was ringing, whilst a red lantern was raised and lowered the height of the mainmast.

"Ought we not to lower another boat, and go in search of Master Simeon?" said I to the captain.

"No," replied he shortly; "there is no occasion to be uneasy yet."

"What distance do you think we are, then, from the land?"

"More than three miles."

I made a gesture of surprise; I thought we were much nearer the cliffs. Nevertheless, in spite of his apparent calmness, the captain walked to and fro with an impatience quite unusual in him. He had the rockets brought out; one of these projectiles, which he suddenly sent up himself, opened a luminous track in the darkness, but it only lighted up the waves. A second rocket, thrown more to the right, occasioned a cry of delight: we had seen the boat exactly in the line of light left by the rocket.

The bell was again rung to guide the rowers. Soon we heard the sound of their voices and the boatswain's sharp whistle. The sailors, understanding this signal, ran to the stern of the vessel, holding several tow-lines, which, thrown with precision, fell into the boat just as it came alongside.

"Keep the boat steady, lads!" cried the voice of Master Simeon; "and you up there throw a rope to the right carefully; we are going to lash a woman to the end." Two minutes later Master Simeon appeared, supporting in his arms a shapeless bundle of furs. A lantern thrown on the new-comer showed us a pale face, with soft frightened eyes buried in a large hood. Whilst Master Simeon made his way to the cabin, the captain gave his orders, and the *Siren* resumed her course through the darkness.

I followed Master Simeon, helping him to support the young woman whom he had brought with him, and very anxious to know the details of his perilous expedition. Scarcely had the shipowner entered the cabin when he seized the tea-pot placed near the stove, filled two cups with the Chinese beverage it contained, and offered one of them to his companion. The latter murmured some words in a guttural tone, drank it greedily, and helped herself at once to a second cup. A ham and sea biscuits were brought, and the large slice I gave the new-comer disappeared with amazing rapidity.

"The poor creature is dying of hunger," said Master Simeon, "and perhaps we ought to give her food by degrees."

"Have you not questioned her?" I asked.

"I have done nothing else for the last hour, and she replies very obligingly; only one must be her father or her mother to understand the language in which she expresses herself. The word *Ouanga* is on her lips every moment; I suppose it is her name."

As though to justify the shipowner's supposition, the bright-eyed young woman pointed to the ham, placed her right hand on her chest, and among other words pronounced that of *Ouanga* several times.

"I understand this time," cried Master Simeon. "Ouanga is hungry and would like some more ham; but Ouanga might choke herself, which would be no better than to die of hunger. Let us give her some tea, that will be acting wisely."

"How did this poor creature come to be on that island where you went to look for her?" I asked of my companion.

"On an island?" repeated Master Simeon. "One judges ill when one judges from a distance. The poor little creature was completely stranded on an iceberg; otherwise she would have gained the land, for she is active enough. How did she come there? How long was she there? This is what she has been fully explaining to me, and which she will explain to you in your turn if you will question her, and we shall soon know what to think about the matter if you know anything of the Esquimaux tongue."

Master Simeon had the food taken away, and Ouanga—we gave her this name—sat down near the stove. She took off the hood which covered her head and shoulders, then a sort of fur jacket, and at last we saw a head adorned with black plaited hair. Small of stature, rather stout, at least as far as the thick petticoat which reached down to her knees allowed us to judge,

Ouanga possessed all the characteristic features of her race; her forehead was low, her eyes large and soft; she had the orange-coloured skin of half-breed Indians, a rather flat nose, a wide mouth, adorned with teeth of dazzling whiteness. Although our presence did not seem to cause her any embarrassment, her gestures were awkward. Suddenly she began to speak, accompanying her sentences with brusque movements. I imagined that she was explaining her misadventure to us: stationed on the ice, she had felt herself carried away, and had ended by being stranded near the islet where Master Simeon had found her. I was not far from the truth, as I learnt three days later.

Ouanga's narration was long; but gradually her speech flagged and her eyes closed. I showed her the hammock destined for her; she immediately stretched herself on the mattress, and soon her loud and measured breathing told us that she was soundly asleep.

CHAPTER II.

The little Esquimaux—The toilet of an uncivilized beauty—An ill-bred child—Civilizing effects of an accordion—Mr. and Mrs. Stewart—A house under the snow—Mrs. Ablouk-Kanik.

OUANGA slept on. Master Simeon was filling his pipe for the third time, when the captain and those of the crew who were not on duty on board came in and grouped themselves round the stove. All were silent, hoping that the shipowner was about to relate his adventure; but Master Simeon, seated comfortably in his easy-chair with his arms crossed, looked at us roguishly without uttering a word.

"Will you not tell us something about your little excursion?" I said to him at last.

"There is little to tell," at once replied the shipowner, "and you partly know it. On leaving the ship we struck out straight towards the peak which, like you, I had taken for a small island; but either we steered our boat badly, or we were carried by the current, for we struck against an ice-bank far above the place we wished to reach. My brave fellows had hard work, I can assure you, for the darkness was so intense beneath the cliffs we could hardly see each other. From time to time we shouted to attract the attention of the person we wanted to help, then we left off rowing and listened for an answer. We had neglected taking a lantern with us, forgetting that night was coming on; and I very much regretted this carelessness, as I began to think we should lose our way, for the ice-banks which from here seem to form a straight line are in reality indented with numerous deep bays. We had just stood out to sea, and I was wondering whether it would not be more prudent to return to the *Siren* and wait for the moon to rise, when we heard a cry. In less than ten minutes we came upon an iceberg, on which, standing close against a perpendicular wall, was poor Ouanga. It was no small affair to get the poor creature into the boat; the snow cracked under her feet, and at each movement she made, the block of ice which carried her shook and threatened to capsize. Our boatswain is a fine fellow, captain; it was he who had the idea of forming a kind of bridge with our oars, and then had the courage to venture on it himself, to go after the poor deserted girl."

"Deserted? Do you think there has been some crime in this?"

"No, no. The Esquimaux are gentle; and, although they do not value their women very much, they would not willingly condemn her to death. It was an accident; nothing more."

We lost ourselves in conjectures, and each one told yarns about Esquimaux carried away on icebergs; no uncommon event, as it appeared. Our captain, whose father had sailed in all the polar seas, assured us that before the arrival of the Moravian Brothers at Labrador, the natives, or *Little Esquimaux*, as they are commonly called, used to strangle their old people who had become feeble and incapable of getting their living. These barbarous acts have ceased, but the Esquimaux is still scarcely civilized. The severe climate in which he lives, makes hunting and fishing necessary, and obliges him to lead a nomad

"WITH THE OARS HE FORMED A KIND OF BRIDGE."

life. Long fasts encourage gluttony; and one can truly say of this people, that they live to eat instead of eating to live.

Before supper, I went up to take a turn on deck. What was my surprise to find myself in a kind of half daylight. High up in the sky, at last cleared of the grey snow-laden clouds which had veiled her for a week, the moon shone brilliantly, and flooded the sea and cliffs with her white, silvery light. Nothing can be grander than these mountains of ice thus illumined—sometimes cut in sharp ridges, sometimes rounded like cupolas; but a vague feeling of sadness crept over me before this stereotyped picture. The air seemed sharper and more biting than in the morning; the thermometer had, in fact, gone down several degrees.

Our evening meal, invariably composed of bacon, salt beef, or preserved mutton, with rice, beans, or lentils, was very quickly despatched. Master Simeon, a firm advocate for temperance, a virtue still more necessary in these rigorous climates than elsewhere, allowed the crew no other drink than tea. It required a holiday or some perilous work to get a distribution of grog, which was the more appreciated on account of its scarcity. The sailors, with their pipes alight, stretched themselves on mattresses around the stove, whilst Master Simeon and the captain undertook a quiet hand at cards, which lasted until nine o'clock. At this appointed hour the lights were extinguished, and I was lulled to sleep by the creaking of the ship and the splashing of the waves against her hull.

The next morning, whilst I was making my toilet, I saw Ouanga's large eyes open and fix themselves on me with artless curiosity. She came and took hold of my hand, as though she were wishing me good morning; then turning towards the basin, full of soapy water which I had just used, she took off a kind of tunic which served her as a dress, and displayed herself attired simply in her fur pantaloons. After a moment's hesitation and a series of comic grimaces, she washed her face and hands with an awkwardness which showed how little she was accustomed to such an operation. I hastened to give her a towel; she took it, examined it, and turned it round twenty times; evidently this white, finely spun linen was a curiosity to her. I handed her a comb; she unplaited her hair and began at once to comb it. When she began to plait it again I handed her a pot of pomade; she smelt it, and turned away with a look of disgust, as though the smell of lemon were very obnoxious to her. To make up for this she tried to dip her fingers in the oil of the lamp which lighted us; and succeeding in her attempt, she copiously greased her hair.

Master Simeon entered the cabin, and Ouanga at once ran up to him and patted him gently on the shoulder. She put on all her clothes except the hood, and then pointed to the tea-pot and cups. As on the preceding evening, she ate with disagreeable greediness; it was not only hunger but a national custom which caused her to swallow the pieces we helped her to without biting them. I had the idea of cutting up her meat as one does for children, and offering her a fork; but whilst I was carefully cutting up the piece intended for her, the nimble young woman robbed my plate, and part of my meat had disappeared before I had time to cry out.

In short, Ouanga was a great, badly-behaved child. She took Master Simeon's pipe without the least ceremony, and puffed away at it in a manner which clearly showed that it was not her first trial. The Esquimaux women do indeed smoke sometimes, but it is by no means a general custom among them.

As soon as she was satisfied—that is to say, as soon as the dishes were taken away—Ouanga prowled inquisitively round the cabin, touching everything, feeling everywhere, and questioning us by gesture and look as to the things of which she did not know the use. My clothes seemed to interest her more than anything else—their shape and cut, but especially the buttons with which they were trimmed and which she tried to pull off. I had the ill-advised idea of showing her the box in which I kept my reserve of buttons; the box immediately disappeared, and was probably stowed away in some hidden pocket of the young woman's clothes. Neither my peremptory demands nor my vexed look could regain me my treasure; either Ouanga could not understand my demands, or else she pretended not to understand them, and I was done out of my box of buttons.

When we went up on deck the young woman at once followed us, but she quickly ran down again when she felt the cold air, and muffled herself up in her hood; then, coming back, she placed herself near me. The weather was fine, and the sun, which was every day getting higher in the heavens, made the influence of his pale rays felt, although somewhat feebly. Ouanga's looks were directed towards the land, which we were now at some distance from, and she uttered an exclamation. After attentively watching the man at the helm, she pointed to the cliffs and tried to make him turn the wheel. Seeing that the ship continued her route undisturbed, she ran up to Master Simeon, seized his arm, and with her right hand pointed first to the ship's boat and then to the land, whilst she talked rapidly. One could not doubt but that the poor creature was begging him to take her back to the shore which we seemed to be leaving behind us. Seeing that they paid no attention to her entreaties and the ship pitilessly continued her course, Ouanga began to groan and then to cry. Her tears flowed freely, and we were all moved at the sight of her despair. The sailors tried to make the young woman understand that she would be on land the next day, that they would then take her back to her tribe, and that she must not cry. All was in vain; she jumped into the boat and tried to detach it.

"Well, really," said Master Simeon, "I doubt whether we ought not to take her back to land. Her tribe is perhaps camped in front of us; and when she sees that we are leaving them behind the poor creature is capable of throwing herself into the water. How can we explain that it is for her good that we are keeping her?"

"Can we not go and look for them?" I asked.

"We should be obliged to climb those cliffs first, Mr. Parisian, and the thing seems to me impossible. Let us leave this poor woman to cry, although her sobs are heart-rending: humanity urges us now to stop up our ears."

Like a child, who, after a long fit of passion and a tempest of tears, sobs, sighs, and then falls asleep, Ouanga, weakened, conquered, and watched, went back to the cabin, threw herself on her mattress, and soon slept soundly. She did not awake until dinner time, and then ate as usual, with a very good appetite. She refused the pipe filled with tobacco which Master Simeon offered her, and crouched down near the stove, where for a long while she watched the red-hot cinders falling from the grate. I persuaded the young woman to follow me on deck. She hesitated at first, and then made up her mind to go with me; but directly she saw the land she began to cry again, and my consolations, delivered in French, English, and Spanish, proved as unsuccessful as ever.

All at once the sound of an accordion was heard in the cabin, played by one of the sailors, who sometimes enlivened us with his Canadian airs. Ouanga was startled, and cast frightened looks around her; then, as though attracted, she went down to the cabin, and stood spell-bound before the musician. When he left off playing, she went up to him, put her hand out towards the instrument, and then drew it back as though afraid to touch it. The sailor began another air, and the young woman sat down by him, examining with curiosity the movement of his fingers. Was she sensible of the harmony, or was it only the noise that attracted her? What is certain is, that when the musician retired, after putting his instrument into its box, Ouanga tried to detain him, and followed him on deck.

The next day, as soon as it was light, I saw that we were approaching land. We passed between two small islands; then we went through a narrow channel, and came out unexpectedly into an extensive bay. In front of us lay a flat shore, and to our left a promontory, surmounted with a pole, from the top of which waved the English flag. I had hardly recovered from my surprise when the sailors shouted repeated hurrahs. The end of our difficult voyage was at last attained.

Soon, and as though they sprang from the plain of snow which extended before us, a score of men appeared, making signals to us. An hour later the *Siren*, perfectly sheltered, dropped anchor alongside a wharf constructed on piles. We were in a kind of narrow channel not unlike that in the hollow of which the town of St. Thomas, in the island of the same name, is built; only, instead of palm trees, orange trees, and pomegranates crowning the heights, blocks of ice with sharp peaks and fantastic forms rose around us.

Ouanga, mad with joy, whirled herself round on deck like a squirrel in a cage. In her haste to leave the ship she would certainly have fallen into the water had I not watched her. At last Master Simeon's employés were able to come on board; they had received no news from Europe for a year, so Heaven knows what huggings, and what an avalanche of questions, we were overwhelmed with. The hunting and fishing had been good, and the *Siren* would go back well laden with barrels of oil, bear skins, and walrus tusks. Master Simeon introduced his principal partner, Mr. Stewart, to me; I say principal, for all the men employed in the station had a share in the profits realized. My character as tourist made these hard-working men smile, but I nevertheless received a very cordial welcome.

Ouanga was not long in attracting attention, and what we knew of her history was quickly told. We then learnt, that the evening before several Esquimaux belonging to a village about ninety miles off, had come to make inquiries about the young woman. The tribe were in great distress, and could not explain her disappearance. Her husband had left her occupied with watching the fishing-lines, and the block of ice on which she was had moved away. They had searched the coast, but in vain, and they thought Ouanga lost.

No one knew the Esquimaux language sufficiently to explain these things to Ouanga, so we were obliged to wait for the return of the interpreter, who was now on an expedition. The young woman questioned each of the workmen; but they could only answer with fragments of sentences, which did not seem to satisfy her at all. One of the new-comers tried to explain to her that the next day she would be taken back to her village. Did she understand him?

Mr. Stewart led us to his house, then imbedded in six feet of snow, like all the other buildings in the trading-station. This trading-station—I use the name given it by the proprietors—was composed of four extensive buildings, three of which served as warehouses, and the fourth as a dwelling-place. One entrance, only communicating with a long corridor, gave access to this house, divided into small apartments. The rooms had no furniture but what was barely necessary; but my surprise was great on being introduced to Mrs. Stewart, a graceful Irish lady, who had bravely followed her husband to this desolate place. Two other women, both Canadians, constituted, with Mrs. Stewart, the whole of the feminine population of the station.

Mrs. Stewart, owing to her position, had a private suite of rooms—that is to say, a bed-room, sitting-room, and dining-room, lighted both day and night by lamps with unclarified oil, the odour of which was anything but agreeable. A large stove, placed in the general sitting-room, heated the whole house; they burnt a kind of peat, gathered in the neighbourhood, which also had a very bad sickening smell, and almost made me ill.

However, I grew accustomed to these disagreeable odours sooner than I had dared hope; only every time I came in from the open air I held my nose for a few seconds in order to accustom myself gradually to the heavy and to me almost pestilential atmosphere, in which my companions were living without appearing to notice it.

They put up a bed for me in Master Simeon's room, and I had the use of half the large table on which he made up his accounts, an occupation which began the night of our arrival. They proceeded without delay to unload the *Siren*, and it was no little pleasure to Mrs. Stewart to have half a dozen cases bearing her name to unpack. Master Simeon had thought about the household and toilet of his partner's wife, and had brought her many pretty and fashionable things. At dinner time, instead of the long fur dressing-gown she had worn all day, Mrs. Stewart appeared in an elegant costume which literally astounded Ouanga.

I spent my first day in visiting all the warehouses of the station, admiring the barrels of oil, the sacks of feathers, and the piles of bear, reindeer, and hare skins, collected by Master Simeon's laborious workmen. What pleased the shipowner more than anything was the sight of a quantity of walrus tusks, an article in great requisition at New York. The property thus accumulated would bring the owner a profit of several thousand dollars.

Ouanga had accompanied us everywhere, and twice she led me to the shed, where were about thirty fine dogs struggling and howling piteously; five or six of them were Newfoundlanders, and were, I was told, the leaders in the sledge team. I admired the Labrador dog, a similar breed to the Newfoundland, with jet black hair, a fine shape, and intelligent head. The rest of the kennel was composed of Esquimaux dogs, so much like wolves that one has to look twice to distinguish them.

I passed the evening talking with Mrs. Stewart and asking her questions. The young woman did not seem to feel her isolated life very dull; she often accompanied her husband on his hunting and fishing excursions. Summer and the long days were coming on; they would at last be able to leave the house in which the darkness obliged them to remain, and this prospect was consoling. As to the cold, one would never have thought where we were sitting that we were under several feet of snow, and that the thermometer outside was nearly twenty-five degrees below zero.

I slept soundly that night and so long, that I had only just finished dressing when I heard some one calling me to breakfast. When that meal was finished I went outside to breathe the fresh air, and Ouanga led me towards the promontory from which waved the English flag. The hardened snow did not even crunch beneath my feet; but I admired my companion's powers of equilibrium as she rapidly climbed several slopes, whilst I was slipping about awkwardly and once or twice almost fell. At last we got out of the inlet which sheltered the station, and by the light of the rising sun I saw a flat, white, extensive plain stretching before me, whilst on my left rose mountains which seemed to me transparent.

In our countries, when the land is covered with snow, bushes and trees rise up here and there, and one feels that there is life, life ready to awaken beneath the great white mantle, the brilliancy of which dazzles the eye; but the vast plain spread out before me was so desolate-looking, that I turned sadly from it. Ouanga, on the contrary, smilingly examined the horizon; she pointed to a spot in the direction of the mountains, and then made a long discourse. She was undoubtedly talking to me of her village, and I again tried to explain to her that she would be taken back there on the following day; but I had some trouble in getting her to return to the station.

My day passed in seeing barrels and bales of goods taken down to the *Siren*; I even helped in the work, as much to pass away the time as to escape from the heavy, sickening atmosphere of the house. In the evening a whist-party was arranged, and Mrs. Stewart helped us to some excellent tea, for which Ouanga appeared to have a special liking. About nine o'clock every one was asleep in this secluded corner of Hudson's Bay, disputed by man with the walrus and white bear.

I was awakened next morning by loud talking, and entering the dining-room, I found Master Simeon and Mr. Stewart in company with a man whom I did not recognize as one of the workmen I had helped the evening before. It was the interpreter, a Canadian, who had been almost brought up among the Esquimaux. He had just returned from his expedition, and he told us that the whole tribe to which Mrs. Oblouk-Kanick (day of snow) belonged, were roaming along the sea-shore in search of the young woman. Mrs. Oblouk-Kanick was no other than she whom we called Ouanga, a word which signifies *I* or *me*, and which we had taken for her name. They called to the young woman. She was not in the house, and no one had seen her that morning. We went to the warehouses, then on board the *Siren*, shouting her name at the pitch of our voices. All in vain. Ouanga did not appear; and after having been round the stores twenty times, searched all the rooms in the house, climbed the promontory to examine the plain where I had accompanied her the day before, we were obliged to give up the search. The foundling had taken flight; but where and by what means? We were lost in conjectures. The sun, which suddenly rose, lighted up the vast snowy plain. Our eyes wandered over this immense desert in vain; not a black spot stained its white shroud.

CHAPTER III.

The sledge drive—A rustic supper—The Oblouk-Kanick household—A snow village—Origin of the Esquimaux—A new use for buttons—Return to Canada.

OUANGA was gone; we could no longer doubt the fact. Through not understanding our explanations, and seeing no preparations made to take her back to her people, the poor young woman, ill-calculating the distance, must have set out during the night. The preceding day, as on the day of our arrival, she had roamed about the dog-shed a good deal, and I mentioned this circumstance to my host.

"The harness is locked up," replied Mr. Stewart; "and if they had harnessed one of the dogs, all the others would have howled in a way to attract our attention; nevertheless, let us go and see."

We went to the shed; the dogs were all there.

"The poor creature will perish," said the interpreter. "There is not a soul on the plain, and her strength will fail her before she can reach the storehouse."

"Have a sledge got ready," cried Mr. Stewart. "Although she has the start of us by a few hours, my dogs will soon overtake her; we cannot leave her to perish."

There was a short consultation held. The interpreter wished to set out again at once, but Mr. Stewart insisted on his taking rest.

"Have the Newfoundlanders harnessed to your large sledge, Stewart," said Master Simeon all at once, "for I shall certainly go with you. Are you in the humour for travelling?" added the shipowner, turning towards me.

"To be sure I am," I cried. "I only wish we were already far on the way, for I feel very uneasy about poor Ouanga."

An hour later two large sledges were ready. I took my place in one with Mr. Stewart; Master Simeon and the interpreter went in the other. All the inhabitants of the little settlement came out to see us start. The dogs, impatient to be off, danced madly about, whilst their companions in the kennel howled dismally. Every moment disputes were taking place between the dogs in harness; they showed their teeth, growled, bit each other, and got entangled in the reins; but at last the signal for starting was given, and with a violent jolt, which almost upset me, I felt myself carried away with a rapidity far surpassing all I had imagined. Our sledge, which was lighter than that occupied by the interpreter and Master Simeon, was harnessed to seven large native dogs, whose black skins contrasted vividly with the white plain. We rapidly took the advance; my companion's long whip served rather as a motive of excitement than an instrument of correction, for it was enough to wave the lash over the heads of our singular coursers to make them bound madly forward.

"At the rate we are going we ought soon to overtake the fugitive," said I to my companion; "but I doubt whether your dogs can keep up this furious pace long."

"They will gallop as long as I want them to; these Labrador dogs are noble animals," replied Mr. Stewart. "However, I shall take care to hold them in presently; if, as I hope, we pick up Ouanga, our weight will force these rascals to slacken their speed."

Meanwhile, we were carried away like a whirlwind, and the interpreter's dogs were left far behind. We followed a kind of beaten path on the hardened snow, most likely traced by the Esquimaux in their search for their lost friend.

We galloped for an hour without stopping over the immense plain, in the midst of which we seemed lost. The jolting was no slight affair; the dogs pulled with jerks, and the leader often made unexpected zigzags; besides, over this frozen ground we had the alternatives of good and bad roads. Sometimes a violent jolt threatened to send me out of our vehicle. I only speak for myself, for my guide seemed to foresee the shocks, against which I stiffened myself in a way which would soon have broken my arms. By degrees I let myself go with the movement of the sledge, and found it decidedly more comfortable; but the cold literally cut my face until my lips were bleeding.

The plain, so flat in appearance, rose and fell in long undulations. We often descended a slope with giddy speed; then our dogs were obliged to make an effort to climb the opposite hillside. When the dogs' excitement began to cool down, their drivers became more masters of them, and the sledges followed each other so closely that we were able to exchange a few words. Soon we came to a hill, where we were obliged to alight to relieve the dogs, and stretch our frozen limbs. Arrived at the top, we found ourselves again in front of a white, flat, interminable plain. The word *desert* ought not be applied to the Savannahs, but rather to these immense lifeless plains, where reigns such terrible silence.

"Are there no herbs, no shrubs, no trees, in this land?" I asked of my companion.

"Certainly there are," replied he; "there is a fine prairie five or six feet below us, where one can see the fresh green grass in the month of July. There are also shrubs, and we shall see the tops of some of them as we get nearer the mountains; as for trees, all the tops of the hills in front of us are covered with woods."

We had been on our way almost two hours, and I calculated that we must have gone over at least thirty miles of ground. The interpreter and Master Simeon had taken the lead in their turn, and I saw the latter point his telescope along the horizon every minute. Suddenly a black speck appeared to our left.

"A reindeer!" cried my companion.

"No," said Master Simeon; "a sledge."

The dogs, vigorously held in, stopped short, then lay down breathless on the snow, which they began to lick. The black speck grew larger, and soon we saw an Esquimaux. His dogs came tearing down upon ours; and at the risk of being bitten, I helped Mr. Stewart to hold in our coursers, who were quite ready to fall on the new-comers.

The Esquimaux was hunting, and I saw three hares and a sable on the side of his sledge. He quite shrieked with delight when he learnt that Mrs. Oblouk-Kanick was living; and, joining in our pursuit, he travelled with us. Suddenly he urged on his dogs, pointing to the horizon, and, thanks to the lightness of his sledge, soon outstripped us. Master Simeon's telescope, levelled in the direction indicated by the native, made him utter a joyful exclamation. Ouanga was in front of us.

For my part, this news acted as a stimulant, and made the blood tingle in my veins; for, in spite of the weight of skins over me, my limbs were beginning to get numb.

An exciting race now ensued, and the Esquimaux would certainly have gained the prize, had not his sledge been sharply overturned in wishing to bar the way to the interpreter. We stopped a moment to help the Esquimaux; but during this time the interpreter and Master Simeon had reached the fugitive, who, exhausted, and perhaps frightened at seeing herself pursued, had just fallen unconscious on the frozen ground.

A spoonful of rum, followed by vigorous rubbing, soon restored poor Ouanga to life, and her first movement was an attempt at flight; but the interpreter and her countryman managed to reassure the young woman. A consultation was held. At about fifteen miles from the place we had reached was a snow-hut, constructed partly by the Esquimaux, and partly by the workmen of the trading-station, which served as a kind of storehouse. It was agreed that we should rest under this shelter, and then pursue our way as far as Ouanga's tribe. It was on my account that Mr. Stewart and Master Simeon had proposed this halt, a kindness for which I warmly thanked them.

In order to make room for Ouanga, the interpreter took his place in the Esquimaux's sledge, and we resumed our journey forwards. The dogs, hungry and tired, were at last gentle and tractable enough, so that we were able to drive side by side. The sun was just setting when we came in sight of the shelter where we intended to pass the night, a simple snow-hut, the entrance to which was an opening hardly large enough for a man to get through. The dogs, immediately unharnessed, were driven before us into this gloomy retreat. Ouanga, guided by the

"OUANGA HAD JUST FALLEN ON THE FROZEN GROUND."

interpreter, was soon able to light a lamp and then a peat fire, before which she cooked the game the Esquimaux had politely given to us.

Constructed, as I have said, partly by the Esquimaux, and partly by the workers of the trading-station, the hut which sheltered us was a kind of inn. It was provided with combustibles, dried fish, cooking-utensils, and some household objects. The heat soon became so intense in this room, scarcely four yards wide at the most, that Ouanga and her countryman unceremoniously took off their cloaks, and we were not long in following their example. I had thus a foretaste of the comfort enjoyed in the dwellings of the Esquimaux, or *eaters of raw fish*.

The dogs, which were looked after first of all, greedily devoured the dried fish thrown to them. After being well fed, they were shut up in a corridor which served as antechamber to the hut, and all of them went quickly to sleep. We ate with good appetites; for a drive such as we had taken, under a rigorous temperature, is worth all the tonics possible. I should not certainly recommend to delicate people the hare-steaks smoked over a peat fire, and still less fish-steaks dressed in the same way; but this evening I found them as savoury as a beef-steak *à la Chabrilland*. Thanks to Mr. Stewart's forethought, we had some excellent tea; and this warm drink, although not sweetened, was as delicious as it was refreshing.

Ouanga and her countryman stretched themselves before the fire, and were not long in going to sleep. The heavy atmosphere we were breathing made us also feel the need of rest. Towards five o'clock in the morning I was awakened by the howling of the dogs; Mr. Stewart, the interpreter, and Master Simeon were feeding them. I learnt that Ouanga and the Esquimaux had already started, and that we were to overtake them. I undertook to prepare some steaks and the tea, a repast to which was added a tin of preserved beef. It was not till seven o'clock in the morning, with a bright moon shining overhead, that we set off at a gallop, in the direction of the hills, at the foot of which lay Ouanga's village.

The sun was just rising when, without any delay, we entered

the encampment. Imagine about thirty mounds of an irregular form sheltered by a hill from the north wind, a snow-clad hill on which here and there were pine trees at some distance from each other. Black smoke was issuing from the tops of a few of these mounds; the Esquimaux burned peat as at the trading-station.

We were hailed by a little, portly man, with a radiant face, who was talking with several of his countrymen, and seemed to be watching for our arrival. It was Mr. Oblouk-Kanick; he had come to invite us to his house. He did not thank us for having saved his wife; in that we had only performed a natural duty. The little man preceded us through a long muddy gallery, which led to the interior of his dwelling. There we saw Ouanga busying herself in households affairs, and talking at the same time with a dozen women accompanied by as many children.

The young woman came and shook Master Simeon's hand, and made him sit down on a bear-skin near the stove. As for me, I coughed enough to kill myself, and was quite blinded. I think I had never been in a more noisome hole in my life than that in which I now found myself. The smoke of a large lamp, mingled with that of the peat, and the smell of rancid oil, joined to that of refuse of all kinds which strewed the ground, suffocated me. I tried to make my way to the door, thinking that it would be impossible to breathe in this suffocating atmosphere, made more unbearable by the presence of unpleasant smelling people.

The hut gradually became empty, and the only remaining occupants of the narrow space were Ouanga's father, her sister, and two sisters-in-law, which was still too many.

My fit of coughing was at last allayed, and my eyes ceased watering; I could gradually distinguish my surroundings. The only room of Mr. Oblouk-Kanick's winter residence was of an oval form, six feet long and four feet wide. The eatables were piled up in a little loft, and a heap of skins served at the same time as seat, table, and bed. Ouanga, her sisters-in-law, and all their friends were naked down to the waist, and did not seem at all disturbed by this simplicity of costume. Besides, the heat became so intense, that, following the example of Mr. Stewart and Master Simeon, I soon reduced my costume to my shirt and trousers.

The Oblouk-Kanick household wished to do us honour, and a large fish, a kind of sturgeon, caught in a neighbouring lake, so I was told, was soon broiling over the peat fire, and renewed my fit of suffocation; nevertheless, I am convinced Ouanga's hut was one of the most comfortable in the village. The leaf-hut of the Indian is a palace compared to the narrow, bad-smelling cellars, in which the Esquimaux shuts himself up.

How little it requires to live, and to live happily; for all the people in the tribe appeared to me to be happy! The Esquimaux has hardly any other desire than that of eating; therefore, when the hunting and fishing are good, his highest wishes are fulfilled. Fish, walruses, seals, and elks furnish all his wants; their flesh feeds him, their skin clothes him, and their bones serve as the chief material for the fabrication of the things he has need of.

Mrs. Oblouk-Kanick would take us to the place where she had almost perished, and I was surprised to find that we were hardly a mile from the sea. They made us visit several dens, all like, except in dimension, the one I had been in. I made inquiries, hoping that one of these dwellings might be unoccupied, and that we could camp there. Vain hope! We were obliged to pass the night in the narrow space of Ouanga's hut; and although I placed myself near the passage, thinking that a little air might enter through the door, the said door was so well shut, that I was forced to resign myself to suffocation, which I considered would be certain.

However, nothing so alarming happened; but directly I awoke I hurried out to get a long breath of icy air. Master Simeon and Mr. Stewart again visited the huts, making exchanges. As evening came on it was agreed that we should set out again for the trading-station as soon as the moon appeared on the horizon.

I had thought for a moment of staying a few days in the

village, in order to study the customs which seemed to me singular, and to get a correct idea of the Esquimaux. Hardly had I expressed this desire, when I received twenty invitations; they were anxious to take me to the hunting and fishing, and to let me witness some of their festivals. The summer was coming on, and the tribe would change about from place to place on the borders of Hudson's Bay, from whence I was told it would be easy to reach Canada. All this was very tempting; but the atmosphere of the huts gave me such violent headaches, and the food to which I should have been condemned was so repugnant to me, that, checking my curiosity and love of adventure, I made up my mind to return with my companions.

On the way I learnt from the interpreter that the Esquimaux say themselves that they originally came from Asia. At a remote period, which learned geographers date as far back as the reign of Ghengiskhan, a considerable emigration of Tartars peopled the Aleutian isles, Alaska and Labrador. Had the fugitives continued a direct line, they would have reached Greenland, and thus peopled the farthest confines of America. What is certain is that the Esquimaux whom I had the opportunity of seeing bore an incontestible resemblance to the Tartar type. Short of stature, copper-coloured skin, stoutly built, eyes obliquely set, large mouth, thin beard, hair more often black than fair, such is the Esquimaux of Labrador. In short, the men are very plain-looking; but the women have a lively air, and their large expressive eyes lend a charm to their faces.

Although the loading of the *Siren* was steadily got on with by all the workmen, Master Simeon had several hunting and fishing parties arranged for my benefit. I killed some hares, a fox, and a seal, but I only saw walruses, elks, and bears in imagination, which I regret even now; for who ever travelled in the polar seas without encountering a white bear? I alone, I believe.

If the truth must be confessed, it was a dull journey, and a trip from which I derived very little good. The vast snow-clad landscapes, always the same, always silent, make me feel melancholy whenever I shut my eyes and see them again in imagination. During the month I passed on the borders of Hudson's Bay, I saw not an insect, bird, or plant. So when the bell for departure rang, I hailed the sound with delight.

Mrs. Oblouk-Kanick came to wish us good-bye, and I saw all the brass buttons which she had stolen from me displayed effectively on the fur cloak in which she was enveloped. The young woman appeared to be very proud of these ornaments, and I very much regretted that I had not another box to offer her. She gave me a fox-skin in token of friendship, and several other little things made of bone, which I had asked her to get for me. In recognition of this service I took her to my portmanteau, and let her choose what pleased her. She did not wait to be asked, but immediately pounced on my looking-glass, a shirt, two towels, a paper collar, and, in short, used much discretion in her choice, taking only the objects she saw were in pairs.

On the 20th of June the *Siren* left her moorings; towed by the sailors and workmen of the trading-station, she quitted the little bay which had sheltered her for a month. I bade farewell to my hosts, whose courage I admired. It is true that after four or five years of this severe exile, they would most likely return to Canada rich enough to live happily. I wished them all good fortune, especially Mr. Stewart and his charming wife.

The channel was soon passed and the mainsail unfurled. The farewell hurrahs were shouted, and our bows cut the waves. The cliffs, the ice-mountains, gradually assumed a bluish tint, and the next day at sunrise we were between sea and sky.

With what delight five weeks later I hailed the flowery banks of the St. Lawrence! I travelled to Quebec by land, so happy was I to find myself among plants and flowers, and to see the birds flying.

Honour to those brave pioneers who seek the still unknown passage to the North Pole! For my part, I have sworn, although perhaps somewhat tardily, that no one shall ever again persuade me to visit those lands of darkness, ice, and snow. There is nothing like sunshine.

A CANADIAN FAMILY.

CHAPTER I.

The Canadian cross-bill—On a hunting excursion—A chance meeting—What a few acres of snow were worth—Montcalm and Wolfe—The St. Lawrence—Quebec—The forests—The storm—An American hat—A wrong direction—Another meeting.

THE Canadian cross-bill (*Loxia Enucleator*) is a sparrow with orange-red plumage and wings edged with white, a specimen of which my friend, Professor Sumichrast, very much desired. On my departure for Canada the learned ornithologist urgently begged me to bring him back two specimens of these beautiful birds, which I ought to find in abundance in the woods around Quebec. My friend had taken the trouble to write out a long description for me in order that I should not confuse the real cross-bill with similar species. Thus I know that in old age the bird in question is of an orange-red, the female brown, and the young ones ash-coloured. But in its first year the plumage of the cross-bill is a deep crimson, and it was a bird in that livery that my friend wished for.

A week after my arrival at Quebec, I provided myself with a gun, and leaving the neighbourhood of the town, went in search of the cross-bill my friend coveted. It would have been a very simple matter to make acquaintance with one of the hunters of the country, who would have taken me at once to the fir tree woods, the favourite resort of the cross-bill; but this was a way of proceeding quite contrary to my custom. It seemed to me much more ingenious to go straight to the encounter until some good fortune helped me to find the bird whose plumage I had promised my friend. I was in a civilized country, so I only exposed myself to taking a longer route than necessary, and at that time a few miles more or less was a matter of little importance to me.

So I started on my way along a road bordered with fine crops turning to gold under the burning sun—a July sun, and, what is more, a Canadian sun.

After walking for a quarter of an hour, the high-road seemed to me uninteresting, so I struck out over a hill crowned with woods, situated towards my left. On my way I carefully examined the bushes from which flew hosts of sparrows. The cross-bills scarcely ever leave the forests; but, in spite of ornithologists, one might have ventured on to the plain. So many birds with brown, orange, and ash-coloured plumage flew before my eyes, that I thought Canada must be full of cross-bills, and for a moment entertained the hope of taking back to my friend a dozen or so of the Canadian species.

Three shots fired successively put me in possession of a robin, a swallow, and a cross-bill. As a further stroke of fortune, the sound of my gun brought up three natives, without large beaks, but whose large eyes regarded me in no very friendly manner.

"Holloa there!" cried one of them to me in English; "are you trying to kill some one?"

The question was made in an impudent, even threatening tone, and I was about to reply with the same amiability, when an enormous Newfoundland dog bounded up with glittering eyes, bristling hair, open jaws, lowered tail, and all the look of an animal of his kind when ready to make a spring.

"Call off your dog," I cried to my questioner. "I am not going to let him bite me, but I should be sorry to kill the brute."

"Ontario will not do you any harm, don't be afraid," said the man, who nevertheless called back his dog on seeing me lift my gun.

The dog stalked behind his master, who came up to me.

My position was rather embarrassing; rid of the dog, it was not without a certain amount of apprehension that I saw its master and his two companions approach me. I lowered my gun and stood my ground firmly, but, to my surprise, the three men bowed to me very politely.

"A scanty dinner," said one of them, unceremoniously handling the game in my hand and examining it.

I explained that my game was to be stuffed, and that I was in search of the *Loxia Enucleator*, the plumage of which I described to them.

"I do not think that bird lives in our fields," said my new friend; "but who can say? Look for it; but do not fire into the bush as you did just now; you might kill or wound some one, which is always an expensive business."

I learnt that my questioners were Irishmen, employed in farming on the land where I now found myself. They very obligingly showed me the path leading to the fir-tree forest, the black foliage of which I could see in the distance; and I set out again, greeted with a good-day by one or two workpeople, both men and women, who regarded me curiously as I passed.

I was quite surprised at the heat of the sun, and the verdure which surrounded me. Two years before I had seen this country covered with several feet of snow, and it had then appeared to me barren and desolate; here and there thin skeletons of trees, a grey sky, and flights of black crows dotting the whitened ground. I was reminded of Voltaire's words in 1763, when the Treaty of Paris ceded our Canadian possessions to England: "We have just lost a few acres of snow." These few acres of snow constitute in reality a country twice the size of France, covered with virgin forests, rich in iron, mercury, and lead mines, and fertile in agricultural productions. This country belonged to France for two centuries; it was made illustrious by Denys, Jacques Cartier, Raimbault, Lasalle, and Charlevoix, heroic explorers, and lastly, by the Marquis de Montcalm, who, by the sole resource of his genius, defended it for several months against the English.

Montcalm, Marquis of Saint Véran, was a grand character;

QUEBEC.

invested in 1756 with the command in chief of the troops of North America, he fought against the English a score of times with only a handful of men, and at last, forced into an unequal struggle beneath the walls of Quebec, he was killed at the onset. His rival, General Wolfe, perished in the same battle. A monument has been erected on the spot where the two warriors fell, and bears no other inscription than their names.

It was in the year 1497 that the Venetian Cabot, then in the service of England, discovered Canada and took possession of it. The Frenchman Denys, sent out by Francis the First, visited the St. Lawrence in 1506. Several years later the Spaniards appeared in this country in their turn. It is said that, not finding on the coast any trace of the gold mines, in search of which they had come, the Castillians returned, saying: *Aca nada* (here, nothing). The two words, retained by the natives, and repeated later on to the French, were taken by them for the name of the country.

Canada is divided into two large parts: Upper and Lower Canada. Upper Canada is separated from the state of New York by the chain of lakes: Ontario, Erie, Huron, Superior, and Lake of the Woods. Lower Canada, bounded on the east by Maine and the Gulf of St. Lawrence, has Quebec for its capital, and its chief towns are: Montreal, Three Rivers, and St. John.

Quebec, the former capital of Canada, and now the principal town of Lower Canada, was founded, in 1608, on an immense promontory formed by the St. Lawrence and the St. Charles. In appearance quite a French town, it contains a numerous population, and is divided into high and low town. The first, protected by a citadel, and built on a steep rock which is scaled by steps cut in the cliff, may be regarded as the old town. The old-fashioned buildings and the irregular streets contrast singularly with the straight streets and the elegant, coquettish, modern architecture of the low town.

The principal buildings of Quebec are the French and Anglian cathedrals, the houses of parliament, the market-place, and the hospital; below the town the river is spanned by the

D

famous Victoria bridge, built by the engineer Robert Stevenson. The St. Lawrence, which at this place is almost three miles wide, renders the Quebec port the central depôt for the productions of the country. Hundreds of ships at a time come here to take in supplies of grain, flour, and wood. The country round Quebec is very picturesque, and dotted here and there with charming mansions. Heat and cold are two cruel enemies to this city, where the mercury freezes in winter, and during the summer the heat is tropical.

Strangers whom good fortune leads to this hospitable town, willingly visit the two cascades, which are quite worth seeing, even after those of the Niagara. First of all, the Montmorency river, which falls from a height of a hundred and twenty feet; then that of *la Chaudière*, two hundred and thirty feet wide. From the height of Fort St. Louis, or from the promontory of the *Diamant*, three hundred feet high, nothing can be more magnificent than the sight of the yellow waters of the majestic St. Lawrence, washing a series of capes or bays whose banks have been transformed into magnificent gardens.

The St. Lawrence, which was first explored by Jacques Cartier, has a length of seven hundred miles; it issues from Lake Ontario, separates Upper Canada from the United States, crosses Lower Canada and falls into the gulf which bears its name. This river, the medium breadth of which is about a mile and a quarter, carries immense quantities of water to the sea, for it is the natural outlet of the Lakes Superior, Huron, Michigan, Erie, and Ontario.

Thus reflecting, I had climbed the hill and found myself on the outskirts of the pine wood, where I hoped to meet with the cross-bill *Enucleator*. I cast a last glance over the uneven country which I overlooked, and Quebec, crowning a summit of fortified rocks, appeared to me like a second Brest.

The forests of North America have nothing in common with those of the tropical regions. No creepers, no birds, no trees with varied foliage; everywhere sombre rows of black, gigantic pine trees. In those fortunate lands where they have the sun shining all the year round, life springs up with an intensity akin to prodigality: birds, quadrupeds, reptiles, insects, one can hardly take a step without meeting a living creature. There is never absolute silence in the tropical woods; both day and night alike one hears the flutter of wings in the branches, the buzzing of insects in the air, or under the bark of trees, and the rustling of the leaves by reptiles, with the howling of jaguars, wild boars, conguars, the screeching of parrots and chachalacas, or the plaintive songs of night-birds greeting the rising or setting of the sun. In the pine-woods reigns profound stillness, uniform monotony; a sterner nature works in silence, and one cannot repress a vague feeling of sadness. The tropical wood is bold, exuberant youth, believing in its eternity; it is the land of illusions: the pine forest, on the contrary, represents old age, dreary, austere, disenchanted, the land of reality.

For a few minutes I followed the outskirts of the wood, then coming across a path, I penetrated the dense forest. A quarter of an hour's walk brought me to the bottom of a ravine, where enormous blocks of even, polished stone revealed the bed of a stream. Here and there were clear pools of water swarming with tadpoles, and a few birds were singing overhead. With my eye on the watch I wended my way alongside the stream in the hope of discovering the bird I had come in search of. I walked for a long while up and down hill until I was almost exhausted, for the heat was overpowering. At last I came to a kind of hollow so wild and magnificent, that I determined to rest and do justice to the provisions I had brought with me.

I passed almost two hours here, botanizing and chasing insects; this wild, lonely place captivated me. The wind had gradually risen and was waving the tops of the pine trees. Suddenly great black clouds covered the strip of sky overhead, and the wood became dark. A rumbling sound was heard; a storm was about to break forth. I thought of going back to Quebec; but it was a two hours' walk and the rain was beginning to fall, so that I had no other resource than to shelter myself under the rocks until the tempest had passed over.

I found a place between two blocks of sandstone, above

which nature had formed a roof of moss, and I had hardly settled myself there when a flash of lightning lit up the forest, and there was a prolonged peal of thunder just overhead.

For three hours I was kept captive between the rocks, blinded by the lightning and deafened by the thunder, in a dense gloom. At first I looked upon this misadventure in a very philosophical light, and compared this storm to those of the tropics. But, however grand the spectacle of which I was an observer might be, I began to grow impatient and almost terrified when, after waiting so long, I saw the tempest redouble its fury, instead of abating. A high wind was rocking the tops of the trees with a mournful sound, and the bed of the torrent I had followed was filled with muddy water, which kept rising higher and higher, dashing over the rocks and mingling its noise with that of the thunder and wind. I left my retreat, determined to brave the rain, and get back to Quebec as quickly as possible.

I was obliged to look for a place where I might wade through the torrent, for, not having foreseen a storm, I had had the imprudence to cross the ravine which separated me from the former capital of Canada. I walked along the banks for half an hour; but far from becoming smaller, as I had hoped, the banks grew continually wider apart. Soaked to the skin, I bitterly regretted leaving my shelter, towards which I mechanically returned. I began to wish my friend Sumichrast at Jericho, and the *Loxia Enucleator* still further, which, however, did not dry a thread of my clothes. The rain continued; and, after another halt, I determined to climb the bank, to look for a path and follow it, at the risk of its being the right one. But climbing a perpendicular bank made slippery by the rain, and covered with pine cones, was an undertaking as difficult as a dozen of Hercules' feats put together. I climbed, I slipped back, I rolled over, I fell and covered myself with mud, before I attained the object of my efforts. Then, obliged to sit down on the ground to take breath, I innocently sheltered myself under a pine tree, as though twenty drops of water more or less could in any way change the state of my affairs. I again thought of my friend Sumichrast, quietly sitting in his armchair, smoking or studying at his ease, whilst I was here, wet to the skin and half blinded, looking for a bird which perhaps did not exist. I set out once more, and after an hour's wandering, came upon a path which led me to a road where I saw the ruts of wheels, so that I was at last getting back to civilized life.

I wore a hat which I had bought at New York, and which, on the shopkeeper's word, I believed was of English felt. But this very curious production of American industry turned out to be simply made of grey cardboard. The rim of my hat, originally turned up, had gradually fallen down under the prolonged action of the rain until sufficiently softened, when it became detached and fell round my neck in guise of a collarette. I was thus left with a kind of softened grey cap, and in my tumbles, not content with soiling my clothes with the yellow mud, I had managed to daub my face all over with it. In this condition, and armed with a gun, I must have looked less elegant than wild, and I foresaw that my entry into Quebec would not be exactly triumphal.

On reaching the road, I thought myself saved; but I quickly fell into another perplexity. Must I turn to the right or the left? That was the question. To turn to the right or to the left is a problem easy enough to solve when one knows where one comes from; but when one comes unexpectedly upon an unknown road, I defy the most skilful to make it out. After demure reflection, calculating that I had crossed the ravine here, followed the bank there, ascended it to the right and descended it on the left, and that since my departure I had kept my back towards the good town of Quebec, I resolutely took the road in a direction which seemed to me to be the right one. The rain had ceased; but the sky was overclouded, and the sun which might have served me as guide was nowhere visible. I had walked for a long while, and was surprised at not meeting any one. It was getting late, and I began to think uneasily that I might be overtaken by night in the midst of this forest. Suddenly I heard behind me the noise of wheels, and it fell upon my ears as the most harmonious sound I had ever heard.

I stood on one side the road in order to hail the driver of the vehicle which was coming along. My presence, perhaps on account of the pitiful appearance I presented, did not seem to alarm the stranger, who was enveloped in a white mackintosh. He stopped his horse, and I saw the fresh face of a young woman, with blue eyes and fair, curling hair, leaning towards me.

"Am I on the right road to Quebec?" I asked of the young woman, who was looking at me with surprise.

"Yes," she replied; "only you are going in the wrong direction. Quebec is over there," added she, pointing with her whip in a direction to which I was conscientiously turning my back; a fact which does not say much for our instinct—or intelligence, if you like it better. But our life is passed in turning our backs on things we wish to reach; and, what is sadder still, we err on our path through the moral, as much as through the physical, world.

I asked the young woman several questions, but, instead of answering, she said, looking at me with her beautiful, large blue eyes—

"Are you a Frenchman, then, sir?"

"Yes," replied I piteously; for I ill represented our country for the time being.

"A Frenchman from Old France?" added my questioner.

"A Frenchman from Old France," I replied smilingly.

"If I were not afraid of making my father uneasy, I would willingly offer to drive you back to town, sir; for you look tired."

I thanked my charitable friend, and again asked her to show me the shortest way back to Quebec.

"You have only to walk straight before you," said she; "but if you are not pressed for time, you might come with me to the farm, and I can give you some one to show you the way."

"I shall be very pleased to accept your offer," I eagerly replied.

And shouldering my gun, I prepared to follow the cart.

"Get up here," said the young woman, making a place for

me; "we have three miles to go, and you could not keep up with my horse."

I looked wonderingly at the handsome young woman who thus gave me such a proof of confidence. What a difference between the countries which we consider wild, and civilized lands! In Old France, as my companion called it, if I had been met in a wood, with clothes covered with mud, a battered hat, and a gun slung over my shoulder, by an individual belonging to the fairer half of humanity, it is probable that that individual, far from offering me a place by her side in her cart, would have urged on her horse, and told her friends in the evening that, being frightened on her journey by a ferocious-looking man, she had only escaped great danger by her self-possession, whilst all the time she would be dying of fright.

I sat down near my companion with all the precaution possible, for I did not want to soil her cloak with my muddy clothes. She whipped on the horse, and we set off at a trot.

"Am I rude, sir, in asking you by what chance you found yourself so far from Quebec in such dreadful weather?"

"It was the fault of that rascal of a *Loxia Enucleator*," I exclaimed.

"A friend of yours, undoubtedly?"

"No; a bird, classed by Linnæus, badly described by Buffon, and which lives in Lapland and in this country."

And as my companion's eyes regarded me with a questioning look, I related my departure from Quebec, and then the misadventures of the day, which gained for me the pleasure of seeing some beautiful white teeth, and hearing such a laugh as only twenty years old can give.

"Please excuse my gaiety over your misfortunes, sir; from the bottom of my heart I wish our sky had treated you more kindly."

"Laugh, madam, as much as you like; I know you are charitable, and that is enough for me."

"If you will be kind enough, you will call me miss—Miss Louise Martin."

We had just reached the foot of a hill, and the horse was

taking its own pace, when suddenly my companion half rose from her seat, and appeared to examine carefully the top of the hill we were near. She frowned slightly, and half closed her eyes, like one in deep thought. I asked her a question, but she did not seem to hear me; her mind was evidently elsewhere. I respected her silence; and, looking to the top of the hill, thought I saw a human form sitting between two trees on the roadside. I seized my gun mechanically. The young girl turned sharply round to me.

"There is some one up there," said I.

"Yes," replied she, and gave two little smacks with her whip.

Aroused by the noise, the horse pricked up his ears and mended his pace. Soon I was able to distinguish a tall young man, dressed in a hunting-suit, with high gaiters. He got up and came slowly along the road as though to bar our way. On our approach he took off his fur cap, which, in spite of the season, he wore over his eyes, and I saw a handsome fellow, with fair hair, an open brow, and regular features.

"Louise," said he, when we were quite near him, "I should like to speak with you."

My companion's face grew serious, and the horse made a few steps before she replied. She heaved a deep sigh, drew the reins in, and the horse having stopped, she got lightly down.

"Good day, Louise," said the hunter, holding out his large hand.

"Good day, Peter," replied the young girl.

"How is your father?"

"Better, thank you."

"Louise, I should like to speak with you."

"Will you take the reins, sir," said the young girl to me after a moment's hesitation, "and be so kind as drive to the top of the hill?"

Then, without awaiting my reply, she took the hunter's arm and walked on with him.

Rather surprised at this scene, I picked up the reins and slowly followed the two young people.

"SHE TOOK THE HUNTER'S ARM."

CHAPTER II.

Miss Louise—Arrival at the Secret Valley—Grandfather Martin—A patriarchal evening—What is Mr. Peter?—A mistake—An *enfant terrible*—Another search for the *Loxia*.

THE rain had quite ceased; the sky gradually resumed its clear deep azure; drops of water were trembling on the fir-cones; and when the sunlight penetrated through a glade in the wood, one would have said that the trees it fell upon were studded with diamonds. The wayside banks, of a beautiful orange colour, reminded me of the ochre slopes in certain parts of Normandy. Was it a freak of my imagination? I do not know; but the trees, the bushes, the paths, the herbs growing by the roadside, carried my thoughts back to France; my misadventures of the morning were forgotten, and I could hardly believe that the broad ocean separated me from my native land.

From time to time, I looked towards the two young people; they were speaking in an undertone. The hunter was making energetic gesticulations, and seemed to be either justifying himself, or trying to persuade his companion, who, with her head bent down, only answered him at long intervals. The young girl had taken off her cloak, and I was better able to judge of her appearance. She was tall, robust, but nevertheless graceful. She wore a grey dress trimmed with blue, which, without being of any particular fashion, suited her well. Her boots were of chamois leather, embroidered with beads, and reminded me of the mocassins which the Indians in this part of the country wear. Her luxuriant golden hair was tied back with a dark blue ribbon something like the large bows with which the Alsacians adorn themselves. Her walk was firm and self-reliant; Miss Louise had an aristocratic look about her.

In short, the two young people formed a charming couple which it was a pleasure to look at. My curiosity had been aroused by this unforeseen meeting, but I noticed that they treated each other with a familiarity which spoke of a long acquaintanceship; I thought I saw before me two lovers trying to make up a love-quarrel.

At the top of the hill Miss Louise stopped and held out her hand to her companion, saying, " Good-bye, Peter."

" No," replied the latter, eagerly taking her hand ; " not good-bye."

" Very well, then ; but it depends entirely upon you."

The young man shook his head, and helped his companion to take her place again in the covered cart; then going back a step to let us pass, he took off his cap and bowed politely to me.

A minute later the horse was trotting down a long slope. Before me lay a pretty valley, at the bottom of which stood some extensive buildings. Miss Louise, serious and absorbed, maintained a strict silence, and I spoke not a word, for fear of disturbing her thoughts. She turned her head quickly, nodded to the hunter who was still standing on the top of the hill, then, the road being sheltered by trees, she heaved a deep sigh, slashed her whip, and said to me, pointing to the buildings—

" The Secret Valley—my father's house."

The Secret Valley! This name had been admirably chosen. The valley into which we were descending was enclosed on all sides by high hills, and at present it was covered with golden harvests. We passed by an old woman occupied with chopping wood and making faggots; she wished us good evening in French, and her accent, her black striped petticoat and her cap, again reminded me of Normandy. I told my companion my impression.

" You are in New France," replied she; " and my family, who have held this property for more than two hundred years, as well as our servants, came originally from Rouen."

" Have you ever been to France? "

" No. I was born in the house you see down there, and I have never been further away than Quebec."

" Were you brought up in Quebec? "

" I have been brought up in the Secret Valley, and I have never slept under any other roof than that to which I am taking you. But why do you ask me these questions?"

"Because you speak French so remarkably well."

"Thank you for the compliment," said the young girl, smiling; "but I beg you to remember that for me, as well as for half the inhabitants of Canada, the French language is our mother-tongue, and although we know English we only speak it when obliged to do so."

"Nevertheless," I said, "all your countrymen do not express themselves in the elegant way which I admire in you."

"I know how to read and write, sir," replied my fair companion; "the secret lies there, perhaps. You are not very polite," added she. "You have seen Quebec, and yet you seem to think we are but half civilized here."

I hastened to do justice to Quebec, whose English and French colleges I had admired, and whose reputation for learning is incontestible. Nevertheless, the Secret Valley was not in the least Quebec, so that I was somewhat justified in showing my surprise on hearing a beautiful young woman, with educated speech and ladylike manners, declare herself that she was only a farmer's daughter.

"Is a farmer's position, then, in France considered as an inferior station, or as a degrading occupation?" asked the young girl, looking at me.

"No," replied I at once. "The culture of the land is everywhere honourable and honoured; but, unfortunately, gentlemen-farmers, as they are called here and in England, are very rarely to be found with us. Our farmers are honest people; but they are often uncultivated, even boorish, and, beyond their business, more ignorant than I dare confess."

We passed through a wide gateway. Two enormous mastiffs chained to their kennels, began to struggle furiously. The cart crossed a courtyard and stopped before the steps of an old house, with windows irregularly placed here and there, such as our forefathers, regardless of symmetry, were fond of building.

An old man, with a three-cornered hat, knee-breeches, and knitted blue stockings, came towards me, leaning on a walking-stick. One might have said he was an ancestor stepping down out of an old picture; he only wanted the curled wig, for he wore the old-fashioned shirt-front and frilling. He took off his hat to me: his head was still covered with curls, but as white as snow; I thought I had never seen such a handsome, venerable-looking old man.

"Welcome to my roof, sir," said he, holding out his hand to me. "You must forgive my forgetting if you have ever been to the Secret Valley before, for I do not remember your features or your name."

I explained in a few words that, being drenched to the skin, and having lost my way, I had met with Miss Louise, who had kindly offered me a seat in her conveyance, and promised to let some one show me the way to Quebec.

"Quite right, Louise," cried the old gentleman. "But our guest must not go away without resting and having some refreshment. See to that, my child."

"Grandfather," said the young girl, "the gentleman is a Frenchman, from Old France."

"Heavens be praised! Is it true?"

"It is true," I answered.

"Then, sir, you are doubly welcome. You are among friends, countrymen, and brothers."

How was it that this simple, cordial welcome moved me almost to tears? It was because I was a thousand leagues away from that dear country, the name of which was enough to call forth so much kindness. How precious and honourable my title of Frenchman was to me when the old man warmly grasped my hand and led me into his house! I had long known of the sympathy the Canadians have for the land of their forefathers, but never had I seen that sympathy exhibited in so touching a manner.

Two hours later I had become the guest of the Secret Valley, and was sitting at table between Mrs. Martin and the grandfather, whilst a servant was despatched to Quebec to let my friends know that I was still in the land of the living.

Mr. Martin, the father of Louise, was forty-eight years old, his wife forty, Miss Louise eighteen, her sister Victorine sixteen, and her brothers Victor and Émile fourteen and twelve.

As to the grandfather and grandmother Martin, they represented between them almost a century and a half. The farm-servants, about ten in number, sat round the lower end of the table; some of the grey-headed ones treated the masters and children of the house quite familiarly. The grandfather having asked a blessing, every one sat down and partook of a large ham and cabbage, followed by a roast joint of mutton.

"Father," said Louise rather suddenly, "on my way back from Quebec, as I was bringing our guest here, I met Peter."

"Did you speak to him, Louise?"

"Yes, I spoke to him," replied the young girl. And I noticed she changed colour.

Silence ensued, and nothing was heard but the noise of knives and forks.

"Very well," said the farmer all at once; "we will talk about that by-and-by."

Then turning to me, Mr. Martin entertained me with an account of his crops, the work he had undertaken, and his plans for improving his property.

I listened absently. Miss Louise's declaration seemed to have cast a gloom over all present. Who was this Mr. Peter, whose name was enough to disturb this good family? A headstrong youth, a prodigal son, perhaps. But no; I had noticed Miss Louise did not treat him familiarly enough for that. I was lost in vain conjectures.

The grandfather returned thanks and all rose from the table. We had supped in an oblong room, furnished with one of those immense chimney-pieces which one still meets with occasionally in some parts of Normandy. The kitchen utensils made a brilliant display on the walls, and great beams ran across the ceiling. The farmer led me out of doors, and Miss Louise, after having poured out some coffee, and placed the cups on a small table, offered me a long slate pipe, a regular calumet, which I was obliged to decline.

The clock had just struck eight; the night was starry and light. The moon, which was still invisible, was rising towards the north, and casting her silvery light over the sides of the hills in front of us. Through the still air came the sound of lowing and bleating from the out-buildings, mingled with the cackling of a few hens late in going to roost. I questioned my host, and he answered me very obligingly; he was a serious, well-instructed, and affable man. I learnt that he and his wife had been their children's only instructors; that six generations of Martins lay in the little cemetery of the Secret Valley, after having lived here as happy as human creatures could be, working, fearing God, and making simplicity the root of their happiness. Mr. Martin dreamt of no different future for his four children, and he strongly hoped that they would never know any other part of the universe save the place where they were born.

Years have passed, and have sprinkled my head with grey hairs, but they have detracted nothing from the pleasing memory of the Secret Valley. I have only to shut my eyes to hear grandfather Martin ask a blessing in the large room in which I was first received, to see the serious features of his son, the goodness beaming on the face of Mrs. Martin, the beautiful eyes of Miss Louise, and the gay faces of her younger sister and brothers. I see again the large sitting-room where my host led me after we had finished our coffee, Mrs. Martin and her daughters sewing by the light of two large lamps, the grandfather reading, and his grandsons bending studiously over their lessons for the next day. Oh! happy, simple family, what never-to-be-forgotten memories did I bring away after a week's sojourn in your midst! If happiness is not an idle dream, if it exists anywhere on our globe, surely it is beyond the sea, between the hills of the Secret Valley.

"Nine o'clock," said the grandfather suddenly, looking at the clock; then, turning to me, he added—

"Do you like music, sir?"

"Very much indeed," I answered.

"You really mean it?"

"I do indeed."

"You hear, Louise?" resumed the old man. "This gentleman will make excuses for your performance."

Miss Louise sat down at the piano and played remarkably

well; she was soon joined by her sister, and by Émile and Victor, one provided with a violin, the other with a flute, and all executed their parts with great exactness. After this improvised concert, Mr. Martin led me to the bedroom prepared for me, and I soon fell asleep, thinking how much chance has to do with our lives.

My first thought on awaking was of the *Loxia Enucleator*, for the birds were singing under my windows, which looked out on to a beautiful garden. Mr. Martin, his father, and Miss Louise were walking along an avenue; the grandfather was holding the young girl's hand. It was evidently a question on the subject of Mr. Peter.

As soon as I was dressed, I went down to wish my guests good morning; when I reached the garden, the father was saying to his daughter—

"You well know, my child, that your happiness is my only care."

"How can I doubt that, father?" replied Miss Louise.

"Ah, well, Louise, you must try to forget, and we will help you."

Miss Louise gently shook her head, as much as to say, " It is impossible." Then, bowing to me, she went away.

Directly they saw me, Mr. Martin and his son came up and warmly shook hands.

"Poor Louise!" said the grandfather, who was looking after his grandchild; "she is crying."

"Father," said Mr. Martin, "do you, then, side with the women against me?"

"Yes, when I see Louise crying."

"We are here to comfort her now; later on, when we shall be no longer alive, whom will she lean upon?"

I was about to walk on.

"Stay, sir," said the grandfather to me; " there is no secret. We are very much troubled just now about our granddaughter. She loves her second cousin, and there is an obstacle between them."

"Is Mr. Peter a bad character, then?" I risked asking.

"No, no," replied Mr. Martin, eagerly; "Peter is the best lad in the world, and I should be glad to call him my son. Louise would have been his wife a year ago, if . . . . But pardon, sir, our family affairs can have no interest for you."

Not knowing precisely whether my host's reticence was in reality only a polite way of changing the conversation, I dared not reply that, on the contrary, I was much interested in Miss Louise and her lover, and that I wanted very much to know the obstacle that prevented their union.

Mr. Martin led me towards the farm, and I was obliged to submit to what I call the landlord's visit, that is to say, going round all the outbuildings, cellars, and granaries. These forced visits are often wearying; this time they were very useful to me, for I learnt more than one particularity of the climate and productions of Canada.

It was twelve o'clock when a bell called us to luncheon. I saw that Miss Louise busied herself with her sister and mother in household affairs, whilst the grandfather was tutor to the boys. During the meal the *Loxia Enucleator* was the topic of conversation. I had become reconciled to it again, as it had gained me an invitation to spend a few days at the farm. Neither of my hosts remembered meeting with a bird of crimson plumage in their walks or hunting excursions; but the hills surrounding the Secret Valley were covered with pine trees; thus I could explore them at leisure, sure of not getting lost again, as it would have been difficult to lose sight of the farm.

The history of their native land was familiar to my hosts, and at the same time they were well acquainted with that of their mother country. When they discovered that the names and the works of missionaries who had been the first to explore North America, and Canada in particular, were not unknown to me, they redoubled their attentions. They complained of being ill-known in France, and of having no return of affection.

"You are mistaken," I repeated, continually. "A Canadian is no stranger in France."

The grandfather Martin smiled and shook his head. He had seen, said he, many Frenchmen come to Canada, and not one of them knew even the names of Cartier or Montcalm. I defended my countrymen as well as I could, whilst inwardly allowing that my host was right, and that we in France are too indifferent to our past glories. The attachment manifested to France by this good family made me commit a singular error.

"It would be a happy day," cried I, suddenly, "which should renew the bonds of the past, and make you Frenchmen."

"God preserve us from such misfortune!" exclaimed grandfather and son together. "We are Canadians first of all, and secondly, we are the subjects of the Queen of England; and we have no more wish to become Frenchmen than Americans, although our neighbours think the contrary."

I was somewhat confused.

"I thought I understood," I resumed, in an embarrassed tone, "that you regretted the loss of your former nationality."

"We are sons of Frenchmen, sir, and we respect the past," said the grandfather to me; "but on no account do we wish to become the subjects of your kings, or the citizens of your republic, for we possess what you are wanting in, constancy. Your cavilling administration of routine, would soon transform the liberty we enjoy into servitude. We love France and French people; nevertheless, as long as we are allowed to remain purely and simply Canadians, we shall remain English by right, by politics, by love of justice, and by true liberty."

I bit my lips. I have since found among all Canadians the same sentiments as those expressed by the grandfather Martin. If the Canadians love France, our political inconstancy astonishes them, and they say that we understand nothing whatever of liberty.

The afternoon was spent in visiting my host's land. He was very proud of his crops of lucern-grass and wheat. There was the same patriarchal gathering in the evening. At my request Miss Louise took her seat at the piano. She had hardly struck a few notes when one of her brothers cried—

"Oh! that is Peter's song."

At this involuntary exclamation, the musician covered her

face with her hands, and the young culprit sprang to her side, throwing his arms around her neck.

"Oh, Louise!" cried he, "did I make you cry?"

Miss Louise got up and kissed the boy, whilst Miss Victorine at once took her place; and, drying her eyes, the elder sister quietly sat down near her mother. This scene had touched every one, me particularly; little Victorine had shown her good sense by taking possession of the piano, for all were thus able to follow their own thoughts. For my part I should have much liked to know what it was that prevented Louise's marriage with the handsome Peter, and to have been able to restore peace in the Secret Valley.

Towards ten o'clock I took leave of this interesting family, for I was going to begin my search again for the famous *Loxia* among the pine-woods early the next morning. My host wanted me to take a servant, but I declined this kind offer; and the grandfather then proposed that his grandsons should be my guides, and their lessons for that day be dispensed with. At these words the two boys looked up eagerly; their eyes fastened on my lips as though trying to guess what the reply would be. I accepted; they jumped up with delight, and came and squeezed my hands.

My little companions undertook to awake me, and at break of day they knocked at my door. I found Miss Louise in the large sitting-room, filling our game-bags with provisions, for we were going to have our luncheon in the woods.

"You have been very kind to me," said I to the young girl, just as we were starting; "can I be of any use to you?"

"No, sir," replied she; "but I am very much obliged to you all the same."

She shook hands with me, and I followed her young brothers, who were impatient to be off.

CHAPTER III.

A panorama—An unexpected meeting—Luncheon in the woods—Pleading in Miss Louise's favour—Return to the farm—Pleading in Peter's favour—" All's well that ends well "—The *Loxia*.

THE morning foretold splendid weather; a white mist hid the tops of the hills, but the sun soon dispersed this light veil. My two guides led me across a corn-field; then, following them, I climbed a steep path leading into the woods.

By the deliberate way in which my young friends walked, and handled their guns, I soon recognized experienced huntsmen. In fact, they told me that for a long while hunting had been their favourite pastime; and their master in this art dear to all Canadians, had been their second cousin Peter, whose skill was quite proverbial in the country.

On our way, my companions asked me many questions about Paris, London, and New York, three cities which they dreamt of visiting. They were lively, gay, and talkative, and yet more thoughtful than boys of the same age with us. We reached a narrow dale, lost between two hills, and my guides opened the hunt by bringing down a black squirrel.

We agreed on a signal-call, and each took a different direction. I was to climb the slope in front of me, whilst the two brothers took the road to the right and to the left, walking in a direction so as to meet me on the top of the hill. We were surrounded by pine trees of different species, among which I recognised the black pine, the wood of which is very valuable in ship-building; the Canadian pine, or white spinet; then the odoriferous pine, which furnishes commerce with a thick, transparent turpentine, of a very agreeable odour.

Three successive reports of fire-arms repeated by the echo told me that my companions were having good sport. As for myself, in spite of the steep slope I was ascending, I walked on, looking about everywhere, trying to get a glimpse of the red plumage of the *Loxia* among the dark or silvery foliage of the pine trees. I killed a fine woodpecker, then a cross-bill, and I just missed bringing down a weasel of no ordinary size.

Arrived at the top of the hill, I found myself on a platform strewn with blocks of sandstone, and elevated enough to allow of my overlooking the ravine we had crossed, the Secret Valley, and its buildings. The sun was flooding the lovely valley with light, and the emerald-green colour of the fruit trees stood out in pleasing contrast with the dark foliage of the pines. I had reached the place of rendezvous, but as yet heard no sound of the approach of my companions. I sat down under an oak tree, which seemed to have sprung up there quite by chance; its foliage looked singular among the uniform vegetation with which it was surrounded.

After waiting half an hour, I entered the wood again in another direction. From this side, the slope which I had climbed was almost perpendicular. I leant over this precipice, and was startled at seeing Miss Louise's lover, sitting on a rock about ten feet below me, with his gun lying at his feet.

The young man wore the hunting-suit in which I had seen him the first time we met; he was looking towards the Secret Valley, which was plainly visible from the place he occupied. He seemed so wrapped up in his thoughts that he did not appear to hear the sound of my footsteps. I could not see his face, but from his movements I guessed that he was looking after some one. He suddenly turned his head to the left, then listening for a moment, he sprang to his feet and took up his gun. I thought of my young companions, one of whom was to come out from that side, and I was going to warn the hunter, when Victor appeared.

"Peter! Peter!" cried the boy in a gleeful voice.

And at the risk of breaking his neck, Master Victor rushed down the hill and fell into his cousin's arms.

At the same moment Émile appeared further down; at his brother's call, the lad looked up, and walking quickly, soon joined the hunter.

"Peter! Peter!" cried the two boys, enthusiastically; and they tried who could make the most of their cousin, who warmly returned their caresses.

"How are they all at the Secret Valley?" asked Mr. Peter at length.

"Very well," replied Victor; "father has had low fever, but he is better now."

"And Victorine?"

"Rather more of a tease than when you saw her last year."

"And .... Louise?"

"Just the same, Peter; only she does not laugh much, and she looks very sad sometimes."

"And she has been like that ever since you went away," added Émile.

Mr. Peter passed his hand through his hair several times, and was silent for a moment.

"How is it you are here?" resumed he; "I know it is not your holiday."

"We are with a gentleman, a Frenchman, who lost himself in the woods. Louise met him and brought him to our house," said Victor.

"The day that she met you," added Émile.

"By-the-by," resumed the elder brother, "where is our friend? He ought to be here."

"Was it you, then, that fired?" asked Mr. Peter.

"Yes. We have each killed a rabbit, and a bird for the gentleman besides. We are looking for a bird with crimson feathers."

"Ah! well, then, lads, you must be quick and find your guest."

"Leave you so soon for that? Oh no! Let Émile go and look for the gentleman."

"Go yourself," replied Émile, unceremoniously; "you are the eldest. Is it true, Peter," added the boy, seizing his cousin's hand, "that you are never coming again to the Secret Valley, and that you do not care for us any more?"

Instead of replying, the hunter took both boys in his arms and pressed them to his heart.

"Ah! my dear lads! How could you think so!" cried he at last.

Victor, looking up at this moment, saw me, and told his companions. Mr. Peter bowed, and following his cousin, who set out at once to meet me, was soon at my side.

He was indeed a handsome, tall young man, with fair hair and beard, and finely modelled features. He talked well, although with a certain honest bluntness. An hour later we were taking our luncheon side by side, and I had described the *Loxia* to him at least three times. After our luncheon he offered me a cigar, and took me to the rock where I had seen him sitting in a deep reverie; he was evidently intent on contemplating the Secret Valley.

Émile and Victor were too restless to sit still long, so they went on with their sport, and left their cousin and myself to finish our cigars and have a little chat together.

"Really, sir," said I to my companion, "if I thought you would not be annoyed, I should ask you what obstacle it is that keeps you from the Martins and separates you from Miss Louise."

"Separates me from Louise!" cried the huntsman.

I thought he was about to continue; but he covered his face with his hands, and was silent.

"I beg pardon for my inconsiderateness," I resumed, after a few moments; "but I hope you will believe it was not mere curiosity which prompted me to speak."

"God forbid, sir," replied he at last, "that I should be offended with your question. I love Louise, and she loves me, as you know. I have been brought up in Quebec, and have studied there in the best colleges. I have an independent fortune, and I should like to be one of those who rule, rather than of those who are ruled; in a word I want to live in town, and take part in political affairs. My uncle and great-uncle are happy at the Secret Valley, and they will not admit that one may be happy elsewhere."

"Does Mr. Martin wish his son-in-law to be a farmer?"

"Just so; but I have other dreams in my head, which he cannot understand."

"Are you ambitious?"

"Why should I conceal it from myself? Yes, I am ambitious, especially for Louise's sake."

"Does she approve of your plans?"

"No; she sides with my uncle against me."

Finally, beneath all the reserve which modesty imposed on my companion, I ended by discovering that he had literary tastes; that he dreamt of a brilliant life in society for himself and his wife. It was an ambition which I found it difficult to blame. Nevertheless, was not Mr. Martin right when he required his nephew to remain in the Secret Valley, and not abandon the peaceful home where so many Martins had lived happily? Mr. Peter was cherishing many vain illusions. I did not hesitate to try and show him the other side of political and literary life, to which many think themselves called, but so few are in reality chosen.

"If I did not succeed," replied the young man, "I should come back to the Secret Valley."

"Yes, disgusted, and embittered; having contracted habits which would make retirement wearisome," cried I. "Besides, you will always fancy yourself on the eve of success, and your return will continually be put off from day to day. But you might succeed, and remember then the words of Madame de Staël: 'Glory and happiness are not synonymous; the first is often nothing but the shroud of the second.'"

The sympathy I felt for Miss Louise made me eloquent, and I talked for a long while with Mr. Peter, to whom I must do the justice to say that he listened to me attentively, and discussed each of my arguments without impatience. The young man was convinced that, if Louise chose, she could quickly dispel her father's and grandfather's objections; but she was determined never to leave the Secret Valley.

"We will live here together," she had said firmly, to her lover, "or we will die apart."

And this dissension had lasted for a year.

Ah! what a wise young woman was Miss Louise! She possessed all the grace and all the accomplishments which would have made her shine in the society where her betrothed fondly dreamed of taking her; nevertheless, she was resolute in her wish to live in the obscure corner where she had been born. How differently people think in France, where the farmer's daughter has only one desire, to leave as quickly as possible the fields which have given her health and riches, to pine away in a lawyer's study, or a judge's cabinet, as though .... Alas, what is the use of my moralizing?

I spent the day hunting with Mr. Peter, for whom I formed a sincere friendship; such excellent qualities did I recognize in him. As night came on, he walked back with me and my young companions as far as the entrance to the valley.

The sun was going down, a yellow mist enveloped the buildings of the Secret Valley, and the neighing of horses, the lowing of cows, the bleating of sheep, and all those sounds so harmonious when heard in the distance at sunset, reached us where we stood.

"There is happiness," said I, pointing towards the farm and turning round to my guide; "try and convince yourself of that."

The young man made no answer.

"There beats a brave heart, which suffers through you," I resumed; "think of that."

Mr. Peter sighed; then he walked off rapidly, without shaking hands with me, or kissing his cousins; who, when they had recovered from the surprise which this abrupt departure caused them, cried out both together—

"Come and see us, Peter!"

A voice came from the depths of the wood, but none of us could make out what it said.

It was night when we returned to the farm. We had captured four rabbits, three squirrels, and a dozen birds; but, alas! the famous *Loxia Enucleator* was not among them.

The two following days I again hunted in the woods of the Secret Valley. It was not only the *Loxia* I was looking for, but Peter Martin, with whom I should like to have had another talk. I had not mentioned my meeting to any of the inhabitants of the farm, not wishing to appear to interfere with affairs which in reality did not concern me. However, the evening before my departure, as I found myself alone with Miss Louise, who was arranging a bouquet of flowers, I ventured to say rather abruptly—

"I have seen Mr. Peter; did you know?"

"Yes," replied she; "I heard my brothers tell about your meeting with our cousin."

"Is it true, then, that you refuse to live in town?"

"I firmly believe, sir, that our happiness will be more certain here, in this dear old place. Peter is fond of books, and we have a library; what can prevent him from reading, or even writing? If he is capable of writing a book, will his work be any the worse for being composed in the Secret Valley?"

"But if he does not like farming?"

"He does like it, sir, as one likes things one has been accustomed to from childhood. Besides, what is he wanted to do? To become master here; and that is no very poor position. For myself, I am a farmer's daughter, and I do not care to be anything different. Good Heavens! what should I do in the large drawing-rooms at Quebec. I should not dare to speak or move. I am giving you my own particular reasons, as well as those of my father and grandfather, and you will understand that I do well in not yielding to Peter's wishes."

"You want him to make a sacrifice for you, and not you for him," I resumed.

The young girl looked at me with her beautiful eyes, which gradually filled with tears.

"I assure you, sir," said she to me in a trembling voice, "in all this I think more of Peter's happiness than of my own."

I was about to reply, to assure my charming hostess that I did not in the least doubt either her self-devotion or her affection; but the grandfather coming in cut short our conversation. Miss Louise went away, and I had no opportunity of again speaking to her in private.

In the evening I looked for the last time upon this good family, sitting around two lamps, the antiquity of which proved that they had lighted several generations of Martins. As usual, Miss Louise sat down at the piano, and I went up to her to justify myself and explain my words of the morning. At their grandfather's request Émile and Victor took up, the one his flute, the other his violin, when the dogs began to bark outside. The noise did not last long, and I listened for an hour to Canadian airs played by the young artists at my request. After this Miss Louise poured out tea.

"Are you angry with me?" I asked her in a low tone, when she came up to give me a cup."

"No," said she; "I only think that you judge me ill."

I was protesting against this insinuation, when suddenly the sitting-room door opened, and what was my surprise to see my hunting companion, Mr. Peter Martin, on the threshold!

The young man held his seal-skin cap in his hand; he came towards Mr. Martin, who had suddenly risen from his seat.

"Uncle," said he, in a voice trembling with emotion, "is there still room at the farm for me?"

"You are under the roof of your father's friend, in the house of relations; it is your home, Peter," replied Mr. Martin. "But have you come simply to ask hospitality?"

"No; I am come to reclaim my place by your fireside, and my title of son."

Mr. Martin could not answer; he took his nephew in his arms, and laid his head for a moment on the young man's shoulder. The grandfather wept, and so did Mrs. Martin. I felt very much inclined to follow their example. As for Miss Louise, she was sobbing violently.

"Peter," said Mr. Martin at last, "we shall have ten workmen to-morrow in the fields, and there are some new ones among them whom I recommend you to keep an eye on. Louise, my child, offer Peter some tea."

"Let her kiss him," cried the grandfather. And Miss Louise gave Peter such a prolonged kiss that I do not know when it would have ended, had not Victor and Émile put up their faces for their turn. Oh, that happy evening, and what radiant faces I looked upon that night!

I was discreetly taking part in the family's joy, when Mr. Peter came up to me.

"You were eloquent, sir," said he, holding out his hand to

"UNCLE!" CRIED HE, WITH EMOTION."

me, "and you have made me happy a few months sooner than I should have been; for it would any way have ended in this," added he, turning to Louise, who blushed up to her eyes, as Victorine roguishly remarked.

I warmly pressed the hand held out to me; and hardly had I released my hold, when Mr. Peter dived into his coat-pocket and brought out a charming little bird, a real *Loxia Enucleator*, which he very politely offered me.

"It is a rare bird," said he to me, "for I have been looking for it ever since I left you. It was the cause of my delay. You had convinced me, and I should have followed you at once, had I not determined to offer you this present."

I hardly know whether I acted loyally; but I will confess my deed as an act of penitence. I never gave my friend Sumichrast the beautiful little bird I had come so far to look for. I have kept it in my own collection, in remembrance of Mr. Peter and Miss Louise.

About two years ago, on returning to my house, I was told that a young man had been waiting to see me for about an hour; he had not given his name. When I entered my study, the stranger, who was sitting near the fireplace, got up quickly, made a few steps towards me, looking at me with apparent surprise.

"Do you not recognize me?" he asked at last.

"No," I replied. Nevertheless, your features remind me of . . . ."

"Do you ever think, from time to time, of the Secret Valley?"

"The Secret Valley!" I cried. "You are a Martin—Émile, perhaps?"

"No, sir," replied the young man, and his face became clouded; "my poor brother is dead. I am Victor."

I took both his hands in mine, and led him back to his seat.

"I hardly dare ask any more questions," said 1 to him. "Fifteen years represent a long space in one's life. Your grandfather . . . ."

"He went before my brother and mother; but my father is living. It was he, Peter, and Louise who told me to remember them to you when I was starting for Europe. I have a niece," added the young man; "she is in some way your god-daughter, for she is called Lucienne, and here is her portrait."

Victor held out to me a photograph, and for a moment I seemed to see Miss Louise again, as I saw her on the road from Quebec. May God continue to bless her!

NIAGARA IN WINTER.

CHAPTER I.

The coasts of Canada—Sir John Burton—Miss Mary's cloak—Halifax—A sledge drive—A restaurant in a cellar—An oyster-fight—American liberty —Sir John again.

ON the 10th of February, 1863, eleven days after leaving Liverpool, the *Scotia*, a fine steamer of the Cunard line, cautiously steered into the Halifax harbour. The passage had been very rough, and we had twice almost disappeared beneath the green waves which wash the coast of Canada. The state of the sea for the last five days had prevented us from going on deck; but, in spite of the waves, the snow, and the ice, we were obliged to leave the heated saloon, from time to time, to get a breath of fresh air outside; it nevertheless required a good quarter of an hour's deliberation before taking this decision, especially on my part.

We were about fifteen passengers on board, among whom were an Englishman, and a young American lady, between seventeen and eighteen, Miss Mary, the daughter of a doctor at Cincinnati. All my other fellow-travellers were for the most part Canadians, who knew from experience the inclemency of the climate, and were well provided with fur clothing. Being accustomed to live in the tropics, I had almost begun to disbelieve in the existence of cold, and had neglected providing myself with a fox-skin cloak, and a pair of waterproof boots lined with fur, with which possessions I saw my companions, the Englishman included, able to brave the weather on deck. Now, whilst Sir John Burton, who represented on board Old

England, just as I was a representative of Old France, was walking from port to starboard, comfortably wrapped up in his furs, I bravely strode from stem to stern in an overcoat, a hat, and shoes. My self-pride forced me to seem insensible to the cruel, biting north wind; but I charitably warn my readers that an overcoat, excellent for the season in London or Paris, is a very poor protection from cold on the coasts of Canada, between the months of October and April.

Whilst trying to disguise my feelings, especially when the son of Albion was on deck, I shivered from morning to night, and mentally anathematized my want of forethought.

" Go and put on your fur cloak and your high boots," they would say to me.

" It is not cold enough," I replied, trying to force a smile from my frozen lips.

They looked at me with surprise, and I got close up against the steamer's funnel to try and get a little warmth; an action which at once belied my words.

At last I was obliged to confess that I had neither fur coat nor high boots, and that I had foolishly relied on the heat of the sun, which generally baked my shoulders in February. Touched with pity, a Canadian, more than six feet high, on the strength of being my countryman—he was, he said, from New France—lent me a pair of gigantic boots, which reached up to my waist. I bought an almost new fur cap from a sailor; and Miss Mary so kindly offered me an opera cloak, lined with fur, that I was obliged to accept it. My costume, although warm, was, it appeared, rather grotesque; for each time I went on deck I was hailed with general bursts of hilarity. I laughed myself as heartily as any one, except when the Englishman was there. This poor Englishman had such a disagreeable way of laughing, especially when he was talking with Miss Mary, that he quite annoyed me.

Miss Mary, who was well-educated and clever without appearing to be so, was returning from visiting England, France, Germany, Italy, and Spain. She was more graceful than pretty; but with a woman grace and good temper are the first qualities, and the only ones which do not fade. My cap especially amused the young lady; however, she made up for her teasing by choosing me almost always as her partner. Her father, the doctor, took little notice of her. The day after leaving Liverpool he had begun a whist-party, which was only interrupted by meals, and was to last till we reached Boston.

Miss Mary was a true American woman, and did just as she liked. She would be on deck all day, walking from one end of the ship to the other, whilst every one made way for her with a respectful politeness which removed all idea of gallantry.

How is it that in France we are not well-bred enough for our customs to permit of this free confidence? Why do we continually forget that we have brothers and sisters? I am no admirer of Americans; they are rough, ill-bred, and their brusqueness is proverbial; but their respect for women, which is perhaps carried even further than in England, makes me envy this quality for my countrymen. A young girl in America may travel from one end to the other of her vast country without having to fear the insolent looks or the vulgar compliments which are so common among French people. We pride ourselves on our politeness and civilization, and yet our country is about the only one where a woman cannot travel alone.

But let us return to Halifax. As we approached Newfoundland, the tempestuous sea, with the enormous blocks of ice dashing against the hull of the *Scotia*, had gradually subsided into calm waves, over which a light mist seemed to float. In front of us was an indented coast covered with snow. We entered a wide channel, and then an immense bay, capable of holding more than a thousand vessels, suddenly opened before our astonished eyes.

I stood for a long while lost in thought. This land, in appearance so barren, had once belonged to France. This magnificent harbour, one of the largest in the world, where five or six brigs laden with coal, and as many fishing-smacks, were now lying at anchor, had long seen the white flag, then the national standard of France, waving from the overlooking fort. Outside flowed the majestic St. Lawrence, ascended for the first time by

Francis Cartier, and which serves as a kind of outlet to those inland seas, called the Lakes Superior, Huron, Michigan, Iroquois, Erie, Ontario; these last two are, as is well known, united by the celebrated Niagara.

Beyond these coasts rise Quebec and Montreal. Above the Gulf of Fundy, and the state of Maine, stretches an extensive country, wrested from France, in spite of the military talents of Montcalm, and the heroic courage of the handful of soldiers he had accustomed to victory.

" Well, Mr. Parisian," said a clear young voice, interrupting my reflections, " are you not thinking of going on shore ? "

" Most certainly, miss; have you any commission for me ? "

" I am going to propose that you take me with you. My father does not care to expose himself to this north wind, which at present is giving your nose a beautiful bluish hue; but I want to pay a visit to the daughter of the judge of Halifax, who is a friend of mine."

By way of reply, I offered my arm to the young girl, and passed triumphantly before Sir John Burton, who was obliged to bow to me. He was newly shaven and splendidly dressed, and his appearance, although somewhat stiff, was not wanting in elegance. I had put aside my mantle and high boots for this visit to the capital of Nova Scotia; nevertheless, Sir John was better dressed than myself; I could not deny the fact, and I was doubly obliged to Miss Mary for having chosen me as her escort.

Halifax in fine weather is the seat of an important commerce, and nothing can then equal the activity which fills its crooked streets with people and noise. In winter the communications with the interior of the country are often suspended, the principal inhabitants emigrate, and the town is in some measure deserted. The snow becomes heaped up around the deserted houses, and prevents all access, in spite of the height of their steps, which look as though they were perched on stilts. Following the advice of a Canadian, I went in search of a sledge; for my companion would never have been able to walk through the four feet of snow with her long skirts.

At last, with a young lad to drive us, we are on our way to the judge's house. The black horse drawing our equipage is a magnificent animal; he gaily shakes the bells on his collar, and trots along with a firm step over the hardened snow. The sledge goes up and down, and from side to side. I cannot see the ground, but have an idea that the streets of Halifax are not very level. Almost all the houses have a gloomy aspect; nevertheless, here and there a long column of black smoke issues from a roof towards the grey sky. My companion joins with the driver in urging on the steaming horse. From time to time we meet a bundle of furs, which stops to see us go by, but there is no possibility of saying to which sex it belongs. We cross an extensive white plain, dotted here and there with villas built of wood, all hermetically closed; their inhabitants are probably frozen, for nowhere is there a living being visible, nor a sound of life to be heard. At last the sledge stops before the door of a large house, with a flight of twelve steps, at present buried under snow. The judge has left for Quebec or Montreal, so we have had our drive for nothing.

Miss Mary is highly amused, and orders our driver to take us back to Halifax by the longest road, if there is one. The young Canadian smiles, he whips his horse, and we are once more gliding over a spotless sheet of snow, whilst large flakes fall around us and obscure our view. From the way that five or six bundles of furs look at us as we pass them, and then raise their hands to the sky, I am convinced that our driver is taking us along an unsafe road. We are going like the wind, we hardly know where, for the snow falls thickly. Just as I am wrapping myself up in the furs as well as I can, we reach Halifax, and our horse stops in front of a house around which the snow is piled like a rampart.

Miss Mary jumps out, and I follow her between two walls of ice. We reach a door, and then find ourselves in front of a staircase lighted by gas, which we descend. Passing through a corridor, we enter a long room in which a table is spread. A suffocating heat pervades this den, where a score of concentrated odours offend my nostrils; but Miss Mary does not seem to

F

notice it. She has given her name to the servant, for she knows the hotel-keeper's daughter, with whom she is invited to dine, whilst I am asked to go into the *dining-room*.

Entering the underground room called by that name, I find most of the passengers of the *Scotia*, drinking, talking, and smoking, and all are anxious to welcome me. I am called from one table to another, and obliged to taste the national drinks which I have heard praised so much during the voyage, but which I think detestable. I am at an hotel; dinner is to be at one o'clock. Meanwhile, I am told of the excellence of the Canadian oysters; I cannot say how many dozen of which are ordered in my honour.

" No one can flatter himself he has really eaten oysters until he has tasted ours," said my fellow-traveller who had lent me the boots; "you will see."

I did indeed see! The palate and stomach want a great deal of training to taste and digest the infinite variety of dishes which man has invented; my education in this respect was almost perfect, thanks especially to my sojourn among Indian tribes. How many pages it would take to enumerate the frightful mixtures under the name of *national dishes* with which I have been regaled both among savages and civilized people! Oh, what trials my palate has been subjected to!—and what stomach can be better inured to this sort of thing than mine? I thus disappoint my friends, who pride themselves on their *recherché* dinners. I like everything, which proves, they say, that I like nothing. The fact is, I have been obliged to accustom myself to eat with my eyes shut; but when I think of it, how foolish man is with regard to his food!

At dinner, who should sit opposite me but Sir John, who had sprung all of a sudden from I know not where. A waiter brings us both deep plates full of clear, gluey water, in which float little black balls. On either side of us are piles of sandwiches, made with brown bread and rancid butter. They provide us with spoons. The Canadians are looking at us, and we look at each other with an air of commiseration for the first time.

NEW YORK.

For want of something better to say, I ask my neighbour on my right for information as to the way of preserving the singular oysters he is devouring. Sir John casts uneasy looks about him. At last he lifts the spoon to his mouth, turns first red, then pale, and closes his lips; his eyes become dilated. Will he swallow it? *That is the question.* He does swallow it; but he immediately seizes a tankard of beer, takes one drink—that is quite enough; he orders the waiter to take away both oysters and beer, and helps himself to a stiff glass of cognac, looking at me rather sheepishly as he does so.

"Come," thought I with resignation, "it seems that it is still worse than it looks."

The lookers-on are sneering at the unfortunate Englishman. I take advantage of this diversion to set to work. By dint of energy and perseverance, I empty my plate and tumbler, and, behold me crowned a Canadian! I am infamous enough to declare the oysters excellent, and they immediately want to give me a second dose. I manage to escape this politeness, which would have been too much for my courage, and I forget the frightful taste of the mixture I have just swallowed, in eating a slice of leg of mutton, which Sir John dare not touch.

Towards nine o'clock I escorted Miss Mary back to the *Scotia*, closely followed by my antagonist. The following morning we were on our way to Boston, steering through a fog, which made it necessary to keep the alarm bell constantly ringing, in order to avoid a collision. Owing to the snow, the depth of which rendered all communication with the interior impossible, I was obliged to give up my intention of reaching the St. Lawrence, to ascend it as far as the Niagara Falls, the principal object of my voyage.

I took leave of Miss Mary and her father, after receiving a pressing invitation to visit them if ever I came to Cincinnati. Just as I was entering the railway-carriage, I saw Sir John. He was not dressed for travelling, but he kept his eye on me, as though resolved to convince himself of my departure. I passed him without the slightest recognition, and he on his part took no notice of me, although we had lived together for twelve days.

True, we had only exchanged contemptuous smiles; if my boots and cloak amused him, his vexation at Miss Mary's preference for me was sufficient retaliation.

Twelve hours later we reached New York, where I found a spring-like temperature. However, far from imitating the Yankees, who were already beginning iced drinks, I walked along the shore of the bay, thankful at feeling the warm sun once again on my shoulders.

The same evening, in the drawing-room of a charming Spanish lady, I announced my intention of visiting the Niagara Falls. My project was received with loud protests. "It is impossible," said they, "to get near the Falls in winter, or to see the islands and walk in the cave of the winds; I ought to wait for the summer to see Niagara in all its splendour." And they were Americans those travellers, *par excellence*, who tried to persuade me to give up my excursion. They told me that it would be mere waste of time, and that I should come back quicker than I thought to do. They even added that I should risk finding a lodging, the hotels being deserted as soon as the snow begins to fall. I had travelled too much to allow myself to be intimidated; besides, as I must shortly start for New Orleans, I had no choice of season left me.

A week later I went to the New York railway station, and took the train for Albany. The waiting-room of this extensive line was nothing but a small, insignificant apartment, scantily furnished with wooden forms so well covered with grease, that I dared not sit down. The dirty state of the termini and the American cars seems to me to have been generally overlooked by European travellers, who, when in the United States, shut their eyes to all but liberty. I have led an existence too free from trammels not to understand the enthusiasm which the love of liberty inspires; but cleanliness is not to be despised. I also confess that when several of my travelling companions shouldered their guns to fire past me from the carriage at an unfortunate crow, which I innocently watched from the window, I should have preferred seats less dusty and brushed, if only once a year, to this proof of national independence.

Hardly had we started, than one of my companions informed me that we were travelling on the best-laid railroad in the United States. It is true a communicative passenger—one is hardly allowed to be silent in America—had told me the same thing of the railroad between Boston and New York. I have crossed the United States from one extremity to the other, and I know that this praise of the Boston and Albany railroads is well merited.

My fellow-travellers were not long in informing themselves of the price of my hat, and travelling-bag, an article then unknown in America. They drew my attention to the little flags which the pioneers held up to show that the line was clear, or to stop trains in case of danger. I was much struck with this happy innovation, and my companions seemed to notice my wonderment with surprise.

* * * * * * *

The train stops.

" Kingston ! " cried the guard.

I smile as I remember that it was at Queenstown in Ireland that Sir John came on board the *Scotia*. I lean mechanically out of the window; a traveller runs along the platform, and jumps into the train. Upon my word, Sir John has a brother, or it is he himself I have just seen.

CHAPTER II.

The palisades of the Hudson—A stolen repast—Is it he?—The Falls—The suspension bridge—Blondin's rope—Under the Niagara—Cincinnati—An introduction.

If there is much unworthy of admiration in the United States, still all is not to be found fault with. The railway cars are made so as to allow of passing from one end of the train to the other, even when it is in motion. As an exception to the rule, the train in which I had taken my place was arranged like our own, so that it was impossible to discover whether my surmise was but an illusion. After all, what did it matter? To my knowledge Sir John had never told any one the object of his visit to America, nor mentioned the place he was going to; and the laws of England, France, and America left him at perfect liberty to go to Albany, even in the same train that I had been pleased to choose for my excursion

The road to Albany, or rather to Troy, is certainly one of the most picturesque in the world. It runs along the right bank of the Hudson, which flows on widening and narrowing, and the celebrated palisades of which a stranger takes at first sight for immense fortifications. In the distance the steep cliffs resemble the black marble of the Giant's Causeway in Ireland. Brigs, steamers, and small boats descend this stream full speed, or ascend it with more difficulty; there was an animation only equalled by that on the Thames below London Bridge. I caught a glimpse of West Point, the celebrated polytechnic school of the United States. But the country seemed bare, the houses were shut up, and one would have thought them uninhabited, except for the smoke wreathing from the chimneys. The buildings, boats, carriages, and inhabitants reminded me of the neighbourhood of London, which I had recently visited—so much so indeed, that I asked myself if I were dreaming, and if I had indeed crossed the Atlantic. It was night, and the rain fell heavily. The engine gave a shrill, mournful whistle; we had reached Albany after doing a hundred and forty-four miles in seven hours.

I sprang out of the train, and from pure curiosity looked everywhere for Sir John. I must have been mistaken, for I saw no signs of my former travelling companion and rival.

The next day, as soon as it was light, I set out again on my journey. In one day I passed through Utica, Rome, Syracuse, and Palmyra, to reach Rochester. The country became more and more desolate, and the snow fell thickly. Yesterday I thought myself in England, to-day I am in Germany; the inscriptions and sign-boards are all written in the language of that country. The train stopped to allow of our getting some dinner. Every one got up, jostled and elbowed each other in a very unceremonious manner, all trying to squeeze through a narrow door. In France the twentieth part of this pushing and knocking about would have brought about a general *mêlée*; not feeling hungry or vigorous enough to take part in the assault, I allowed the crowd to pass me.

At last I entered an immense room, almost filled by a large table, around which most of the places were taken. I installed myself as well as I could, and a waiter placed boiled turkey before me, with the traditional English paste-like sauce. I asked for the bill of fare: it was composed of ten *entrées*, but the best had already been demolished by the first comers, whilst I was washing my hands. I had hardly sat down when my fellow-travellers rose from the table, and were ready to start again; and yet people say that the French are quick! I have seen steam and electricity perform marvels in the way of speed, but they are surpassed by the rapidity with which an American will gulp down a meal;. it is legerdemain applied to gastronomy.

A bell rings, and I run out at once. It is only the first signal. A snow-storm is whirling round five or six locomotives. One of them is shunting, and getting ready to start; is it the train that I should go by? There is not a railway official or placard from which I can get any information. I question three or four gentlemen in vain. What am I to do? I catch sight of a grocer standing at his shop-door, and as I do not care to be taken back to Batavia, Tonawinda, or Canandaigna, I address myself to him, and, being a polite and obliging man, he directs me to my train.

We make our way through a terrific storm, which quite obscures our view. Night comes on, and the travellers get out at the different stations, until I am left alone in my compartment. At Lockport most of the carriages are taken off, including the sleeping-car, from which a man descends. He seems in a bad humour, and the guard is obliged to tell him three times that he must get into my compartment if he wishes to go to Niagara. The door opens, and Sir John makes his appearance.

Our eyes meet. He arranges himself in a way so as to give me his back; I imitate him, and thus we proceed on our way.

Has chance thrown us together? It is most probable. In short, the English tourist is a man of my own age, well-educated, and able to speak French fluently. Everything should draw us together, and so much the more as we are fifteen hundred leagues from the Channel; but it appeared that we were not meant to come to a friendly understanding.

The locomotive stops. What has happened? The darkness is intense. A continual noise, like the rustling of leaves in a forest caused by a hurricane, reaches us. The guard makes his appearance.

"Do you gentlemen wish to cross the bridge?"

"What bridge?"

"The great suspension bridge. We can take you to the other side of the Niagara, but travellers generally prefer to get down here, and cross over on foot."

I did not understand the motive for this preference until the next day; nevertheless, I followed my rival's example, and jumped out of the train.

Nothing was visible around us save a far-off light, which marked the place of our destination. Directly we had started we found ourselves sinking in a quagmire at every step. Sir John grumbles, whilst I laugh, and our troubles are mutual.

"Where are we? where can we find an inn?" I asked of the guard.

"I am going to shunt the train; will you wait for me?"

I was obliged to resign myself to my fate. After waiting a quarter of an hour, and when I was beginning to shiver with cold, the guide appeared. He took me to a stove, and then led me to a table amply provided with food, and lastly, showed me a comfortable room where I should have slept soundly had it not been for the unceasing roar of the cataract.

I was up next morning before daybreak, which only resulted in trying my patience to the utmost. To pass the time away I went all over the immense hotel, now deserted and silent, but in summer filled with six hundred travellers at a time. As soon as it was light I took up my station at a window, and looking in the direction from which the thundering noise I had heard all night seemed to proceed, I expected to see the first rays of the sun illumine the Falls. However, nothing of the kind was visible. I could only see a few houses, and roads seamed with ruts; the hotel was more than a mile from the Falls.

I left my post after making this grand discovery, and went downstairs just in time to see Sir John start off alone in a fly; he had been more thoughtful than myself, and had made inquiries and ordered a carriage the evening before. He looked at me, and his smile caused me a slight feeling of vexation. It was ten o'clock before I was, in my turn, in possession of a carriage and guide. The sun showed itself at rare intervals through the clouds: a bleak north wind swept the six inches of snow which covered the ground, and the horses could only get slowly along. The dull thundering sound, which no comparison can give an idea of, became more marked. I ensconced myself in the cushions of the carriage until my guide said, in a phlegmatic tone—

"The Falls."

For a long while I remained lost in ecstasy, silent, overpowered. I did not think, I simply gazed with awe on the falling mass of water, and the yawning abysses, in this weird scene. It was a fine spring day when I first saw the ocean; the peaceful waves were gently rippling over the shore: my expectation had been deceived. Here, on the contrary, as when I first entered a virgin forest, the spectacle surpassed all that I had dreamt of: my imagination was outdone.

An hour previously I had admired the fine engravings on the walls of the hotel representing Niagara under aspects familiar to all; clumps of green trees, gravel roads, pretty villas, fine ladies and gentlemen walking about, grounds as well kept as an English park. Winter had effectually transformed this scene; before me stretched a desolate, rugged, gloomy landscape. The rocks which on the United States side are seen at intervals, their black masses standing out boldly through the clouds of spray, were now hidden under a sheet of ice, whilst the snow-covered peak of Goat Island was hidden by the foaming water, boiling and dashing against it. I here saw nothing but a liquid mass, more than a thousand yards wide, advance majestically, and then precipitate itself with overwhelming force into a gulf below. One would have said it was the sea breaking its bounds and deluging the land.

It was some time before I followed my guide, who no longer felt any enthusiasm at the sight of this magnificent spectacle. His first proceeding was to take me to see the rope, still stretched across the water, on which Blondin had crossed, not the Falls—which would be impossible—but the Niagara, where its deep, swift water rolls in great, swollen waves.

I afterwards went on to the suspension bridge, a marvel of architectural daring. It is more than seven hundred and fifty feet long, and overhangs the river from a height of about two hundred and seventy feet. I followed the side-way for foot passengers, the centre being a railroad, and I then understood that the railway officials were right in consulting the wishes of travellers before taking them over this aërial road, wider, but perhaps less firm than that on which Blondin made his omelette.

On reaching the Canadian side I saw the before-mentioned American fall to my left, and in front of me the horse-shoe of the principal fall. The banks along the side of the river rise perpendicularly to the height of at least three hundred feet; the continual spray showered from the foaming torrent covers the snow with a mantle of glazed frost, and wherever the water trickles slowly, it forms fine needles of ice, sometimes several yards in length. An unexpected ray of sunlight illumined the scene; a rainbow spanned the whirling eddies; the rocks sparkled beneath their icy coating; the falling water assumed a bluish tint; the transparent needles, coloured by the variegated light, seemed to encase the falls in a gigantic setting of diamonds.

A negro came up unexpectedly, and offered to take me under the curve described by the waters of the lake as they form the Falls. The whirlpools possess a fascination which I could not resist, and I accepted the offer, in spite of the remonstrances of my first guide. Enveloped from head to foot in a waterproof dress, the soles of my boots provided with climbing-spurs, and a staff in my hand, I ventured on the bank as firm and polished as a mirror.

The first few steps were easy enough; then I had to walk close against the perpendicular side of a smooth rock, to which I tried in vain to cling to preserve my equilibrium; but in order to do that, I should have wanted fingers provided with cupping glasses like flies' feet. The least false step would have precipitated us into the abyss; my negro repeatedly reminded me of this, and I was not in a position which authorized a contradiction of his words. Before inviting a traveller to attempt this perilous walk, the guides ought at least to ask whether he is subject to giddiness. The negro told me, that beneath the bed of ice on which we were treading, there was a path cut in the rock, which visitors took in summer.

We were soon under the ice-needles, and I was able to understand their formation. The edge of the bank overhangs, and allows the water to trickle drop by drop, which thus freezes in the form of stalagmites. The path became more practicable if not easier; a false step would no longer have been a fatal condemnation to death. We ventured between the transparent columns; suddenly a formidable noise, which not even the roar of the Falls could quite stifle, caused me instinctively to lower my head. It was occasioned by one of the ice-needles which my guide had disturbed with his staff, and which crumbled to pieces, awakening a thousand echoes. A few steps further on, we met a mulatto supporting a benumbed traveller. I uttered a cry of surprise on recognizing Sir John, enveloped in a waterproof dress like myself.

"Do you come from the cave?" cried the negro to the mulatto.

"No."

"Are you going there?"

"It is impossible to get there."

I gave my guide a questioning look. He showed me two rows of white teeth, from ear to ear, and hastened to reply—

"It is difficult; but, nevertheless, it is to be done."

I continued my way; whilst the Englishman regaled himself from his flask, and sat down, following me with his eyes.

It was indeed a difficult enterprise. I no longer risked falling into the Niagara, but many times escaped plunging into the fathomless basin, hollowed by the Falls, the depth of which increases every day. Clinging to the ice by the aid of my iron-pointed staff, or my climbing-spurs, crawling sometimes at full length, sometimes sideways, rolling to the right and to the left, not without bruises, and unable to hear a single word of my guide's directions, I came upon a column of water barring my passage, but which I must nevertheless pass. I sprang forward; and I confess I should have been knocked down, had it not been for my companion's firm grasp.

I came off with nothing more than a formidable shower-bath, and found myself on a black soil in semi-obscurity, and in a comparatively warm atmosphere. The negro never let go of me now, and we advanced cautiously together along a narrow path where two people could not have stood abreast. Before me the water was rising and falling in mad fury, and covering me with icy spray. I leant with my back against a rock; above my head arched an immense bluish-green vault: it was the Niagara. After a while the deafening roar caused me unbearable torture. I wanted to sit down to contemplate, to reflect. Vain efforts! One determined, imperious, maddening thought alone possessed me, which was to silence the cataract, and prevent the water from whirling around me. A stone from the rocks fell at my feet, on the very verge of the abyss; I stooped down to pick it up, and then made a sign to my guide that I wished to return. I passed under the waterfall again, and directly the sky was visible I stretched myself on the ice and breathed freely, whilst my negro smiled placidly.

Was the kind of nightmare, which had filled me with the mad longing to struggle against the Niagara, occasioned by the cold, by the want of air, or by a low state of the spirits? I am not subject to giddiness, and I think a deafening and continuous noise should be ranked among the infernal punishments.

When I had again passed the needles, I caught a glimpse of

"THE WATER COVERED WITH FROZEN FOAM."

Sir John near the bank, and was childish enough to wave my handkerchief, in sign of triumph.

I slowly made my way back, with only a momentary fear when crossing for the second time the mirror of glazed frost, from which I could so easily have slipped into the river. Once again on the bank, I vowed never again to go under the Niagara—at least, not in winter.

I afterwards visited Goat Island. I also went up the famous tower, which American newspapers from time to time announce as having been swept away into the gulf which it overlooks; a catastrophe which must happen sooner or later. From the top of this tower I gazed down into the abyss. I saw the water advance with giddy swiftness, as though preparing for the leap, precipitate itself, rise in columns, fall again, finally sweep on down the slopes, called rapids, and then flow calmly and clearly beneath the great suspension bridge.

I did not fail to visit the banks of Lake Erie, whose yellow waters, lashed by the wind, are continually adding new waifs to the trunks of trees heaped up on the shore.

I did not get back to my hotel until evening. There I learnt that Sir John had just started for Buffalo. I was vexed at this, and felt like a conqueror disposed to abuse his victory.

Buffalo, which I visited next day, is a large, fine city, with regularly built streets, which undoubtedly, on account of their width, are somewhat monotonous and dull. At the beginning of the present century Buffalo was only a village, with scarcely a thousand inhabitants. Although situated at about three hundred and twenty miles from the sea, this city, through Lake Erie, and the canal which connects it with New York, is now a port of the first importance, and a centre of manufacture and trade. It is the great place of resort for all German emigrants, who have gradually turned this part of the United States into a new Rhine-land.

From Buffalo I went to Pittsburg, where the rivers Alleghany and Monogahela unite and form the Ohio, one of the principal affluents of the Mississippi. The Ohio, with its yellow water, flows between two flat shores, and is subject to periodical inundations. This grand river, twice as wide as the Seine at Paris, falls into the Mississippi at Jefferson, after a course of 1180 miles.

Fifty years ago the country watered by the Ohio was almost a desert. Travellers scarcely ever ventured on these plains, formerly inhabited by an industrious people, traces of whom are found at every step. From the American archæological point of view, Ohio is the richest of the United States. Unfortunately, up to the present day the researches of the learned have thrown little light on the mysterious people who covered it with buildings, and whose name is not even known among the Indians.

The steamer, on board which I had been making my voyage of exploration, landed me one fine morning at Cincinnati. I at once went in search of the house where Miss Mary and her father lived. The doctor received me with all the warmth of an old acquaintance. His daughter was not at home, but he invited me to dinner, and sent at once for my portmanteau, which I had left at an hotel, declaring that I should sleep under his roof as long as I stayed in his native town.

"We often talk of you, Mary, John, and myself," said the old gentleman to me; "to say the truth, I hardly expected to see you again."

I was going to ask the doctor if he had a son, when a carriage stopped before the house, and, to my great surprise, in came Miss Mary, leaning on Sir John's arm.

"My husband," said the young lady to me after having shaken hands.

Then she gave my name to Sir John Burton; so at last we were introduced to each other.

At dessert I learnt that the young baronet, attracted by Miss Mary's charms, had not hesitated to leave England and take a berth on board the *Scotia* at Queenstown. He followed the doctor as far as Cincinnati, and there formally demanded his daughter's hand. The doctor having required a week's delay before giving an answer, Sir John had taken the journey to Niagara to pass that time as quickly as possible. It was for the sake of propriety that Miss Mary had always accepted my arm on board; the good Englishman thus regarded me as a rival, and naturally had a grudge against me.

"Who would ever have suspected this little romance?" said I to my new friend, warmly shaking his hand.

"True," cried the doctor. "Who on board would ever have thought that you were aspiring to become my son-in-law?"

"No one but myself, perhaps," rejoined Lady Burton blushing, whilst her husband kissed her, and her father hummed the American national air of " *Yankee doodle.*"

SAN FRANCISCO.

The Chinese theatre—A fellow-countryman—The El Dorado of Cortez—The village of San Francisco—A rich proprietor—A gaming-room—A Yankee, Yankee, and a half—"A bird in the hand is worth two in the bush."

It was five o'clock in the afternoon, when, beginning to feel uncomfortably inclined to yawn, I made up my mind to leave the Chinese theatre of San Francisco, where curiosity had led me. Were the actors indifferent? I do not think so; for the Chinese by whom I was surrounded were approving the tirades recited for their benefit, with very significant nods. As for the piece—an exaggerated drama, as well as I was able to judge from the length of the spears with which the actors threatened each other—in order to appreciate its dramatic and literary merits, I ought to have understood the Chinese language, a knowledge in which I was entirely wanting. At first the costumes, the stage-scenery, the music, and the spectators, had all interested me; but after watching for two hours some awkward clowns making grimaces, brandishing their swords, defying and occasionally assaulting each other without my having the least idea of the reason of their incessant quarrels, I began to detest the theatrical art—in the Chinese form of course understood.

Whilst doing my best to try and understand for what crime the young Chinaman who filled the *rôle* of the princess was continually threatened with death, I mechanically climbed one of the numerous hills on which the capital of California is built. Leaving the houses behind me, I soon espied a large isolated tree with moss-covered roots, forming a luxurious seat, on which I comfortably ensconced myself. From this spot, whither chance had led me, I had a magnificent view of the city and bay of San Francisco, which soon banished the incomprehensible Chinese drama from my mind.

The sun was low in the horizon, and its rays, gilding the blue waves of the Pacific, reminded me of that vermilion sea which washes the coasts of Lower California, and which also bears the name of the *Sea of Cortès*. Here and there white sails filled by a gentle breeze wafted a fishing-smack over the golden waves, or indolently bore a vessel to the open sea. Below me lay the immense bay of San Francisco bristling with masts, from the top of which floated the ensigns of all maritime nations; whilst the noises from the city, with its quays, its up-and-down-hill streets, and its temporary buildings, sounded in the distance like an immense bee-hive at work.

I was lost in contemplation, when a voice above me, politely asking for a light, interrupted my reverie. The new comer held a cigar in his hand, and spoke in French. He was a man of about fifty, with a fair complexion, a firm, energetic countenance, and piercing eyes. In reply to his request I gave him my fusee-case. He thanked me, and after taking a few puffs at his cigar, seated himself quietly beside me.

"A fine view, and a beautiful country," said he, stretching his arm towards the sea and gradually bringing it round to the hills.

"Are you a Frenchman, sir?" I asked, in lieu of reply.

"Certainly. I am from Boulogne-sur-Mer; and what is more, I am your next-room neighbour at the hotel *de la Sonore*. It was on the strength of being your countryman that I took the liberty of asking you for a light."

"Do you live in San Francisco?"

"Yes, for the present."

I again looked towards the bay, across which a steamer was passing, and my companion seemed to be absorbed in contemplation of the city.

"I almost think I am dreaming when I carry my thoughts

G

back ten years," said he all at once. "At that time, sir, you would see a vessel once a month in this bay, where now thousands are crowding together. As to the great city lying at our feet, it then consisted of about fifty houses."

"Did you ever visit California before it belonged to the United States?"

"Yes, in 1845. I had read the old Spanish authors, and I knew that Cortez, after the conquest of Mexico, had explored the coasts of the Pacific in search of the El Dorado. Charles the Fifth encouraged the conqueror in this enterprise, but the latter scarcely went further than Lower California. Urged by I know not what instinct, I set out in search of the land of gold, sought for in vain by Cortez, and one fine day I landed on this apparently barren coast. I lived here almost six months. Convinced that the soil was fertile, the country pleasant, and the climate healthy, I resolved to settle here; and, in company with one of my friends, I bought all the land you can see before you."

"All the land before my eyes!" I repeated, turning towards my companion.

"All," replied he, taking short puffs at his cigar; "the land on which this city is built included."

"Did the land on which San Francisco is built belong to you?" I resumed, slowly scanning my words.

"It belongs to me still, if you please, and in such an incontestible way that the American Government are now offering me ten million dollars in exchange for my title of proprietor."

"And are you going to accept the offer?"

"No; I refuse, as I want twenty million."

I thought I must be talking to an individual slightly deranged in his mind, like several I had seen at the time the gold fever was bringing so many emigrants to California; but my companion spoke so quietly and seriously that I hardly knew what to think of him.

"Yes," he resumed at last, " do what I will, I continually see behind this populous city the miserable village founded by the Franciscan missionaries in 1776, which, notwithstanding its good position, had so ill prospered, that when first I came here it had a population of scarcely two thousand inhabitants. I have seen the poor Indians disappear one by one from this coast where they used to live; everywhere and at all times civilization is fatal to the coloured races."

"By what chance," said I, "did you become possessor of this land? Did you foresee the future of California?"

"Not the least in the world. As I have told you, I came here in search of gold, of which there is abundance, as we now know; but I did not know how to find it. After buying the land which surrounds us, I was discouraged and weary of wandering about, so I determined to cultivate the vine, which has always flourished wonderfully in California. I dreamt of providing the two Americas with wine, and entering into trading negotiations with Europe. Unfortunately, I reckoned without considering the indolence of the natives, and, for want of help, I was obliged to give up my plans. Having made up my mind to go back to the Sonore, I tried in vain to sell the lands I had bought, even at the most insignificant price. I could find no purchaser. I went away, taking my title-deeds with me; and again I set out in search of the El Dorado dreamt of by Cortez, and near which I had just been unconsciously living."

"How was it you did not put forward your rights directly after the cession of California to the United States, on the rise of San Francisco?"

"You forget, my good friend, that the rise of this city has been in some measure startling. In less than six months the village, the greater part of which was in my possession, became a considerable town, and if I had dared mention my rights to the first emigrants, I should soon have had a bullet through me. Nevertheless, I could have made good my claims if, as I have just told you, I had not then been lost in the wilds of La Sonore. At the present day the right of the strongest is no longer the only law which governs this fine country, and I confidently await my twenty millions of dollars."

Night was coming on. My companion got up, and I followed him. We returned to the town by the Chinese quarter, and in passing between two rows of little shops lighted by coloured lanterns, I could quite fancy myself for the moment in a city of the Celestial Empire.

San Francisco is the most dusty city in the world, for the hills on which it is built are downs, from which fine white dust rises with the slightest breeze. Built hastily and at hazard, the houses are cramped together on the steepest hills without any regard to the convenience of foot passengers. The town, at first built of wood, has been several times destroyed by fire, and is gradually being reconstructed of stone. It is of no use to work continually for the edification of new inhabitants. San Francisco is always too small for the population it contains. One must be very rich to have a house of one's own in this city; thus it is that the majority of the inhabitants live at hotels. But every day civilization accomplishes its wonders here; the streets are laid out in straight lines, paved, and provided with side walks. If the police still leave much to be desired, they are nevertheless beginning to protect the public against the bands of ill-doers of all nationalities, who from the first made this a place of resort. The gold fever has given way to that of agriculture, and California grain is now to be seen in European markets. There is no thought of misery in this fortunate city, where paper-money is unknown; and at the time at which I am writing the dollar might be considered as the equivalent of the French franc. Will this prosperity last? Yes, if one considers that but a third of the whole country is cultivated, and that vast tracts of land where European grain and tropical productions might grow, still remain to be cleared.

After having taken me through the districts of a city, too often described for me to hazard giving a slight sketch, which would no longer be true at the present day, my companion invited me to dine with him, and told me his history more at length. He bitterly complained of his partner, whose exigencies, he said, prevented the Washington Cabinet from closing the credit which the incessantly growing city rendered every day incalculably more valuable.

My companion had accompanied me to my room, where we talked together until about ten o'clock, when our conver-

"I ENTERED THE ROOM."

sation was interrupted by the sound of cries and a pistol-shot below us.

"What is happening?" I cried.

"Oh! some dispute between two gamblers."

We went down; the report which we had heard proceeded from a revolver which its owner' had let fall, and which had discharged itself. I entered the gaming-room, brilliant with gilding and lights. A score of men with neglected beards, dressed in woollen shirts, and pistols in their belts, were sitting at a table covered with green cloth, gambling and paying their stakes with gold-dust. Chinamen were taking round grog, consisting more of brandy than water, and often receiving from the fortunate gamesters a pinch of the precious metal. In short, it was a sorry spectacle, and I did not stop long in this den.

I was obliged to start for Mazatlan the next morning, and at break of day my friend of the preceding evening awoke me, and accompanied me to the American schooner on which I was to embark.

"Now you know all my affairs," said he to me, "what would you do in my place?"

"I should accept the ten millions already offered," I replied, "and then make for Europe as quickly as possible, to live there in peace."

"Pooh!" said he. "With my ten millions, which, in fact, would be reduced to five, since I have to share them, I should be nobody in London or Paris. Yes, I must have the twenty millions; I have nieces to portion."

Five years later, when riding through Cordova, a small town situated on the high-road from Vera-Cruz to Mexico, I alighted before a grocery shop, where I wanted to buy a box of fusees. What was my surprise on seeing behind the counter my San Franciscan acquaintance. The Mexican newspapers had spoken of his lawsuit, then of his imprisonment; some had even said that the title-deeds he produced were false. Jonan—I think I may mention his name without indiscretion—took me into the parlour behind his shop, and again related his history to me.

He had, in fact, been in gaol, and after two years of imprisonment, had succeeded in escaping.

"I ought to have followed your advice," said he to me; "but in order to secure my ten millions, I had the bright idea of changing the square roods on the title-deeds into square acres. This little game would have succeeded, and it would have been a smart piece of business to do the Yankees out of fifty million dollars; but, unfortunately, I had a quarrel with my partner. He wanted the lion's share, declaring that if I would not yield to his demands, he would expose me as a forger. I forestalled him, and made a clean breast of our little business to an American judge. We were imprisoned, but my partner managed to escape; and taking advantage of circumstances, in retaliation the Yankees at once declared all my title-deeds false, and pocketed the ten millions, which, if I had listened to your advice, I should have now possessed."

This confession, made very innocently, showed me that a twenty-years' stay in California can singularly deaden the conscience of even a Frenchman.

"After all," said the proprietor of the ground of San Francisco, "I still have several square miles in La Sonore, which the Americans will want to seize, sooner or later; but I shall have my revenge then, for this time my title-deeds are drawn up in good form: all the same, those Yankees are notorious scoundrels."

I have nothing further to tell you, dear readers, than that this is a true story.

TORTOISE ISLAND.

CHAPTER I.

Departure from Havre—Deerfoot—Señor Bandoin—Count Monistrol and Baron Martin—The trade winds—Equatorial calm—The Phaeton—An arrest.

Love of one's country is no imaginary feeling, as modern utopians pretend. Seven times from the deck of a steamboat I had seen the coast of France standing out clear against the horizon, and then disappearing again in proportion as the wind and steam bore us away from the land, and each time my heart beat painfully, and I felt a strange feeling of oppression. On these occasions I always take refuge at the stern, and there, unnoticed by any one, with moistened eyes I gaze on the shore and cliffs of my native country until there is nothing to be seen of them but a far-off bluish vapour. I shuddered at the thought that death might suddenly overtake me when far from this beloved land, and that my body would lie in strange ground; but I soon roused myself from these melancholy thoughts. I was twenty when I went on my first voyage, and I thought myself more master of my life than it was mistress of my destiny. It seemed to me impossible that my desires should not, sooner or later, become realities; it was only a question of waiting.

I have waited, or rather the hours, days, and years have rolled on without being waited for. How many buds, on the verge of blossoming, have perished without blooming! how many, which should never have withered, now strew the paths I have trodden with their discoloured petals! One must blend the ideal with the real in our lives; but if one would avoid a painful fall, ideas and dreams must not be too lofty. We should try as much as possible to remember that life never begins again, and that of the two faces she shows us, the past and the future, the last only really belongs to us.

On the 4th of January, 1853, I was standing on the poop of a brig, *en route* for Yucatan. Provided with a telescope, I watched Havre disappear behind Francis the First's Tower, which was pulled down several years ago in order to enlarge the entrance of the harbour. It was three o'clock in the afternoon, the sky was black, and the sea rough. After having taken us out to sea, the pilot lowered himself into his boat, and left us to our fate; and the *Zampa*, tossing and rolling, began bravely to cut through the waves, which seemed to try their utmost to bar her passage. A mist soon hid the land from view, and I turned my looks towards a sea-gull, which was following in our wake, uttering hoarse cries, and sometimes dipping its wings in the white foam. It was almost night when the bird flew twice round the ship, and then was lost in the mist.

For twelve days the *Zampa* struggled with this rough weather. At meal times, although feeling very uncomfortable, I took my place opposite the captain and the second mate. The cold was intense, and the deck, continually swept by the waves, afforded no shelter. Groans were continually rising from the depths of the cabin; and, being able to walk about, I was an object of envy to my fellow-travellers. Our crew was composed of eight sailors, who, through working night and day, were almost overcome with fatigue. No one on board was lively except "Deerfoot," who was continually humming to himself, and who might be seen almost at the same time at stem and stern, in the cabins or in the yards, as though he had the gift of being in two or three places at once. I followed his example as much as I could—that is to say, I ferreted about everywhere; but with a marked disadvantage. If, for instance, I started for the capstan the same time as Deerfoot, I invariably got there last; and when I thought I had reached him, I heard him whistling over my head, or answering the captain's call from some corner or other. It was a curious fact that every one on board was allowed to

order about Deerfoot, and the fragile little fellow found means
to satisfy every one. Never did I see such an active little being;
and yet he did not belong to the monkey tribe.

Deerfoot was fourteen years old; he had well-opened black
eyes, regular features, and a rough head of hair. He was born
on the coasts of Brittany, not far from Piriac. During the three
years in which he had sailed as cabin-boy, Deerfoot had visited
India, Brazil, Newfoundland, and Oceanica. When I could persuade him to talk for a minute, I led him on to tell me about
his voyages, and nothing was more amusing than the remarks of
this keen observer; and after all, of all the countries he had seen,
one only seemed to him beautiful, fertile, gay—his own. He
knew of nothing superior to the cottage where he was born,
where his mother was waiting for his return. The voyage to
Yucatan, where the yellow fever is so prevalent, is always well-
paid, and an increase of salary had tempted the cabin-boy to visit
Campeachy instead of New York. Deerfoot had his theories: he
firmly believed in God, and not at all in the yellow fever; or
rather, according to him, the disease would only attack silly
people. He only thought of one thing, which was the seventy-
five francs which his voyage was to gain him. He regarded his
seventy-five francs as an inexhaustible mine, and the *Zampa*
would not be able to contain the things he intended buying for
his mother with this sum so hardly earned. Deerfoot had
hardly reached the age I spoke of, when one thinks one's self
master of one's life. It is an undeniable fact that I quite forgot
the bad weather when I was able to get a few minutes' conversation with the little sailor. He repeated his words a little,
as blunt honest hearts have a way of doing, but one was never
tired of listening to him.

The life of a passenger on board ship is insupportable; the
idleness to which one is condemned makes the time seem
doubly long, and the unfortunate traveller carries his weariness
from stem to stern, and from deck to cabin. One cannot always
read, the walks backwards and forwards become irksome; nevertheless, exercise is beneficial. Thus it is that directly I go on
board a vessel, I place myself in apprenticeship and try to make

myself useful for my own sake. I go up into the yards, I learn the names of the rigging, how to manage the helm, and the hundred and one ways of tying a knot. Provided with this knowledge, I help the sailors in their work—at least, I look as if I were helping them, which gains their friendship. Without counting the captain, the second mate, and Deerfoot, I soon had other friends on board the *Zampa;* these were Mathurin, John, and Pornic. I do not know whether I ought to reckon Baudoin among the number.

Baudoin lived on deck in the boat placed near the mainmast. He was rather bad-tempered, and never left off grumbling. Gifted with a formidable and not at all delicate appetite, he was never satisfied. Deerfoot often reproached him on this account. However, this sulky, surly Baudoin was very good friends with me. I often obtained leave in the mornings for him to be allowed to walk about the deck; and the poor creature, as little accustomed to the pitching as to the rolling, tried to follow me, stumbling, picking himself up, and then, infuriated, taking refuge in his last resource of grunting. We had to use force to get him reinstated in his boat; for the captain, a strict observer of rules, would never allow a passenger of the 'tween decks to ascend the steps leading on to the poop. The reason of this rigour is not wanting in logic: a cabin passenger pays about twenty pounds, and a passenger of the 'tween decks only twelve; now, a sum of six pounds makes a gulf between two men, the depth of which is only known to those who have experienced a long sea-voyage.

At first sight one might think that a second-class passenger was necessarily an inferior being in every respect to a first-class passenger. Well, it may be strange, but such is not the case. In my seven voyages—I do not recall them for the sake of boasting—I have met with as many well-educated and intellectual men below the poop as above. I err: Baudoin was superior to no one; he was less a passenger than a victim, and the captain was right in excluding him from the reserved enclosure.

Baudoin was a victim! The shipowner's orders allowed of

no weakness on the part of the captain; he was to have the prisoner executed as soon as we should have reached a certain degree of latitude. What was the crime of the unfortunate creature? Alas! that incident to his race: he was good to eat. One evening, a fortnight after leaving Havre, as the wind had subsided for the moment and was content with filling out the sails, the captain, smoking his pipe on deck, answered Baudoin's grunting by bragging to me of his cook's talents. The bad weather had so far prevented the head steward from making a display of his culinary science. After the execution of Baudoin, I should eat—so the captain assured me—black puddings, sausages, ham, brawn, and bacon, such as I had never eaten before. This little enumeration is, I suppose, enough to let my readers know that Baudoin belonged to that class of pachydermous animals of which Mr. Isidore Geoffrey had made the family of the *Sulliens*, and which are called boars, sows, or hogs, according to their sex or age.

In passing, I may remark that, with fowls and turkeys, the animal that served as a dog to St. Antony is one of the greatest resources in long voyages. It is known at what epoch turkeys were civilized; but no one can tell the original type of the pig, so well-modified and transformed by English breeders. As for the fowl, it is thought to be a native of Persia, and what is known for a fact is, that India from the remotest times has furnished us with this useful species of bird. On the other hand, Europeans were greatly surprised to find domestic fowls in all the South Sea Islands. At Oualan, an island situated between the group of the Carolines and the Mulgravian Archipelago, although fowls were very plentiful, they were not used for food by the natives, who only learnt that they were good to eat from the crew of *la Coquille*. Fowls, turkeys, pigs, dogs, cats, horses, in fact, all domestic animals, vary very much in form, plumage, or skin, which greatly perplexes naturalists.

Climate has undoubtedly a great deal to do with these transformations, and it is to this that must be attributed a peculiarity met with on the south coast of the Gulf of Mexico, where one finds fowls with black flesh. Although disagreeable to look at, these negro fowls are quite as tender and savoury as any others. Do you doubt, my reader, that there is a country where black fowl is served up at table? I have many times been asked to take some, and have helped others to it.

Five weeks after leaving Havre, we were sailing on a tepid sea in splendid weather, and every one on board the *Zampa* had forgotten the hardships of the first fortnight. Four good mothers of families, with their children, had successively made their appearance on the 'tween decks, accompanied by four working-men, the fathers of this little colony.

At the table where I had for so long kept company with the captain and the second mate, I now found the widow of a planter, a good lady, but rather affected; then a fat gentleman, who, from his thick gold chain, his trinkets, studs, and rings, I took at first for a jeweller. I was mistaken. I was in the presence of a banker, who, having bought some land at Yucatan, was going to inspect it with a view to colonizing.

Twenty-four hours after Mr. Martin, Count Simeon de Monistrol made his appearance. He was young, well dressed, neither plain nor handsome, but a great fop. As soon as he had taken his place next to the widow, he talked to me of hardly anything else than his horses, his shooting-grounds, his estates, and, in lieu of ancestors, of his money. Noisy discussions took place between these two passengers, who had no sympathy with each other. The captain listened to their discussion with a knowing look, only interfering when it verged upon a dispute. As for myself, I found Monsieur Simeon too aristocratic, and Mr. Martin too wealthy, not to keep me at a distance.

In revenge, I paid attention to Doña Mencia and her daughter Clara, amiable Spanish ladies, living in Yucatan, but who had been brought up at Paris. Doña Mencia was a relative of one of my friends at Mexico; so we willingly enough formed an acquaintance. Nevertheless, we were much amused at our companions' discussions, especially when Monsieur Simeon de Monistrol styled Mr. Martin the *baron;* a title which we all soon adopted for the Crœsus.

The confidence shown me by Doña Mencia, drew on me from time to time a sarcastic remark from these gentlemen, especially when they saw me talking familiarly with the passengers of the 'tween decks. These good people knew nothing of America, thus they were glad of any information I could give them; and I prepared them somewhat for the difficulties and annoyances which they would be sure to meet with in this foreign land. Doña Mencia and her daughter took great interest in the women and the children, and every day distributed some of their own wardrobe among them.

Deerfoot, who had been obliged to serve as general valet to every one, rose still higher in my esteem. The sea no longer amused itself with playing him bad jokes and doubling his work, so that the cabin-boy had now a little leisure. I undertook to teach him to read; but soon Miss Clara replaced me at the lesson hour, as, taking the advice of the second mate, I profited by the fine weather to devote myself to fishing, or rather to letting out lines, which, after having floated from sunrise to sunset on the surface of the golden sea, returned fruitlessly to their box.

One day, a sailor of the name of Lambert, the only one with whom I was not intimate, brutally struck little Deerfoot. I snatched the lad from the coward's grasp, which action drew upon me a volley of coarse insults. Stunned by the blow, with a bleeding face the poor little lad crept up to Baudoin's boat, and there wept in silence, his sense of honour preventing him from making any complaint. This was not the first time Lambert had ill-treated the poor cabin-boy. In the evening, when all was quiet, and the captain and I were smoking together on the poop, Lambert came up to take the helm. I at once took the opportunity of speaking in a loud voice of the sailor's brutality and insolence; and the captain, who was ill-satisfied with the man's service, severely reprimanded him. Lambert made no reply; but when he was relieved from his watch, he passed close by me and swore that he would throw me in the sea on the first favourable opportunity. The threat did not frighten me; nevertheless I had received a warning, and not caring to take a bath in the open sea, I kept on my guard.

Three days after this, the captain came on deck just as Lambert was again ill-treating Deerfoot. The commander of the *Zampa* was a kind man, but he strictly enforced discipline. Lambert received a rough shaking in his turn; and the captain threatened to give him over to the first man-of-war we met, where he would learn obedience. Grumbling fiercely between his teeth, he declared, that not only would he throw me into the sea, but that he would send Deerfoot and the captain after me; which threat very much alarmed Doña Mencia and her daughter.

We were in search of the trade winds, which always blow in the direction of the diurnal movement of the sun; that is to say, from east to west. This phenomenon very much terrified the companions of Christopher Columbus; for seeing the wind blow persistently in the same direction, they feared they should never get back to Spain. Science now explains the natural cause of these trade winds. They are composed of an upper and lower current, produced by the unequal heat of two bodies of air, which thus glide one over the other to recover their equilibrium. Before this discovery, the cause of the wind was attributed to the rotation of the earth, the movement of which was thus almost palpable.

If sailors are eager to find the trade wind, they feel, nevertheless, some apprehension in approaching the equator; they dread the equatorial calms, which seem as though of eternal duration. There is not a breath of wind; the ship lies motionless; the sun's rays fall vertically on the deck, melting the pitch which joins the planks of the ship, and the sea is as smooth as glass, without the slightest movement. A month may pass thus before a tempest liberates the ship from this too placid serenity. Water and provisions become exhausted; the sailors, wearied by this monotonous calm, intently watch the horizon, and pray for the storm, which may prove so formidable to them.

Nothing in the way of disasters and vexations seemed to be wanting during our passage, and one morning we found ourselves caught in one of these disastrous calms. The captain

"SEIZE THAT WRETCH........"

became irritable; the count and the baron, being unable to breathe, were at last obliged to postpone for a time their interminable discussions. The ship, transformed into a furnace, was uninhabitable; thus we were obliged to live on deck. Assisted by the second mate, I made a sheltered seat on the poop for Doña Mencia and her daughter, who were stifled in their cabins; and every evening, turning towards the setting sun, we whistled for a breeze—an infallible means of obtaining one, according to the sailors.

We whistled for a week; and the cloudless sky tinged the sea with a deep blue. Seated at the stern of the *Zampa*, I spent many hours examining the transparent water, and gazing into its fathomless depths. Sometimes a sea-monster would make his appearance quite close to us: a whale, according to some, and a shark according to others; but it never stayed long enough for us to determine its real form. The *Zampa*, more motionless than if she had been lying at anchor in a river, creaked mournfully. There was not the slightest current; the things we threw overboard floated round the ship, and I was invariably unsuccessful in my fishing.

One afternoon we received a visit from a phaeton, commonly called a ring-tail. The phaeton lives between the tropics of Cancer and Capricorn; its manner of flying is graceful, and very powerful. The magnificent bird at first hovered above us, with outstretched wings, as though it were fastened to the sky; then, swooping gently down, it flew round our masts, and again soaring upwards, disappeared from our sight with a few strokes of its wings.

On the same day, hastily ascending from the hold where he made frequent inspections, in fear of a fire through spontaneous combustion, the captain ran to his cabin and reappeared, armed with a revolver. On a sign from him, Deerfoot violently rang the bell on board, to give an alarm. Passengers and sailors hurried on deck.

"Seize that wretch!" cried the captain, pointing to Lambert, "and bring him to me."

Lambert turned pale, and tried to get into the shrouds; but

seeing Mathurin in his way, he threw himself into an attitude of defence. On a second order, the sailors soon secured their companion.

"Put him in irons!" said the commander, sharply.

Then, whilst they were obeying him, and we looked on at this strange scene, the captain spoke rapidly to the second mate, who, whilst he listened, shook his fist at the prisoner.

CHAPTER II.

Scarcity of fresh water—The calm—Flying-fish—Dorado—Tropical grass—St. Domingo—Tortoise Island—Freebooters and pirates—An unexpected meeting.

HAD Lambert killed one of his mates? They were all capable of defending themselves, and none of them disposed to be ill-treated. Deerfoot was walking about the deck, so that he was out of the question. Although the sailors had unhesitatingly obeyed their captain's orders, they did not seem very ill-disposed towards their companion; they even smiled after having exchanged a few words with the helmsman, who had just come up after the captain from the hold.

"The beer ration will be doubled now," said Mathurin to Pornic. "If the shipowner had an idea of this, it would be enough to prevent him from sleeping."

"Provided there is enough on board."

"There is too much," replied Mathurin. "For my own part, I stowed away forty or fifty barrels."

"To the pumps!" cried the second mate.

The work at the pumps was an exercise in which I always joined; so I ran to my post. The *Zampa* had been recently repaired, and seemed proof against anything, and the work at the pumps might be considered as a simple precaution. This time, to my great surprise, water was flowing from the ship's sides; and I afterwards learnt that Lambert, in an excess of mad folly, had bored holes through all the reservoirs containing our supply of fresh water, and it was this precious reserve that we were throwing into the sea!

Nevertheless, the offence, grave as it was, did not seriously annoy me. I knew what an enormous supply of wine and beer the ship contained, and the idea of thirst and its intolerable sufferings was done away with. The culprit, humble, dumb, and struck with consternation, was placed at the foot of the mainmast near Baudoin, who protested against this by energetic grunts.

At dinner time we found the dishes rather salt, and the cook was accused of having a heavy hand. The poor steward justified himself by saying, that for want of fresh water he had been obliged to use sea-water, to which—he assured us quite seriously, —we should accustom ourselves in a fortnight. Mr. Martin drank the wine pure, M. de Monistrol did the same; but the ladies, from habit, were wanting water every minute, and sadly turned away their heads when Deerfoot roguishly offered to draw some from the ocean for them. The passengers of the 'tween decks were as pleased as the crew at the double ration of beer distributed among them. The captain was the only one who seemed at all anxious.

Next morning, at the time Deerfoot usually filled our cabin cans, he was less parsimonious than usual, and generously distributed a liquid full of salt, soda, potash, magnesia, chalk, iodine, etc. By reason of which numerous ingredients, sea-water has the vexatious property of neither cooking meat nor vegetables, and of stoutly refusing all combination with soap.

I must confess that Lambert's trick now appeared to me in a new and disagreeable light. At the end of a week, we were literally dying of thirst, doubly intensified by the air, and the enforced use of pure wine. One afternoon, guided by Providence, a score of flying-fish settled on our deck. The steward at once seized the clumsy creatures, and cooked them, and we found their white, delicate flesh a great luxury.

The flying-fish, or *exocet* (a word derived from the Greek, meaning *out of its house*), is about the size of a herring. Its back has a beautiful bluish tint, and its pectoral fins, which are large, allow of its not only rising in the air, but of its skimming over the ocean at a distance of about a yard from the water. The flying-fish is often seen under the tropical rays darting like an arrow, flying from the pursuits of the hungry dorado, which often snaps up the fugitive just as its dried fins oblige it to fall back into the water.

When the sea is calm, the *exocet*, which almost always flies horizontally, goes for several hundred yards; but when the water is rough, it springs from wave to wave, and seems to bound like the flat stones with which children amuse themselves in making ducks and drakes. They almost always swim in shoals, and they spread themselves out by millions around ships, the enormous bulk of which probably astonishes them.

Twenty-four hours after the capture of the *exocets*, just as I was drawing in my line, which floated from morning to night at the stern, I felt something heavy at the end, which augured well. Little by little, with Deerfoot's assistance, I landed a dorado, a yard long, the brilliant colour of which was a cause of general admiration. The fine fish struggled for a long while in painful agony, and its body assumed successively all the colours of the rainbow, a phenomenon well known to sailors.

A slight cloud was at last seen on the bluish horizon, and was hailed by loud hurrahs from the crew. It floated along, grew larger, and then was lost in the golden mist of the setting sun. I awoke in the middle of the night; it seemed to me that the ship, leaning on the port side, was creaking more than usual. I was not deceived; we were moving, and the masts of the *Zampa* were furnished with sails. Setting foot on deck, I uttered a cry of surprise; we were surrounded by *tropical grass;* we might have thought ourselves in the midst of an immense prairie.

The onward progress of the vessel enlivened us a little, and we wanted something to cheer us up, for we felt low-spirited and dull enough. The crew had begun to feel the bad effects of the want of fresh water, and to complain of it. Our lips were parched and bleeding, and the wine, far from appeasing the intolerable thirst to which we were a prey, only served to increase it. The women especially suffered from this state of things. Mr. Martin would have willingly given a thousand crowns, and M. de Monistrol one of his castles, to any one who could have offered him a glass of pure fresh water, as each of them remembered having quaffed with delight.

Campeachy, the place of our destination, was still too far off for it to be possible for us to reach it without renewing our supply of fresh water; our health would have failed, and the captain thought of putting into port. He resolved to take us to Tortoise Island, in order to avoid paying anchorage, pilotage, and tonnage dues, required of every vessel which enters a harbour open to commerce. Thus the bow of the *Zampa* was turned in this direction.

I was pleased with this slight alteration of the ship's course, and not at all sorry to visit the ancient fortress of the bold pirates who, in the fifteenth and sixteenth centuries, were the cause of so much harm to Spanish commerce, and gave St. Domingo to France. On the 25th of February, the day on which we ought to have reached Campeachy if our passage had been accomplished regularly, we came in sight of the French cape, and, coasting alongside the large island of Hayti, we saw rising to our left, the crests of the Cibao Mountains. The Island of St. Domingo, called Hispaniola by Christopher Columbus, was, in 1495, the seat of the first European settlement in America. It became legally French at the peace of Ryswick—that is to say, in 1697. A century later, the National Assembly having decreed the emancipation of the negroes, the result of this liberal proceeding was the massacre of the white people, and Hayti proclaimed its independence.

The sight of land increased our sufferings, and the captain had hard work to resist the passengers' entreaties that we might land at once; but he had the shipowner's interests to consider before us. So he shut himself up in his cabin to avoid our complaints. The wind was favourable, but still the *Zampa's* progress did not satisfy our impatience.

Under any other circumstances, this unexpected *détour* in our voyage would have been full of interest, and we should have left the land behind us without any feelings of regret. As fishing-boats were sailing between us and the shore, we hoped to see one come near enough to sell us fruit or to give us a supply of water. Vain hope! In order to get what we wanted, we should have been obliged to make signals and heave to; and our captain had but one care, which was to advance and make up for lost time.

Often very pretty birds, led by their own caprice, or carried by the wind, would perch among our rigging, and then as unexpectedly fly away again. I even met with a poor butterfly, with purple and blue wings, which I presented to Doña Clara. Placed by the young girl in a luxurious bed of cotton wool at the bottom of a little box, the beautiful lepidoptera succumbed during the night; which I believe cost its new mistress a tear.

Crouching at the foot of the mainmast, a victim, like ourselves, to his wicked prank, Lambert would look at us with wild, hopeless eyes. Discipline, without which a long voyage would become impossible, required that he should be given over to the first man-of-war we met; and there the unfortunate creature would have to serve for a year or two, in addition to the corporal punishment he would receive. The women, notwithstanding their sufferings, were the only ones who had self-denial and goodness enough to pity the prisoner.

I am wrong. Deerfoot, under pretence of attending to Baudoin, who owed a prolongation of his life to the want of water, often lingered near Lambert and talked to him.

"If he had the chance, sir," said the good little cabin-boy to me, "he would not do it again, for he is dreadfully sorry for his wickedness. He has already served on board a man-of-war; and with the bad character he will get from here, he will scarcely be able to find another berth. He says it was not his fault, it was his bad temper. He has asked me to forgive him for having beaten me, and he is even sorry at having insulted you. Do you know, sir, we ought to try and beg the captain to let him off."

Doña Mencia and her daughter had soon drawn up a petition; but the second mate, to whom I spoke of the proceeding, assured me that it would be useless. The captain would be obliged to give strict account to the shipowner of the events on board, especially when they had such serious results as those which at present were taking us to Tortoise Island. On the other hand, to allow such an infraction of discipline to go unpunished, would be to make the captain appear unworthy of his position as commander. Nevertheless, far from being discouraged by these reasons, Doña Mencia resolved to wait until the reservoirs should be full of water, and the nearness to port make all hearts less implacable.

"I shall beg the captain so hard that I shall obtain at least an alleviation of this poor sailor's punishment," said Doña Clara. "I ask you as a favour," added she, looking at me beseechingly, "not to complain so loudly nor so often of being thirsty before the captain; I have noticed that it irritates him still more against Lambert."

I promised, and kept my word.

At last the coast of St. Domingo disappeared; a bluish line, which grew rapidly larger, stretched before us. It was Tortoise Island. The followers of Columbus must certainly have experienced a lively joy when they first discovered America; that is to say, the Island of Guanahani, or San Salvador. I doubt, nevertheless, whether their joy was greater than ours at the sight of the tall Mimosas which border the northern coast of the ancient pirate stronghold.

Although about thirty miles in length, Tortoise Island is only accessible by the channel which separates it from Hayti. All its northern coast is surrounded with rocks; but our captain, whom I then suspected of having once been a smuggler, seemed to know all the ins and outs of the coast lying before us. Towards five o'clock the *Zampa*, skilfully steered, entered a little creek and cast anchor about a mile and a half from land.

The long-boat was got ready, lowered, and loaded with empty casks. My reputation as a worker gained for me, as well as two of the passengers of the 'tween decks, the good fortune of taking part in this expedition. This favour provoked energetic protest from Baron Martin and the Count de Monistrol, who seemed to consider this privilege as a want of respect to them. The captain left these august persons to grumble to their hearts' content, and got into the boat where three sailors and Deerfoot had already taken their places. Night came on as we landed.

Rolling the barrels along, we began to climb the rocks, which was no easy matter when, like the burden of Sisyphus, the casks were continually threatening to fall back on us. When we had reached the summit of the rocks the captain seemed to hesitate for a moment; then, giving us the order to halt, he descended the hill-side. After a quarter of an hour's absence he returned, visibly satisfied. Following his steps, at the risk of being crushed by the fall of our barrels, we came to the source of a small stream gushing from a rock, into the basin of which I unceremoniously plunged with a cry of delight.

The first cask was filled, an operation which took no less than two hours. Not wishing to lose time, nor be surprised in the act of landing, the captain was anxious to set sail again at break of day; thus he urged us on to work without intermission. But if the barrels were filled without any trouble, it was no slight work to get them back to the shore. I had to remain and watch the thin stream of water which a zinc gutter, brought for this purpose, conveyed straight to the bung-holes of the casks; whilst my companions, perspiring, panting, and relieving each other from time to time, were occupied in rolling the casks to the shore. On their return, they told me that the captain, Deerfoot, and Mathurin had gone back to the ship, taking the water, which we found so delicious, to the poor creatures so anxiously waiting for it.

When the sun rose, only three of our barrels were embarked. The workmen, overcome with fatigue, stretched themselves beside the fourth cask and went to sleep. I had neither the courage to blame nor oppose them taking their well-earned rest, and in the mean time amused myself botanizing.

The island being well-populated, I was surprised to see no

"ROLLING THE BARRELS......."

trace revealing the presence of man, and more astonished still that the approach of the *Zampa* had not attracted any of the inhabitants. We were at the bottom of a gorge, where only a few Mimosas were to be seen growing here and there. I climbed the slope in front of me, and as soon as I reached the top, I looked down into a deep valley which I could see, as well as another low range of hills. I caught sight of a hut in the distance, and was rather startled by suddenly hearing a cock crow, and then a dog bark.

I sat down, happy at being able to see trees, flowers, birds, and butterflies, after spending so many days between sea and sky; it was an infinite pleasure to tread on firm ground, and inhale the fragrant odours. It seemed strange to be on this island, which owes its name to its form, and plays an important part in the history of France. I recalled to mind the names of the bold pirates whose histories have been related by Oexmelin and Archenholz, heroes who, after having taken Panama in 1670, Maracaibo in 1677, Vera-Cruz in 1683, Carthagena in 1697, would perhaps have conquered America, had their policy been equal to their courage.

I remembered that the first adventurers who settled on Tortoise Island came from the Island of St. Christopher, then possessed both by the English and French. After disembarking, the new comers at once divided themselves into three classes, which are often mistaken one for the other: the *buccaneers*, or hunters; the *filibusters*, or pirates; the *inhabitants*, or cultivators.

The buccaneers took their name from the wooden hurdle, *boucan*, which they made use of in drying the flesh of animals killed for their skins. It was at the expense of the Spaniards, who made no scruple of occasionally killing them, that the buccaneers exercised their industry. Bold, brave, and accustomed to a life of hardships, the buccaneers were easily transformed into filibusters.

The latter, who were true pirates, often gave chase to the Spanish vessels, and sometimes ravaged the coasts of Mexico and Peru, and made the cities pay ransom. As to the *inhabitants*, a people of more regular habits, they slowly and honestly heaped up fortunes through their agricultural employments.

The greater part of the French and English adventurers were driven from Tortoise Island by the Spaniards, who were inconvenienced by their proximity. But the buccaneers, under the command of the Englishman Willis, regained possession of their fortress, firmly established themselves there, and resumed their excursions on the Island of St. Domingo. The French, thus consigned to the second rank, demanded aid from their compatriots, settled in the Island of St. Christopher, and the Chevalier de Poincy, who commanded in these coasts, listened favourably to their request. M. le Vasseur, engineer to the king, embarked on Tortoise Island in 1640, at the head of forty soldiers, and as many volunteers. The English decamped without offering battle, and the conqueror at once employed his men in building the fort of La Roche, which still exists.

Thus master of a little kingdom, Le Vasseur busied himself in duly administering the government. He repulsed an attack of the Spaniards; but the desire to enrich himself made him hard, cruel, and unjust, and he was assassinated by two of his officers. The Chevalier de Fontenay then took his place, and the freebooters, sure of finding a protector here, resumed their marauding expeditions. Exasperated by the losses from which they suffered, the Spaniards had recourse to strong measures, banished the chevalier, and were soon after dislodged by M. de Rossey, who gave up the island to M. d'Ogeron, the representative of the French Company in the West Indies.

The filibusters reckon the Englishman Morgan as one of their most celebrated chiefs; it was under his command that they took Panama. Pierre Legrand, whose adventurous life was quite a romance, one day, with a boat equipped by twenty-eight men, took possession of a Spanish ship carrying fifty-two guns. Nau L'Olannais and Michel le Basque, at the head of four hundred filibusters, accomplished marvels of daring; unfortunately, they were as cruel as they were brave, and animated with undying hatred against the Spaniards, they more than once dishonoured their victories. Finally, Montbars, surnamed the *Exterminator*, pillaged Vera-Cruz in 1683; he was the last of the great filibusters.

I was in the midst of my reveries, and as the sun rose above the horizon, I saw the plain stretching at my feet display its healthy and varied vegetation. Suddenly a rustling of leaves and sound of broken branches was heard. I got up, expecting to see some animal make its appearance; but it was no other than the prisoner of the *Zampa*, my enemy, the sailor Lambert.

CHAPTER III.

Return to the ship—The captain and Doña Clara—A man-of-war—The pursuit—Prisoners!—Baudoin's departure—The spermaceti whales—Campeachy—Lambert again—André-Marie.

I QUICKLY sprang to a tree, and stood with my back against it. I confess I felt some misgivings, as I had no weapons; and a hand to hand struggle could only show me in a very practical manner a truth which I had not the least doubt of in theory: the muscular superiority of a sailor's arms. Nevertheless, I put on a brave face, and made up my mind to give blow for blow, as far as possible.

Lambert had stood still, and was deliberately watching me. Seeing me pick up a dry branch, which would have been a very inferior weapon, he held out both his hands to me.

"I do not wish you any harm, sir; on the contrary, I have come to beg of you."

"How is it you are free?"

"I escaped this morning by swimming. The ladies on board took off my irons."

"There," thought I, "that is generosity, which will cost me dearly."

Lambert drew nearer.

"I have done wrong," said he to me. "You can see I do not hesitate to confess my wickedness; but I don't want to go on board a man-of-war; I want to get my living. I mean to go to St. Domingo, and take service on board the first American coasting-vessel that wants a sailor, and to make up for my wickedness by behaving well."

"Does not your desertion expose you to some severer punishment in the future, than that from which you are now flying?"

"It condemns me to exile; but I have got my liberty, which I want, as I have told you. Besides, time settles many things."

"What do you want?"

"A little money, a loan," said Lambert to me, turning red. "I have some way to go before I reach the Cape, and the negroes are not always hospitable."

I had not been thirsty since the preceding evening; I was happy at being able to tread the ground, and to hear the birds warbling; added to this, the penitent look of the sailor, from whom I had at first dreaded violence, disposed me to be compassionate. I could not help pitying the unfortunate creature, whom an outbreak of passion placed in a position which might end in a long exile for him. I thought I ought to give him a little advice, which he listened to patiently enough, whilst at the same time on the *qui vive* for the slightest sound. He was afraid that his escape was perceived; that the captain in his wrath would have a search made for him. A sharp whistle was heard. I ended my lecture by giving the sailor my purse, which contained five pounds. He pressed my hand warmly, and at the sound of a second whistle darted off, running down the wooded slope towards the valley.

I turned round to go back to the spring, and met Mathurin. The whistling was for me. The last cask ought to have been embarked, and the captain was signalling for us to rejoin the *Zampa*. Mathurin did not say a word to me about Lambert, and I took care not to speak of my meeting with him. On reaching the crest of the rocks overlooking the sea, I cast a last look on Tortoise Island, which I had no hopes of seeing again; then I embarked, taking with me a wonderful bouquet of wild flowers for Doña Mencia.

It was about ten o'clock, and the captain, attributing the delay to me, when it was really caused by the fatigue of the workmen, accosted me rather gruffly on my return to the ship.

I was silent; the most prudent conduct in dealing with an irritated man, but my reticence was really due to Doña Mencia and her daughter, who from the poop were making signs to me to be silent, and to go to them.

"Has Lambert spoken to you?" asked the young girl rapidly, in a low voice.

"Yes; he is now in safety. Has the captain discovered his escape?"

"Not yet," said Doña Mencia; "and we are not quite easy about the poor man."

I glanced in the direction of the old salt, who, anxious to lose no time in setting sail again, was busy giving the crew countless orders.

"You would do well to go to your cabins, and shut yourselves up there," said I to the ladies. "The captain does not seem in the least humour for joking; and there will be a tremendous storm when he finds out the prisoner's escape."

"Do you think he will be seriously angry?" asked Doña Mencia of me.

"I am quite sure of it," I replied.

"I shall remain, then," said Doña Clara resolutely; "his anger might fall on some innocent person, and I am ready to answer for my deed."

"For our deed, my child," eagerly added Doña Mencia, kissing her daughter.

The *Zampa* had just left the creek, and, with sails spread, was making for the open sea. The sailors were busy in the rigging when one of them, perched on the topmast, cried—

"Ship in sight."

The captain sprang on to the poop, seized a telescope, and scoured the horizon.

"A man-of-war," said he, after a steady examination, "and she is bearing down upon us. If she is French, I will let her have Master Lambert, although I lose another half-day by it."

Whilst speaking, the captain had turned towards the mainmast.

"By all the powers!" cried he, "where is the prisoner?"

The brave captain was the only one on board who was not aware of the sailor's escape. Every one felt a slight tremor as his infuriated glance rested successively on all the bystanders. As nobody uttered a word, the name of Deerfoot came like a thunderbolt from the captain's compressed lips; and this imperious call was answered by a voice from the top of the mainmast.

"I beg your forgiveness, sir," said Doña Clara, advancing towards the captain with clasped hands and tears in her eyes.

The commander took the pipe from his mouth and stood still, expecting an explanation.

"Forgiveness for whom?" asked he at last.

"For the poor sailor whom I assisted to escape."

"To escape!" repeated the captain, looking at the sea which surrounded us.

"Lambert swam to Tortoise Island in the night," said I, in my turn.

"Not with his handcuffs, I suppose?"

"I took them off him," said Doña Clara, with a slight tremble in her voice.

"Then, is every one captain here except myself?" roared the old seaman.

"No, no, captain," I said eagerly; "you are the sole master on board the *Zampa*. You have the right to put Doña Clara in irons, and not one of us, I swear, will say a word against this just punishment."

"By Heaven! sir, this is nothing to joke about, and you may learn to your cost that discipline is no idle word on board the ship I have the honour to command. Who gave her the key of the handcuffs?"

"I did," bravely answered Deerfoot, turning as red as a bullfinch.

Without making any remark, the captain began to stride backwards and forwards, taking vigorous pulls at his pipe, and muttering incoherent words to himself. Now, when two ships are making for each other, they meet with incredible rapidity, and the ship we had hailed was already clearly visible to our right. The captain examined her several times through his telescope and seemed perplexed.

"Hoist the ensign," said he to a sailor standing near the steersman.

In less than five minutes the tricolour flag was waving in the breeze. The vessel in sight at once responded to our politeness, and the red and blue Haïtien flag was displayed from her masts.

"That makes all the difference," muttered the captain. "To the sails, lads," he shouted.

In less than ten minutes the *Zampa's* course was slightly altered, and we were sailing parallel with the little man-of-war. Almost at the same time, the sides of the schooner were enveloped in a white smoke and a cannon-shot was heard. It was an order to continue our first route or to heave to and wait.

The captain, humming a French ditty, again carefully examined his vessel, and then returned to his study of the schooner.

"This fine tropical bird," said he after a time, "would like us to give account for our landing. Unfortunately, I have not time to satisfy her curiosity. They are too impatient to see us at Campeachy. The wind is good, and we are out of gun-reach; we will make acquaintance another time. Leave the flag on the mast, Mathurin; if we do fly we are not ashamed of showing our colours."

The captain's attention being thus suddenly distracted, his wrath had time to cool down. He spent an hour directing the sailors and convincing himself that our speed surpassed that of the man-of-war. This was an incontestible fact, and the captain again hummed to himself with an air of satisfaction. We were going a little out of our way; but we should resume the right direction again under cover of night, when we should pass within gun-shot of the enemy without his seeing us. Thus it was that the captain, rubbing his hands, came up to Doña Clara to reproach her for her felony, in a voice which, in spite of his intention, was not very terrifying.

The young girl at first threatened with having her little wrists handcuffed, had not much trouble in obtaining pardon. One of Deerfoot's ears was lightly pulled just for the satisfaction due to discipline, and Doña Mencia had to submit to a long lecture which was indirectly meant for my benefit. After all, it was quite a relief to the passengers and crew of the *Zampa* to lose sight of the unfortunate Lambert from the deck. Baudoin was the only one who had to complain; his sentence was pronounced, and the hour of his execution fixed for the moment we should have lost sight of the Haïtien ship.

Following our manœuvres, the schooner tried to interrupt our route; the wind was favourable to her and she slowly but surely bore down upon us, greatly to our captain's disgust. The wind suddenly changed, and without the slightest hesitation the captain ordered to tack about; and as in the time of the filibusters, there we were flying before the wind from a ship which suspected us of smuggling, and wanted to know our reason for landing on Tortoise Island.

The *Zampa* was not a good vessel for speed except on a certain tack; but our captain understood his business, and we took an infinite amount of pleasure in the chase which was given us. Our excitement could not have been greater had we been flying before a privateer; one would have thought that certainly our honour and liberty were at stake. The enemy, being better manned, was making more speed than we did, and driving us towards the coast. What had at first seemed to me a good joke soon became a serious matter. If the schooner reached us, she would undoubtedly oblige us to go to the Cape, there to explain our conduct. This would cause a delay and a series of complications which somewhat troubled the captain. For a quarter of an hour he regretted his whim, and thought of making towards the schooner, in order to come to a friendly understanding with the Haïtien commander. But having weighed the different chances of his plan, and being convinced by further calculation that the schooner could not reach us before nightfall, he determined to continue his flight.

Dinner was soon over, and returning on deck, we were dazzled by the rays of the setting sun. Our vessel was enveloped in a golden mist; the sky was red, and magnificent clouds hovered over the hills on the coast; but this grand spectacle was lost upon us, as our attention was riveted on the schooner. The little ship was still following in our wake, and had gained enough on the *Zampa* for us to be able to distinguish her rigging and see her crew at work. When the sun disappeared, another cannon-shot again intimated an order for us to heave to; to which injunction Deerfoot replied by disrespectfully putting the thumb of his right hand to the end of his nose, while the other fingers were rapidly moved up and down. This vulgar piece of impudence, practised between sea and sky at more than a thousand miles from Paris, amused us more than I can say.

M. de Monistrol gaily took part in the chase; but Mr. Martin seemed very uneasy.

"Bullets will come after the powder," said he; "and who will guarantee that one of their balls may not reach me?"

"No one, certainly," replied the captain; "so in your place I should take refuge in the hold."

This question of bullets, brought up by the rich banker, did not fail to make Doña Mencia and her daughter rather uneasy. I reassured them by saying, that if our pursuer thought of saluting us with a cannon-ball, he would take care to send it so as to frighten, but not to send us to the bottom. The truth is, the schooner had perfect right to lodge a ball in the hull of the *Zampa*; and if she had not already done so, it was because the distance between us was too great.

Night came on, a dark night with no moon, under cover of which our captain hoped to make good his flight. He ordered perfect silence on board, and no light was allowed. Towards midnight the *Zampa's* course was again changed, and with the wind favourable, she again sailed in the direction of Campeachy at a medium speed of not less than eight knots an hour.

I went to bed late, and awoke with a start, at the noise of a formidable report. Day was breaking. I was dressed, and I hurried on deck. At less than two hundred yards, a little in advance of us, was the Haïtien schooner, which this time had just given us an imperative order to heave to, which would have been dangerous to brave.

The sails of the *Zampa* were one by one lowered, but the ship continued her onward course, carried by the force of impulsion, and then became stationary. Half an hour later, a boat, manned by six negro rowers, came alongside of us; and a mulatto, dressed in an overcoat, white trousers, and blue necktie, stepped on our deck. The new comer, of gigantic stature, wore an immense epaulette fastened on to his chest in token of his position as lieutenant. He came in quest of our captain, who at this moment was deep in thought and visibly annoyed.

A glass of rum was offered to the Haïtien officer, who, after having helped himself to a second tumblerful, unceremoniously passed the bottle to his sailors. We could see from the poop all that was going on on board the man-of-war, whose half-naked crew were in their turn watching us with no small curiosity.

The captain of the schooner was a negro. Near him stood a European, dressed in English uniform. They had taken us for a slave-ship, and it was a question of reconducting us to Tortoise Island to make inquiries. As a consolation, the lieutenant, showing his white teeth, told me that I should have for my prison the palace built by the sister of Napoleon Pauline Bonaparte, then the wife of General Leclerc, when the latter, at the head of twenty thousand men, who were soon brought low by the fatal climate, tried, in 1802, to restore St. Domingo to French dominion.

Just as they were returning to the boat which was to take off our captain, he suddenly gave orders for Baudoin to be embarked. The unfortunate guest of the long-boat, disturbed by such unusual proceedings, began to utter such shrill cries, that a certain amount of agitation was visible on board the strange vessel.

"They will think that we are killing their lieutenant, and will fire upon us!" cried Mr. Martin, in a state of alarm.

Fortunately, nothing of the kind happened; and in less than an hour after his departure, our captain came back triumphant. Baudoin had served as ransom for us. The gift of his elegant person compensated, in the eyes of the commandant, for the infraction of maritime laws we had committed, in landing where there was no port opened to commerce.

"Ah, well!" said a voice; "I should have been sorry to have seen poor piggy killed."

The speaker was Deerfoot, and the poor piggy alluded to was Baudoin, who passed a sad quarter of an hour, judging from the cries carried back to us by the breeze.

The *Zampa's* sails were unfurled, the crew of the Haïtien vessel gave three hurrahs, the French and Haïtien flags were hoisted as a polite farewell, and, towards nine o'clock in the morning, we had lost sight of the schooner and the coast of Tortoise Island.

A fortnight after this adventure, without any other incident worth notice occurring, except meeting with two sperm-whales, we were sailing in Campeachy Sound.

At last we entered the harbour of Campeachy, where European ships come in quest of the precious wood so valuable in dyeing.

Campeachy did not escape the marauding attacks of the filibusters of Tortoise Island, who pillaged it twice; it then had an extensive commerce in wax, which at the present day is much diminished.

I was obliged to go to Tabasco in a coasting vessel, and the day following our arrival I reluctantly parted with my fellow-travellers. But see what human greatness amounts to! A letter from Doña Mencia, announcing that she and her daughter had arrived safely at Merida, informed me at the same time that M. Simeon de Monistrol was a clerk in a dry goods store, who had an opening offered him by one of the best houses in Merida, and that the banker, Mr. Martin, exercised the honourable functions of head steward. I now understood our captain's sly smiles, who, knowing the social position of these two gentlemen, chuckled to himself at their pretentions to nobility, their grand disdainful airs, and their visible contempt for us.

Years passed on. One evening, when at New Orleans, I was sitting in a small tavern near the harbour, where I had been taken to taste a plate of fried oysters, the national dish of the capital of Louisiana, when a sailor entered, and directly he saw me, came up to me. I had already recognized Lambert.

"How glad I am to see you again, sir," said he, holding out his hand to me. "How is it that I have happened to find you here?"

I answered his question, and motioned to him to take a seat near me.

"Have you made your fortune?" I asked him.

"No, but I have earned a good deal of money; for the Americans, who are in want of sailors, pay much higher wages than our shipowners. But my foolish freak made me, and still makes me, very wretched."

"How is that?"

"For two years I have been dreadfully home-sick. I would give anything to see France again, but I dare not show my face there. Nothing enlivens me, sir; I feel low-spirited and have no appetite. The doctor on board says that I suffer from melancholy. I am home-sick, I know that, and I can't get over it."

Lambert spoke in a dejected tone, and, suddenly bursting into tears, refused the oysters and beer which I had ordered for him. I was deeply touched. He possessed excellent certificates from the American captains under whom he had served. So the following day I set to work. Seconded by the lieutenant of the French man-of-war stationed at New Orleans, I was fortunate enough to obtain pardon for the deserter, with only a slight penalty.

"By-the-by," I asked, whilst accompanying him to the vessel which was to take him back to his country, "do you know what has become of Deerfoot?"

"Little Jack? He is dead, sir; died from the yellow fever. Poor Jack! it was his example that made a better man of me. For two years I have forwarded to his widowed mother a sum equal to what her son would have gained. I never thought to see you again, and I gave the poor woman the money you lent me."

I pressed Lambert's hand, and saddened by the news I had

just heard, returned on shore. The memory of the little cabin-boy had done me good as well as the rough sailor. Whenever I have anything to find fault with in my fellow-creatures, I think of the generous child, whose coffin is rocked beneath the waves, and for his sake I forgive or forget.

A WATERSPOUT AT SEA.

St. Thomas—The Reverend Mr. Smith—The waterspout at sea—A wish realized—Fears calmed.

A FORTNIGHT after leaving Southampton, on the 17th of June, 186—, the fine English steamer, *Magdalena*, sighted the Island of St. Thomas. This is about one of the longest passages that steamers make without calling anywhere; thus their supply of coals becomes exhausted. Passing between two hills crowned with forts, we were saluted by the garrison, composed of a score of Danish soldiers, and we found ourselves in a kind of chasm formed by perpendicular rocks. At the bottom of this chasm the houses of the town were built in five rows, in the shape of an amphitheatre. Europeans landing for the first time on American soil go into raptures at the sight of the stunted palm-trees which grow on this stony soil, barren enough in reality.

St. Thomas Island is only about two leagues in extent, and possesses no other drinkable water than that which falls from the sky during the storms. It is, nevertheless, the centre of an important and extensive commerce, for the Danes have made it a free port. It is to this island that the merchants of St. Domingo, Cuba, Jamaica, Guadeloupe, Barbadoes, Trinidad, in a word, all the West Indian islands, come in search of European merchandise.

Whilst the *Magdalena* was taking in her supply of coal, I visited the town, which had been recently shaken by a violent earthquake. With the exception of the quay, which runs along in front of the sea-shore, the streets of St. Thomas are only accessible by narrow flights of steps. Negroes and mulattos make up the majority of the population in these streets, and it is a curious spectacle to meet at every step negresses dressed in the latest Parisian fashions, and affecting the manners of grand ladies. There are enough caricatures here to employ the pencil of a Cham or Daumier for years; in short, these ladies play with their fans, in imitation of Spanish graces, firmly believing themselves models of elegance.

The day following our putting into port, the *Magdalena* again continued her route, carrying with her several new passengers, among whom were a Spanish pilot who was to take us to the Havannahs, and a Protestant clergyman who was going to Jamaica. I had dined with him the evening before, in the same hotel; he spoke French very well, and I was glad to have him as my cabin companion.

It was daybreak at half-past five. The eastern sky was streaked with fiery red, and for a quarter of an hour it seemed as though we were sailing through a sea of blood. The atmosphere was heavy. Not a wave disturbed the surface of the slumbering sea; not a breath of the wind which every morning freshened, in some degree, the burning soil of the Island of St. Thomas was to be felt.

"We are now on the coasts where waterspouts are almost daily occurrences," said the Reverend Mr. Smith to me; "nevertheless, this is the fifth time that I have sailed in these waters, and I have never once happened to see them disturbed by the least storm."

"Neither have I," I replied; "and I consider myself all the more fortunate."

"A waterspout at sea," resumed the pastor, "must be a marvellous spectacle! One of my friends assured me yesterday that he had never left St. Thomas without seeing one in the distance. He will be disappointed to-day, for that is his ship following in our wake."

The sun rose in gorgeous splendour in the clear azure sky; the sea lay before us like a vast sheet of glass; not a cloud to be seen, not a breath of wind. The sails of a small schooner lying to our left, were hanging limp against the masts.

I followed my companion to our cabin, to help him arrange his luggage, and then we were summoned to breakfast.

All at once the wheels of our steamer ceased turning.

"They are going to sound," said the clergyman to me.

"It is neither the place nor the time," I replied. "I am inclined to think that there is something amiss with the engine."

We hurried on deck. The sea was still calm, and there was no breeze. I saw the captain standing at the bows with his telescope in his hand, and the crew grouping round him. On examining the horizon from the starboard side, I thought I saw foam-crested waves, and a thin black column rising upwards to the sky.

"What is it?" I asked of a sailor.

"A waterspout!" he replied, pointing to the western horizon.

The clergyman seized my arm, and our eyes were riveted on the thin column, looking in the distance like a gigantic mast. A sudden squall filled the sails of the schooner, which, taken by surprise, lay on her side. She did not right herself until a sharp gust of wind covered our deck with a fine rain, carrying away some of our rigging. A low, rumbling sound was heard, and the column, which grew larger as it became more distinctly visible, rapidly approached us. The sea grew rough, and the deck was covered with flakes of foam. The schooner had reefed her sails. We saw her rising and sinking, leaning sometimes to the right and sometimes to the left, and tossing about like a nutshell; whilst the terrible column, now like two funnels placed end to end, came steadily onwards.

All the steamer's crew—officers, sailors, engineers, stokers, stewards—were on deck, whilst most of the passengers had taken refuge in their cabins, especially the ladies, whose sobs and frightened screams seemed to increase the horror of the terrible shipwreck to which we were apparently condemned.

"Why do they not fire the guns to break down that pillar of water?" asked the clergyman of a sailor.

"THE COLUMN SEEMED TO HAVE TWO TUNNELS."

"Our guns are good enough for signals, but they have no calibre to be of any use in this case," replied the latter.

"Why don't we tack about?"

"What would be the good of that? The waterspout would go as far in a minute as we could go in an hour."

"But if it reaches us we are lost!"

"Yes, unless God comes to our help," replied the sailor in a serious tone.

The clergyman turned pale, but repeated a psalm in a steady voice. Almost at the same moment we were lashed in the face, and almost blinded by a body of water which rose at a few cables' length from the *Magdalena*. The thin, barely formed column of water dashed against the steamer's poop, broke away part of the bulwarks, tumbled us over each other, and then continued its furious course. There were now two waterspouts in view. The sun hid itself; the sea and the sky were the colour of steel. We were in semi-darkness, deafened by the roar of the wind and the dashing of the billows. Suddenly the two funnels separated; one sank down, whilst the other seemed to rise into the clouds. For two minutes, which seemed to us all like a century, we were plunged in black darkness and drenched by a deluge of water. For my part, I thought my last hour had come; I seemed to feel the steamer sinking into the sea, and the waves closing over us. Light came back gradually, revealing our piteous condition as we stood on deck—livid, drenched, dishevelled, and awe-struck.

"The danger is over," said the captain; "but, by Heaven, it was a narrow escape! Steer for the schooner," added he, addressing his lieutenant; "I heard sounds of cracking which make me think some harm has happened to her."

Our wheels were once again in motion, and we soon saw the little ship; she had lost her masts, and her deck was battered in. Fortunately, the five men composing her crew were safe and sound. Our captain offered to tow the schooner as far as St. Thomas; but a small steamer which had just left port speedily came up to offer her services. We continued our route, and an hour later were sailing on a sea as calm and smooth as a mirror, reflecting the azure of the cloudless sky. Had it not been for the numerous damages of which the *Magdalena* everywhere bore traces, the terrible danger we had just escaped would have seemed like a horrible nightmare.

"You are satisfied now, I hope," said I to the clergyman, who was imbibing his third glass of orange water.

"More than that," replied he. "I am quite cured of my fancy for seeing a waterspout at sea. Has my hair turned white?" said he, taking off his hat and showing me his head.

"No," said I, smiling; "your hair is as brown as ever."

"Then it will never turn grey. Man feels very small before such workings of the Almighty."

"You are right," I replied; "but I confess I did not want to be brought so near a waterspout to be made conscious of my nothingness."

During the remaining week of our voyage, Mr. Smith slept with one eye open. The sight of a small island, the masts of a ship, or a sperm-whale, would make him turn pale and uneasy; everything seemed to him to foreshadow waterspouts and storms. When once at Havannah he recovered his spirits, but he assured me that he would return to New York by any other way than St. Thomas. He had seen a waterspout, and now sincerely hoped never to see another.

CHRISTMAS DAY AT HAVANNAH.

CHAPTER I.

Havannah—Preliminary formulas—A good dinner—In search of a lodging—A restless night.

THE Island of Cuba, called *The Queen of the Antilles* since St. Domingo freed herself from French rule, is almost three hundred leagues in length, and scarcely forty in breadth. It is, with Porto Rica, the last strip of the immense empire possessed by the Spanish in the New World; and even this magnificent jewel is ready to detach itself from the crown so long without a rival. I cannot think without regret of this beautiful island, which I saw so peaceful and prosperous, now devastated by civil war, the most terrible of all scourges—blood flowing in the plains and valleys, in the forests, whose rich vegetation I admired so much; the feet of horses, the wheels of cannon, disturbing the clear brooks where I have so often quenched my thirst. The first time I visited the Island of Cuba, it had just been devastated by one of those terrible hurricanes which, from time to time, sweep over the Antilles and threaten to submerge them in the waters of the Atlantic. But what are these disasters compared to those caused by man? What, for instance, does a broken tree signify—damage which time will repair—compared with the ruin of the Tuilleries and the Hotel de Ville? And then, however cruel and implacable the rebel Creoles showed themselves, they had at least an honourable end in view—the attainment of liberty.

But let us leave this melancholy subject, and enter the famous harbour of Havannah—a spectacle which greatly surprises Europeans who see it for the first time.

The harbour of the capital of Cuba is only attainable by passing under the line of fire of a fort, built on a rock, called *Moor's Fort*. Vessels glide between two high, bare, desolate cliffs, and then, by a sharp turn to the left, come in view of the town embosomed in a hollow.

With the exception of the fort, boldly placed on a pile of barren rocks, there is nothing at first to strike the traveller's attention particularly. Two or three palm-trees with their tall, slender stems astonish European travellers; but one can scarcely believe one's self in the country so far-famed for good cigars, or in the general *entrepôt* of Spanish commerce, with her ancient colonies. There is little or no verdure; the muddy water is covered with thousands of white sea-birds. The sky is of a pale blue, and a kind of vapour hovers over the town, of which one can only get a glimpse. Strong sea odours impregnate the air. One feels saddened by the dismal, severe aspect of the landscape. The atmosphere is almost burning. One thinks of yellow fever, which makes so many victims here. The cruel malady has well chosen its place of resort.

The American steamer in which I had made the voyage had hardly cast anchor, when we were surrounded by numerous small boats. Nevertheless, not one of the people in them dared set foot on our vessel. They were obliged to wait for the government and police boats, which appeared sailing side by side. I had nothing to show the government officers. As for the police, they granted me permission to go about the town for forty-eight hours. If it pleased me to stay beyond this time in the capital of the pearl of the Antilles, I should be obliged to apply to two officials who could prolong my leave. If the fulfilment of this formula were neglected, the police, horse or foot soldiers, had the right to take me by the collar and put me on board any of the ships lying at anchor in the harbour, whether or no it was the one I had the intention of embarking in.

What was the reason of these strict precautions? Was I so formidable, that they thought my presence capable of turning the town upside down? or had I such a suspicious appearance, that the police thought it prudent to warn me that they had an eye upon me? Nothing of the kind. I was only submitting to the letter of some old regulations which for centuries have closed the Spanish colonies against strangers. Thanks to friends at court, Humboldt was one of the first to obtain permission to visit Mexico and Peru, in 1803. One can understand the success of the stories and descriptions of the learned German. He had the good fortune to appear as though he had discovered the countries of which he spoke, and which stern laws had kept closed more hermetically than any town of China.

After I had formally promised not to get intoxicated, to avoid all scandal, not to preach liberty to the slaves, and to respect the rights of the crown of Spain, they gave me a little square of yellow paper. I hailed a boat, whose proprietor was quite willing to take me in on the presentation of my passport; and, ten minutes later, I landed on a quay, built on piles—a construction as ugly as it was primitive. It was on the 24th of December, 1863, Christmas Eve, that I set foot, for the first time, on the soil of the town founded, in 1511, by Diégo Velasquez.

As soon as I entered the narrow, bad-smelling, ill-kept streets, I was almost stifled by a sickening odour, something like the emanations from dried codfish, olive oil, heavy Catalogna wine, and I do not know what else, which make a Spaniard's mouth water, and sicken a Frenchman. I thought that the houses had a holiday aspect; and I learnt that for a week the inhabitants of Puerto-Principe, Santiago, Fermando de Jagua, Nuevitas, Santa Maria, and Matauzas, had made the metropolis their resort, and that to find a room at an hotel was a difficult matter. I had the address of a French hotel given me, and at once made my way thither.

The hotel, situated in the modern promenade of Tacon, was clean and lively. Whilst waiting for dinner, I stood at the door; and about five o'clock, when the sun was disappearing behind Punta Fort, I saw all the fashionable world pass before me.

Now the fashionable world of Havannah—I speak from what I saw—exactly resembles that of London or Paris. The same coats for the men, the same style of dress for the women; head-dresses, hats, canes, boots, eye-glasses, all come from Paris. Unfortunately, the public watering-cart is an unknown luxury in this dusty Cuban city. It was the month of December, and the heat was as great as in July with us; dust and perspiration mingling on the faces of the fair sex, obliged them to make a speedy retreat.

One of the peculiarities of Havannah is the *volanta*—a kind of cab drawn by two mules, the wheels of which, before and behind, are ornamented with silver, and are of the same height as the hood of the vehicle. On one of the mules sits a negro, smartly dressed as a postillion, with gold lace, and prouder than Artaban of his grand attire. Two or three young women, with flowers in their hair, take their places in the carriage; the postillion cracks his whip, and away they go, jolting over the uneven pavement of the town. After having been a dozen times round the promenade, the strange equipage brings the indolent Creoles back to their houses. It is only in this way, or when going to the theatre, that the fair sex of Havannah is visible. The rare beauties that one runs against in the streets, are only small tradespeople or servants.

Enlivened by watching this marvellous promenade, after having conscientiously remarked that there was no lack of beauty among the women, and that large, dark, expressive eyes are as common in Havannah as Mexico, I determined to have my dinner. My countryman knew how to manage things well, and my dinner, frugal enough, only cost me about two pounds. For this I had neither truffles, blackbirds, nor a plump ortolan; not even a pheasant. Some chicken, a bottle of claret, a salad, which I was told was something excellent, was all that I got for my money. At dessert, they offered me strawberries. Strawberries in the month of December! It was a tempting dish, and I eagerly accepted it. In about five minutes they triumphantly brought me some strawberries preserved in syrup. Judge of my deception! These strawberries, which came from Europe, added another ten shillings to my bill; and never, I think, did I pay more for my dinner than on that day.

Living is expensive in all tropical countries; but my countryman looked sharp after his own interests, and did not treat me altogether as a friend. I thought it useless to exclaim against the exorbitant price of the chicken and salad, and contented myself with changing my quarters. Four years later I was again in Havannah, and allowed myself to be drawn into the coquettish French hotel. It cost me three pounds this time. I suppose one can hardly dine there now under five pounds; decidedly a rather expensive repast.

Late in the evening I went to the principal square, where the governor's palace is situated, and entered one of the famous restaurants, which are the luxuries of Havannah. There is not a sweet nor a refreshing drink that these skilful natives do not know how to prepare; their restaurants surpass anything of the kind to be found in Paris or London, and the coffee, ices, and liqueurs are of the best quality. But I ought to say something about Christmas Day; and if I do not do so at once, I shall lose myself—as I am rather in the habit of doing—in details, which may be of no interest to any one except myself.

I had dined, but did not feel any inclination to spend the night in the open air, and I had convinced myself, by investigation, that all the hotels, even the small inns, were crowded. Whilst I was lingering over a delicious ice-cream, and reflecting how I was to get out of my difficulty, some one touched me on the shoulder, and I found myself face to face with a Mexican gentleman of my acquaintance. We directly began a tête-à-tête, talking of Vera-Cruz, Puebla, and Mexico. I told my friend of my unsuccessful attempts to find a lodging, and of my unwillingness to return to the steamer, which was taking in her supply of coal. He offered to have a bed made up for me in his own apartments, and we set out for them together. An hour later, a sofa was arranged for me, and I took possession of a small sitting-room on the ground floor, with windows looking out into the street.

About midnight, feeling grateful to Providence, I had fallen asleep, when I was suddenly aroused with a start. All the bells in the town began to ring at once. They were silent at last; but a distant rumbling sound still kept me awake. It was like the noise of an infuriated crowd. All the dogs in the neighbourhood began to bark. The noise came nearer; there was no longer any doubt but that it was a wild, disorderly, noisy rabble. They yelled and screamed in a most unearthly manner. I opened one of the windows; and by the light of torches, carried by frightful-looking vixens, I saw a disorderly band of negroes and negresses, running, quarrelling, and making a din with tin kettles, in lieu of tambourines. Never had I heard such a frightful uproar. What was the meaning of it? Had the slaves revolted? Several hundred individuals had passed before me, and in countries where slavery reigns, they would hardly allow the African race to make such an uproar at such an unseasonable hour.

The barking of the dogs died away after a while, and gradually all was silent again, and I could only hear faint and far-off sounds. I had looked up and down the street, and was surprised at seeing no window opened; there was not even a sound in the house where I was lodging. But the noise of revelry again drew near, and another band of negroes, running in the same direction as the others, passed down the street, making more noise if possible. Reports of fire-arms were heard in the distance, and put an end to my doubts—the negroes had revolted. I opened my door, which led into a passage, to make some inquiries as to the meaning of the riot, when a fine mastiff, which had sniffed at me the evening before with a good deal of curiosity, now bounded forwards, and I had only just time to shut my door again, and save myself from his rough embrace. The animal growled, scratched at the door, and whined; perhaps he did not want to do me any harm, and there was only a misunderstanding between us. Nevertheless, I thought it prudent not to open the door; and so, there I was a prisoner.

All was once more silent. A world of ideas filled my brain. The garrison was numerous; but there were twenty-five thousand slaves, and as many mulattos in the town; and the white people, to which party I had the honour of belonging, seemed to me to be in a rather critical position. I lay down again, imagining that the governor's palace was being pulled down; but soon fatigue overcame my fears, and I fell asleep. A saucepan, suddenly rattled against the iron bars of my window, made me spring up with a jump. I heard voices and laughter. A woman was striking a tin kettle, and ten negroes were dancing round her, whilst the one who was making use of the bars of my window, tried to rattle them in time, as though he were playing on a guitar.

"Holloa there!" cried I to the musician; "what on earth is the meaning of this uproar?"

He slunk off, rather amazed, and turning up the whites of his large eyes, answered triumphantly—

"Me free!"

Although a sworn enemy to slavery, I felt a shudder run through me at this reply. How many lives had not this liberty already cost, and how many more might still fall victims to the treacherous slaves of Havannah!

"Has much harm been done?" I ventured to ask the musician, who was rattling on my window-bars with renewed energy.

His eyes opened wide, and, instead of answering, he sang a song, the words of which were quite incomprehensible to me.

"Where is the governor?" I again asked.

"He asleep."

Asleep! That is to say, dead; undoubtedly massacred in his sleep. I went back to my sofa. What could be the reason of this strange riot, and how was it the soldiers of the garrison had made so little resistance? There were several men-of-war lying at anchor; Moor's Fort, and the fort of the Peak, contained a large body of troups. Were they waiting for daylight to fire on the town? But no; the rebels must have made themselves masters of these places first of all. What a fearful catastrophe! Towards four o'clock, the noise having almost ceased, I again yielded to fatigue, and fell into a troubled sleep, dreaming of the black Haïtien heroes, Dessalines, and Toussaint-Louverture.

When I awoke, it was broad daylight. I ran to the window and saw groups of negroes everywhere; not one white man among them. I drew back again, and mournfully proceeded with my toilet; then I cautiously opened the door—the mastiff had been chained up—and a little negress carrying a tray cried out to me—

"Make haste, sir: they are at breakfast."

I went towards the end of the corridor, which, ornamented with plants, served as a dining-room. Four ladies, a priest, and my Mexican friend were quietly breakfasting together, waited on by a fat negro, who at once attended to me.

"Have you been able to sleep?" my friend asked me.

"A little towards daybreak, I confess it to my shame. But tell me quickly, what is the cause of this riot?"

"The slaves are free. Did you not know it?"

The Mexican, an enthusiastic abolitionist, and from his bronzed skin partly allied to the conquerors, told me this news in a careless tone.

"What have we to fear?" I asked.

"Nothing. However, it will be prudent not to show yourself much in the streets, in order to avoid insults, for brandy loosens the tongue."

"Are there many people killed?"

"Three at present; there will be more to-morrow. Last year there were eight."

"What! was there an attempt at rebellion last year?"

They all stared at me with such surprise, and I asked my question with such manifest astonishment, that it was clear there was a misunderstanding between us.

Thus, getting an explanation, I learnt that in observance of an ancient custom, the slaves of Havannah have one day in the year of perfect liberty, and that holiday is Christmas Day.

Notwithstanding the warnings I had of the imprudence of venturing into the streets, especially of mingling with the slaves, nothing could keep me from trying to get a glimpse of their curious proceedings. They predicted a thousand accidents which would happen to me; I should be obliged to take thumps and knocks without complaining, or having the right to revenge myself. I was determined to run all risks, and directly after breakfast I set out, following a troup of negroes, who, dressed in their masters' cast-off clothes, were dancing and singing as they went along.

CHAPTER II.

Fraternity—Sons and daughters of kings—Abuse of saffron—A negro ball.

It was a splendid day, the heat almost unbearable, and one had to think twice to believe that it was the month of December. All the large warehouses and shops were closed, with the exception of the wine-merchants, cigar shops, and especially the spirit stores, which seemed to be doing an active business. Negroes, mulattos, and quadroons, dressed in their finest clothes, were strutting about the streets and noisily applauding the masqueraders.

Having reached a large open square, my party suddenly formed a ring, in which I was enclosed. I was jostled, pushed about, and shaken, but I took it all good-naturedly. A tall negro, dressed in very wide pantaloons, and a coat too small for him, all at once began a dance, which, with its fantastic steps, grimaces, extraordinary leaps, and contortions, I cannot pretend to describe. The dancer sang an African song, whilst some of his companions joined in the chorus. Never did a more discordant, guttural, disagreeable hubbub torture human ears; unfortunately, mine were destined to hear a good deal of the same thing.

K

They stared and pointed at me. I was an intruder. Two young men of a remarkably black skin, more shiny than the best polished leather, came skipping up to me. They were armed with formidable-looking clubs, and began brandishing them in a most uncomfortable manner over my head. The skill of the two cudgel players was indisputable, but they came so close to me that I began to feel uneasy. I thought that perhaps these fine black fellows, whilst apparently only playing, might be tempted to caress European shoulders with their cudgels, and taking advantage of my good nature, might pay off some of the blows they had received from the white people. As I thought it prudent to beat a retreat, I wished to do so as honourably as possible, and I offered the cudgel players some refreshment. My politeness was accepted without the slightest hesitation, and the clubs, ceasing their evolutions round my head, came down roughly but pacifically to the ground. Here was I now walking arm in arm towards a spirit store with two wretched slaves, and followed by the band whom I had at first mingled with.

At Havannah as well as New Orleans, to associate with a negro is at once to shut all doors of polite society against one. I had perhaps chosen my new acquaintances rather thoughtlessly; but I could never accustom myself to despise coloured men, and I could mention more than one who, in intelligence, morality, and goodness, is far superior to many white men. I had only to pass through Havannah, so it mattered little compromising myself with the race of Ham, and I bravely entered the spirit store.

It was kept by a Catalonian, who, seeing my followers, thought at first that I was a victim of the masqueraders, and ordered them to leave me alone.

I hastened to inform him that they were my friends, and that I had brought them there.

"Take care," said he to me; "these familiarities may lead you into serious trouble."

"Do you think these poor creatures are capable of ill-treating me?"

KEEPING CHRISTMAS IN HAVANNAH.

"They will not scruple to take advantage of any opportunities you may afford them. And that is not all. The police are on the watch, without appearing to be so; they may make you account to-morrow for the scandals which you have caused, and you will be punished for having exposed yourself to the outrages of the coloured people."

I remembered the oaths which I had taken in exchange for my passport, and as my proceedings were not in contradiction to any of my promises, I begged the Catalonian to have my guests attended to. The latter were unanimous in asking for brandy, the only refreshing drink they cared for; but my two guests multiplied in some miraculous way, and I had a considerable amount to pay the wine-shop keeper.

In exchange for my hospitality, I received the most intimate confidences; the women especially were open-hearted. I thought I was condescending, and yet here I was surrounded by noble lords, unfortunate princesses, the sons and daughters of kings. The queens, of the number of three, were less resigned than the men at the loss of their thrones; and I only succeeded in drying their tears by redoubling their refreshment. All that these poor creatures told me in their broken language might be true. It was beyond doubt that they had been brutally torn from their cabins, from their native land, and their friends, and had been embarked by force, and carried to Cuba, the name of which they had never even heard, there to be sold as vile cattle. They comforted themselves with the hope of some day returning to their homes, a consoling illusion which I was careful not to dissipate.

The majority of my new friends were negroes born in Havannah. They also dreamed of liberty, but they did not complain of their masters, and the invisible chain which bound them to a white man and a dwelling did not seem to weigh very heavily upon them. At the invitation of the shopkeeper, who told me that it would be unwise to go on walking under the burning sun, I rested in his shop; and my companions, resuming their fantastic dances, continued their way.

My host sold grocery and woollen goods, as well as wine

and spirits; and I watched the customers, from the slave who had become an important housekeeper, down to the little negro girl. These were the aristocratic negroes, who looked down upon the masquerading troops in the streets. From time to time a coquettish mulatto would come into the shop, who, although herself a slave, spoke of the negroes with proud disdain, and ranked herself undoubtedly with the white people. Workmen, tradespeople, masons, and carpenters, came one after another and sat down in the shop. They belonged to a master, who for a certain sum of money allowed them to follow their own occupations, and being skilful workmen, they often succeed in getting a ransom.

I spent nearly three hours here looking on, listening and convincing myself of the sad truth, that however distressing the material condition of the slaves may be, it is a thousand times better than that of workmen in our large cities. But the subjects of slavery and pauperism are far too serious to be treated lightly. I will therefore continue my walk.

Wherever I went through the town, I encountered the same noisy masquerades. I came unexpectedly upon a fair, and the grand display of paintings which struck my eye told me that France had not the exclusive monopoly of bearded women, skeleton men, and learned hares, still less of Hercules and somnambulists. I entered one of the largest booths, where young acrobats were executing their performances with marvellous agility. Five of them, perched on balls, undertook a most amusing race, performing a series of perilous jumps; in fact, monkeys could not have done it better.

I noticed that, with very few exceptions, all the shops in the fair were under the patronage of *Maria de Lao*, who must have been a celebrity, for each of the establishments declared themselves her true and only successor. I questioned successively a negro, a mulatto, a creole, a quadroon, and finally a European about this remarkable divinity, and each time they laughed in my face, thinking that I was jesting. *Maria de Lao* is so well known in Havannah, that I could not succeed in finding out who she was.

I determined to consult a somnambulist, and I asked the young person who went to sleep for my benefit, to give me some information about the celebrated *Maria*, whose portrait, full length and vignette, was everywhere to be seen. My question awakened the somnambulist as though I had fired a pistol close to her ear; that is to say, she started up. They looked at me suspiciously, refused my money, and I even think the showman mildly swore at me. An inquisitive person in Paris or London, who asked a passer-by for the history of Punch and Judy, would most likely meet with the same success as I did.

About five o'clock, tired of seeing the negroes romping about in their grotesque clothing, of swallowing dust, and being deafened by the screeching and noise, I went in search of an Havannah restaurant. I wanted to taste the cookery of Cuba in all its purity.

The dining-room which I entered was neither luxuriously nor meanly furnished, neither clean nor dirty; and the persons whom I saw round the tables looked like small tradespeople or merchants' clerks. They gave me a bill of fare, which I studied attentively, and on which, among ordinary dishes, figured several which I did not know. I began by asking for a soup, which appeared to me to be a queer combination of peas, tomatoes, rice, and pumpkins, with very little broth. This mixture, if well pounded, would have been very good, had the cook been less prodigal with the saffron.

After this they brought me vegetable-marrows, dressed with cayenne pepper, which was enough to set one's mouth on fire. I managed to demolish it, thanks to the ten years' long and painful apprenticeship I had gone through in the Spanish colonies. These marrows, moderately spiced, would be very much appreciated in Europe, but the saffron might well be dispensed with.

A slice of fillet of beef, garnished with rancid bacon, an imitation of the French fricandeau, was brought to me. I allowed myself to be influenced in partaking of this dish. Seeing me steadily consulting the bill of fare, my opposite neighbour said to me—

"Take some fillet; it is very good."

And I asked for some fillet. I do not deny that rancid bacon may be an excellent thing, but I never eat it without being absolutely forced to do so. That which was brought to me was so far gone, that I was obliged to draw myself up to prevent making a grimace when swallowing it. Not wishing to look like a simpleton before the waiter, nor to tacitly declare that my obliging neighbour had detestable taste, by sending back my slice of meat untouched, I ordered a hot sauce, which I thought might neutralize the distasteful qualities of the bacon; but this only added fire to my already burning mouth and throat.

Having sufficiently hacked my slice of beef for the sake of appearances, I gave up all further attempts at swallowing it, and contented myself with a wing of chicken. I thought I was safe in ordering this simple course. Alas! the chicken was placed on a dish of rice, cooked, I firmly believe, in a saffron-box. I dared not ask for a salad; the Cubans would be sure to flavour it with saffron oil.

I set out in search of a *café*, and the comforting beverage soon made me forget the torture I had suffered at dinner. At dusk I went towards the promenade, which I found deserted, so I turned hap-hazard into ill-lighted streets crowded with negroes. All trace of pavement had disappeared, heaps of refuse barred my way, and the houses were low, dirty, and squalid-looking. I heard singing in the distance, mingling with the noise of a guitar and drum, and I soon came out into a street where a series of public balls were taking place. I was the only European anywhere visible.

Elbowing my way and being jostled about, I gradually succeeded in reaching a low room, dimly lighted by two smoky lamps. A young negress was performing an epileptic dance with frenzied gesticulations. Five or six other negroes, seized with the same mad fit, were noisily shaking leathern bags filled with shells and pieces of broken bottles, whilst another was beating a tambourine without any regard to time. The dancing-girl, at last exhausted and foaming at the mouth, fell fainting on the ground. They rolled her in a blanket and carried her away, whilst one of her companions took her place, and whirled about in the same mad fashion. Suddenly, without any warning, I was gently seized, lifted up, and carried out of this dreadful den. I had unduly entered a private party. I was conscious of my offence, and at once went off, without offering the slightest resistance.

The miserable hole I had just been excluded from, was one of the lowest dancing-rooms; and I soon came to another, larger, better lighted, and filled with better-dressed people. Two negroes, armed with cudgels, and wearing immense white neckties, stood like black marble caryatides at the door of the establishment. Emboldened by the ceremonial neckties, I drew near; but the two terrible clubs barred my passage. I spoke to the two Cerberuses, who only showed their white teeth, and gave me a fine example of incorruptibility by pocketing the money I offered them. Whilst they were explaining to me in remarkable Spanish, and with perfect Castillian courtesy, that it was a private party, and that no white man, even though he were their friend, as I pretended to be, was allowed to interfere with them, I saw about a dozen negroes, and as many negresses, dancing, twirling, and hopping to the sound of music even more discordant and primitive than the first. Having exhausted my arguments, and seeing that I was looking on at the spectacle which I had no right to do, the two negroes began to brandish their clubs over my head, which dangerous familiarity I had already experienced in the morning. I retired, thinking it unwise to risk further parley with these black door-keepers, and I had the consolation of seeing them refuse admittance to a mulatto who they thought was not well enough dressed. Are there, then, social distinctions among slaves? Man is born a despot.

I am obstinate, and I succeeded in squeezing among a crowd through the door of another mixed establishment. The *bambula* were performing their escapades, whilst at the same time a very well-executed square dance was going on; the different music made a frightful discord, which did not seem to disturb the dancers in the least. Sometimes the whole room joined in the chorus of a song in honour of *Maria de Lao*. I had found such a comfortable place in a dark corner, that I ventured to sit down, and was innocently enjoying the forbidden fruit, when I saw two soldiers, led by a mulatto, making their way up to me. The soldiers were no mere lookers on, for they wore their muskets, the butt-ends of which came down sharply at my feet.

"You have no business here," said one of them to me; "follow us, if you please."

The music had ceased, the dancers were interrupted, and every one was staring at us. I got up at once.

"Am I committing any infraction of the laws of the country?" I asked.

"Yes," replied the soldier; "and the people by whom we are surrounded, and with whom you are interfering, have the right to turn you out as roughly as they like."

"I am a stranger, señor, and I did not know I was doing any harm."

In the street I found a police-sergeant, who asked for my name; instead of which, I showed him my passport.

"What mad spirit could have possessed you to go into such a wasp's nest?" said the under-officer to me. "People of your class do not usually come into these quarters, where you are not safe even in daylight."

I explained as well as I could, that I liked to see everything in the countries I visited, high as well as low life.

"You may thank God that you are still alive," said the sergeant to me; "and remember that he who goes in search of wool often gets shorn. Where do you want us to take you?"

"It is not worth while troubling you, sir; I am going back on board the steamer in which I came here, and which leaves to-morrow."

At a sign from their principal, five or six soldiers surrounded me, obliging me to walk between them. The sergeant gave me no more answers to my questions, and even imposed silence on me. I was a prisoner, but, strong in my innocence, was preparing the explanation of my actions, to give the officer before whom they might take me.

We went through the town, more deserted and silent as we

approached the aristocratic parts, replying to the *qui vive* of the sentinels whom we met. On reaching the harbour, a boatman was hailed, and received an order to take me to the ship to which I belonged. The sergeant bowed politely to me, wished me adieu, and, turning back with his men, was soon out of sight, whilst I was carried back to the *Solent*.

I stood gazing for half an hour on the sleeping town, from which rose a subdued murmur of sounds. The palm trees stood out clear against the star-lit sky, and now and then the sound of a guitar, wafted over the water, struck my ear. The hour, announced by the deep-toned bells of the clock tower, was hailed by the sentinels on the forts with a *garde à vous*, which, repeated from distance to distance, made one think of customs long gone by. In short, Havannah, with its commerce, pleasures, activity, luxury, and vices, would be a most agreeable town were it not for the terrible yellow fever which is constantly throwing a veil of mourning over the whole island.

The following day, when I went up on deck, we were out of the channel, and the town was already invisible. Black vultures, of a smaller species than those of Mexico, were hovering over the bay, and the cannons of fort *del Mora* shone in the sunlight. On a promontory to the right, might be seen a mansion shaded by palm trees, a magnificent building, which was soon to be destroyed by a formidable hurricane. All the morning we were continually passing Spanish, American, and English vessels, on their way to Havannah. By breakfast time, the island was lost in a mist, and my adventures of the preceding day seemed to me like a dream.

FROM HAVANNAH TO NEW ORLEANS.

CHAPTER I.

Departure from Havannah—The slavery question—The Gulf Stream—The Mississippi—A kidnapping business.

ALTHOUGH Havannah is but a commercial town, with narrow, winding, and dirty streets, the tourist, after a month's sojourn here, does not leave without regret. By what secret ties the capital of Cuba attaches itself thus to the hearts of its visitors, is a question I cannot pretend to answer. I must confess, however, that it was not without a real feeling of regret that, on the 10th of April, 186—, leaving the *Pearl of the Antilles* for the second time, I went on board the American steamer bound for New Orleans.

The sun set just as the anchor, yielding to the efforts of the capstan, was heaved to its place on the deck of the *Texas*, and restored her to liberty. Before long, the screw, beating the stagnant water of the bay, disturbed the peace of thousands of *medusæ*, whose soft, whitish, transparent bodies made such strange arabesques on the waves. I gave a last look at Moor's Fort, then I turned towards the ocean, or rather the Gulf of Mexico, which at this moment, gilded by the last rays of the magnificent sunset, looked like a fiery furnace.

One of my fellow-travellers, General Dumont, came up quietly and placed his hand on my shoulder.

"You are very thoughtful," said he, "and yet you do not leave any friends or relations at Havannah."

"True, general; but it is ten years since I came here for the first time, and I am comparing my impressions then to those which I now feel."

"May I, without indiscretion, ask you the result of that comparison?"

"I have come to the conclusion that it is a fine thing to be only twenty, if it were only for the reason that at that age one thinks one's self master of the future."

The general shook his grey head.

"Nonsense," said he. "Age is more in disposition than in reality. You seem to me very melancholy for a Frenchman."

"Fortunately, I only feel so at certain times; but the generous dreams of youth are worth a feeling of regret when they have never been realized. It is ten years since I landed at Havannah for the first time . . . ."

"Bother the man!" cried my companion, gaily; "he is going to tell me his history."

"Nothing but a memory, general."

"Well, since the memory makes you sad, get rid of it; that is the advice I give you."

My companion walked round the upper deck, and then came back to me.

"I lay a wager," said he, "you were smitten by the beautiful eyes of the Creoles, and that you thought you would die from the terrible wound."

"Nothing of that kind. I dreamt the freedom of the slaves was not far off."

"Good gracious me! And by what means, if you please? By the aid of the pen, the tongue, or the sword?"

"I minded very little, so long as the negroes were restored to freedom."

"And you have not been hung?" said the general, turning round to examine me.

"Not that I know of," said I, laughing.

"One word more: are you cured of this fit of slave-freedom?"

"I shall never be cured of it till the last slave has been set at liberty."

"You are seriously ill, then, young man," continued the general, in a grave tone. "Take my advice. Do not go ashore at New Orleans; the air is very bad for those with your ideas, especially just now, when the Northern States, breaking the compact of the Union, threaten to subjugate us."

"I know how to respect the laws of the countries of which I ask hospitality, general. If I happen to preach, I do not address myself to the slave, but to his master."

"And naturally you lose your time."

"One never loses time in defending a just and humane idea, in strict conformity to the laws of morality."

"Take care," replied the general. "I have about thirty slaves, and I believe I am as just and as humane as you can be. It is the name that deludes you. My negroes are my children, and wear no chains."

"You are an exceptional master. But one swallow does not make it summer, and . . . ."

My companion cut short my words, led me in to tea, and then invited me to spend a week at his house, situated about thirty miles from New Orleans. I had known General Dumont at the Italian consul's house at Santiago, in Cuba, and had met him by chance at Havannah. He was of French origin, as his name manifestly showed, and I very much liked his frank, jovial character, though it was a little rough. I accepted his invitation, and the evening was spent in listening to him talking of his only daughter, Miss Arabella, who, having been sent to a boarding-school at New York after her mother's death, was now finishing her education at home, under the direction of a learned North American lady, Miss Angelina Henderson.

The next day, a little before dawn, I strolled about the deck, watching for the sun to rise, which is always a new and magnificent spectacle in the tropics. Slowly it freed itself from the golden mists, and then bursting forth, shed its glory over the heavens, whilst its bright beams fell vertically upon us. Almost at the same time, hundreds of porpoises covered the sea and began sporting around us, even in the white foam of our steamer's wake. Leaning over the bows, our captain seemed to take a lively interest in the gambols of the capricious fish. I went up to him, and although the commander of a ship does not always care to be questioned by the passengers, I ventured to ask him if he had any news.

"Not yet; but we must have some before long," replied he, without raising his head.

"Do you fear bad weather?"

My companion glanced hastily along the horizon.

"No," said he.

"Are you studying the gambols of the porpoises?"

"Not exactly. I am watching the *Gulf Stream* which we are about to cross, and I want to ascertain its temperature."

Without further preliminary I took my place by the captain's side, and with him gazed into the depths of the sea, where, from its different colour, we could distinguish the great stream of warm water, which, penetrating the Gulf of Mexico, between Cape Catoche and Cuba, washes the shores of Campeachy, Tabasco, Vera-Cruz, Florida, and the Bahamas, and then, following the coasts of North America, goes as far as Newfoundland, and bathes the icy regions of Norway with its still tepid water.

Whilst I was looking, the colour of the water, until then greenish, became gradually deep blue, and the screw of the steamer beat against banks of *fucus natans*, a kind of sea-weed, food which sailors do not despise. A quarter of an hour later the captain gave the order to heave to. We were in the middle of the current.

The trunk of a palm tree was swept rapidly past us. The tropical tree would most likely be stranded on the coast of England. It was thus the mainmast of the *Tilbury*, burnt on the coast of St. Domingo during the seven years' war, was found on the northern coast of Scotland.

Humboldt states that barrels of olive oil, washed from a ship which foundered on a rock near Cape Lopez, in Africa, were likewise stranded on the coast of Scotland. These *débris*, carried by the Gulf Stream, had thus twice crossed the Atlantic.

Learned men were led to make calculations from the fact

of the Gulf Stream carrying stems of bamboo-cane, carved wood, and corpses of men belonging to a particular race. More than one dreamt of an unknown world beyond the seas. Columbus was aware that bold fishermen, in sailing westward, had encountered covered boats rowed by strange-looking men. "That the natives of America," said Humboldt, "most' likely the Esquimaux of Greenland or Labrador, driven by the currents or tempests, have landed on our continent, is a fact attested by the most convincing proofs." James Wallace relates, that about 1682 a Greenlander came sufficiently near the coast of Eda Island to be seen by the inhabitants.

The captain had several soundings made, and filled twenty bottles with the water of this singular stream—water remarkable for the quantity of salt it contains; then the *Texas* continued her route towards New Orleans. The following day, in the afternoon, the sea became suddenly of a yellowish colour. We were no longer in the Gulf Stream, but sailing through the muddy waters of the celebrated Mississippi.

"You will now see a river rather more majestic than the Seine," said General Dumont to me, with a touch of national pride; "a river that has a course of three hundred and thirty-five miles, and receives rivers still more considerable than itself."

"I shall not see it without pride," I replied, adopting the slightly ironical tone of my companion. "It was Lasalle, my countryman, who first explored the course of the Mississippi, the source and mouths of which were once in the possession of the French."

"Humph! The name which I bear does indeed prove that your countrymen formerly crossed my country," resumed the general, gaily. "I even believed that they settled there, and that New Orleans was founded by them in 1717. Frenchmen know how to take; fortunately, they do not know how to keep, or half the world would belong to them. Do not say a word," hastily added my future host; "allow me to act as your chaperon and do the honours of my country, for we are at this moment entering one of the principal arms of the *Meschacébé*, discovered, in 1541, by the Spaniard Ferdinand de Soto."

FROM HAVANNAH TO NEW ORLEANS. 143

"All the shores we can see, appear to me very barren."

"They are, being marshy and covered with shifting islands; for the Mississippi diverges very much from its course before falling into the sea."

"Is that another of its superior qualities?"

"Not for sailors, at any rate; they often mistake its course, to the great damage of their ships. You are undoubtedly aware that until 1832, the Mississippi was thought to take its rise in Lake Cass; in reality, it rises in Itacca Lake, as I proved myself ten years ago. The majestic sheet of water which you see here swollen by affluents, such as the Missouri, the Arkansas, the Ohio, the Red River, and the Illinois—I mention the most important—is twenty feet wide where it issues from Lake Itacca."

We were constantly passing ships of all nations, with their flags floating from the masts, making for the open sea, there to disperse in a hundred different directions. When night came we were still about fifty miles from New Orleans, and our captain paced the deck with an uneasy look. The heat was overpowering; sharp gusts of wind quickly lashed the yellow water of the river into heaving billows, and the sky was gradually covered with black storm-clouds. Suddenly the *Texas*, veering round, entered a bay in which were two schooners, and a cry of consternation escaped from the passengers when they heard the anchor-chains unwound, and knew that they were condemned to be stationary until the morrow.

No one expected me at New Orleans, so I placidly accepted the turn in events which would delay our arrival by twenty-four hours. My travelling companions were less complacent. The general fumed away, and offered to take the direction of the steamer through the darkness; a proposition which was not even listened to. He asked for a boat, talked of swimming to land; but finding it all of no avail, he ordered a bottle of Madeira and entered into a game of whist, which allowed him to vent his wrath on his unfortunate partner.

About nine o'clock I was driven from the upper deck by a formidable deluge. The sky seemed literally dissolving into water. The air was full of ominous sounds; angry gusts of wind mingled with the continuous surf of the waves. Flashes of lightning almost blinded us, and at short intervals the majestic voice of the thunder drowned all other sounds. When I entered the grand saloon, I was dazzled by the brilliant lights; the passengers were playing, talking, working, and reading. The contrast between this peaceful scene and the fury of the elements outside, was singular enough.

Towards midnight I again ventured on deck. The thunder was rumbling in the distance, the wind had sunk, but it was still raining heavily. I went back to my cabin, and did not get to sleep before two o'clock.

I awoke with a start.

"Get up, get up, you lazy fellow," cried the general, cheerily; "in an hour we shall be in sight of the capital of Louisiana."

I rubbed my eyes. The sun was gilding the glass of my small port-hole.

"Now then," cried the general again, "you need not be afraid of putting on your best things. You are going to land in a populous city, endowed with a bishopric, a court of justice, two theatres, and a school of medicine . . . ."

"And a slave-market," I interrupted, smiling.

"Yes," replied my friend, not in the least disconcerted; "one of those markets not to be found in your European cities, where the poor masters find themselves at the mercy of inquisitive, gossiping, insolent servants, who, if the least thing is said to them that they do not like, at once leave their employer, whilst he innocently thinks that it is the wages he pays that really give him the right to command. Here, in less than an hour, you can be in possession of a valet, who . . . . But enough of that now; we will talk about it again at my house, over a bottle of Bordeaux, such as you could not drink, even at Bordeaux."

I found the deck of the steamer already crowded with visitors. The great secession war was about to break out, and the last news from Europe or Washington was being commented on. I had scarcely taken one look at the great city I was about to visit for the first time, when the general, giving me a gentle push, sent me back to my cabin.

"When do you mean to have your luggage brought up?" said he. "Have you forgotten that you are to be my guest for a week, and that we must be on the way to Méssangère in an hour's time?"

I exclaimed against this. I could not pass New Orleans before, as it were, setting foot there. I had, besides, several things to buy, and four letters to leave at different houses.

"That is not of the least consequence to me," replied the general, with undisturbed tranquillity. "You can make your purchases next week; and as for your letters, a servant will take them with a note from you which you will date from Méssangère; for you will sleep there to-night, as true as my name is Dumont."

"But...."

"Silence in the ranks! I will show you an hotel where you can leave your heavier luggage. In an hour's time—I am impatient to see my daughter, and it is your duty to do all you can to assist me—in an hour's time, then, I shall be at your hotel with a carriage, and at twelve o'clock precisely we shall be at Méssangère. I have made up my mind for that."

"But once again...."

"What is the good of useless observation? It is all perfectly understood."

And so it was. An hour later I was sitting beside the general in a fly which was taking us to his house. There I was to see a miracle of Creole beauty, Miss Arabella Dumont, and a well of science, bearing the name of Angelina; and I was assured that I should speedily be convinced that the best condition in life is that of a slave, when one cannot be master.

CHAPTER II.

Departure for Méssangère—The unfortunate Thomas—The danger of letting a dress get wet—A New Yorkist, and a native of Louisiana—A curious way of getting a husband.

For a quarter of an hour we followed a dusty, ill-kept road, from time to time meeting with heavy waggons, or bands of negroes laden with burdens. These poor people, scantily clad, touched their hats to us as we passed, which politeness I returned. My companion, with a cigar in his mouth, watched me do so with an amused look.

"I ought to tell you," said he at last, "that it is not the custom here to raise your hat when you say 'good day' to a negro."

"I have always been of the opinion that one man is as good as another, whatever is the colour of his skin or his condition in life. Thus, contrary to the rules of etiquette perhaps, I always return the bows of servants of the houses I visit. I should be sorry to think that although these people are slaves, they are more polite than I am."

"That fine speech is not your own; it comes from one of the governors of India, whose name I have forgotten," said the general, smiling.

"I confess it does; but I think like this governor, and being unable to say anything better, I repeat his words."

"For goodness' sake, do leave your hat alone!" said the general to me, seizing my hand just as I was going to bow again. "Although I know how precious you hold your illusions," added he, "just notice that these people are not touching their hats to you any more than they are to me."

"Are they paying this homage to your fly, or to your horses?"

"Not more to one than the other. Oh, short-sighted Frenchman! They are wishing our coachman good-day, that is all."

I bit my lips. My host was right, as I convinced myself with a little attention. Accustomed as I was to the polite courtesy of the peasants of the old Spanish colonies, there was a natural excuse for my mistake. I was the first to laugh at my blunder, and I promised to be more careful in future to whom I raised my hat.

The rich vegetation of Mexico was too vividly impressed on my mind for me to show as much surprise at the beauty of the surrounding country as my companion expected. The plants, bushes, and trees which I had seen growing in wild luxuriance were here trimmed, fenced in, and cultivated. But, as I have since convinced myself, one ought no more to judge of Louisiana from New Orleans than of Mexico from the barren, sandy, desolate coast around Vera-Cruz.

We skirted the border of a wood, and then turned into a cross road, seamed with deep ruts, hardly wide enough to allow our carriage to pass. After half an hour of rough jolting, our vehicle suddenly stopped short.

"What has happened?" asked the general of our coachman.

"It is impossible to go on, sir."

We alighted. A small cart was lying across the road surrounded with cases, bales, and parcels, and an old unharnessed horse was contemplating the disaster with a melancholy eye, whilst he solemnly munched a mouthful of grass.

"Ah, Thomas! poor Thomas!" said a plaintive voice near us.

My companion ran towards a negro, who, seated on the ground, his face hidden between his hands, was repeating, in tones of deepest despair—

"Ah, Thomas! poor Thomas! unlucky Thomas!"

"Are you hurt?" asked the general.

"No," replied Thomas energetically. "No, I am not hurt. The truth is, sir, if you must know, the horse has been drinking, the cart has been drinking, the parcels have been drinking— even the small ones—and they could not hold themselves up."

"Get up."

The thing was easier said than done, seeing that Thomas

was in exactly the same condition as the cart and the packets: he had been drinking, and could not hold himself up.

"Plague take the drink!" cried the general. "Here, all through this booby, I shall be delayed getting home for an hour."

"You need not have asked me for the truth," murmured Thomas.

"Come along, blockhead that you are; try, at least, to help us."

It was no slight work, setting up the cart and then piling in it the cases, parcels, and small barrel of brandy, the contents of which, in escaping, had wetted the parcels, the road, and above all, Thomas' throat. Fortunately, we were assisted in our work by two negroes who were passing by. As to "poor Thomas," he sat down and calmly watched us, declaring all the time that our efforts were useless, seeing that as the cart and parcels were quite tipsy, they would only roll over again, as soon as they were put up.

For a trifle, the two negroes who had helped us undertook to take Thomas to his place of destination, and we were once more driving along the narrow road. During the whole of this scene I had admired the general's goodness and patience; and I told him so.

"To be angry with a drunken man, would be to show yourself as senseless as he is," replied my companion.

"How many lashes will the unfortunate Thomas get?" I asked. "His escapade will doubtless cost him dearly."

"That depends on his general conduct, and his master's character; however, as I have before told you, we do not walk about here slashing our whips from right to left, as people in Europe seem to think. There are laws to protect the negroes; and the slave unjustly treated by a brutal master, can oblige the latter to sell him."

"Is it true, that it is forbidden to teach these poor wretches to read?"

"It is. But tell me, do all the peasants and workpeople in France know how to read?"

"¡HOLD!"

"No; but they are free."

"So be it. I suppose their liberty feeds them when they have no work to do, and takes care of them when they are ill, does it not? But stay; do not let us discuss this matter. We are looking at it from an opposite point of view, and have no chance of coming to an understanding. To you Europeans, the negro is a man; in our eyes, he is only a child—a child whose intelligence will never develop, do what you may. If you can bring forward an exception, I shall answer you that it confirms the rule, and we shall have gone as far into the matter on our arrival as when we set out."

We had left the narrow road and were crossing an undulating common interspersed with clumps of mimosas. Before long houses bordered the roadside; and entering a fine avenue of plane trees, we drove up before the door of an elegant house, built on a slight eminence, its windows commanding a good view of the surrounding neighbourhood.

Five or six negroes, and as many negresses, surrounded our carriage. The general was not expected, and his servants kissed his hand with every demonstration of delight, whilst three fine greyhounds jumped and gambolled around their master.

"Where is Miss Arabella?" asked the general eagerly.

"In the garden, sir," answered a tall negro, dressed in white clothes, as though to set off the ebony of his skin to greater advantage.

"Come," said the general, "I am going to introduce you to the queen of my little kingdom."

I followed my guest, who, after having crossed a wide hall leading into the garden, went towards a clump of pomegranate trees.

"Hold!" cried he suddenly, in a stentorian voice.

On one of the rocking-chairs so generally used in the United States, sat a young woman, her eyes sparkling with anger. Near her stood a beautiful girl, who seemed to be begging for mercy for a negress, who, kneeling down with hands clasped entreatingly, was threatened by the whip of a mulatto standing over her.

The girl sprang into the general's arms, whilst the young woman, rising slowly and majestically from her seat, said in a voice trembling with suppressed vexation—

"Goodday, sir. Has your journey been pleasant?"

"What is the matter, Miss Angelina?" asked the general, turning pale.

"I was exercising the authority you allowed me, sir, and was about to punish one of your slaves."

"What crime has she committed?"

"She has been away from the house for two days, and was only brought back by force this morning. Besides this, sir, I have more to speak to you about when I can see you privately."

Miss Angelina bowed, as Juno might have done when she left Olympus, and went away. The general at last kissed his daughter, introduced me to her, and turning to the slave who was still kneeling, said to her kindly—

"Get up, Manon. Is it true, that you wanted to run away, my girl?"

"Me afraid of Miss Angelina, massa," replied the negress.

"Afraid of Miss Angelina! Have you offended her, then?"

"Miss sent me to town to fetch her beautiful dress. The rain came, it spoil the beautiful dress, and me was afraid to come back."

"There is a misunderstanding in all this, father," said Miss Dumont. "Miss Angelina thought that Manon had let her dress get wet on purpose."

I was greatly embarrassed during this scene. Not knowing where to go, and not wishing to appear to be listening, I studiously examined a fine shrub, until at last the general had pity on me.

"We will settle this affair presently," said he. You, Manon, go back to your work; and you, my child," continued he, addressing his daughter, "go and see about the arrangements for our guest."

"Did you build this house?" I asked the general, who was silent and thoughtful.

"No. My father had it built.... I have lost my wager with you," continued he, in the rough tone he sometimes assumed; "nevertheless, I can assure you that for the last fifty years not a slave—not one—has ever received corporeal punishment on my estate."

"Had we not better let that subject drop?"

"No. We should then be obliged to talk with reserve, which for my part I am incapable of. I told you, did I not, that Miss Angelina is a New Yorkist? Well, now, if we Southerners look on the negro as a child, our Northern neighbours regard him as nothing better than an animal."

"Nevertheless, the Northerners are against slavery."

"Only out of opposition to us; not in the least from conviction or humanity. There is not perhaps another part of the globe where the coloured man is more spurned and despised than at New York. This is a fact which you will see for yourself by-and-by, and which will explain Miss Angelina's conduct."

"A spoilt dress is enough to explain feminine anger, general, and Miss Angelina undoubtedly belongs to the race of coquettish Roman women, who at their toilet would run pins into their maids' shoulders, when the latter were not skilful."

My host led me back to the house, and I was shown into a most comfortable room, the windows of which looked over the park. There was an extensive view; but, probably owing to the season, the country had a dusty and rather gloomy aspect. The sun was sinking below the western horizon, and the long shadow of the house fell over a terrace planted with orange trees. Suddenly I heard Miss Angelina's voice, talking with her pupil. The two young people were sitting on the terrace before a small table, on which a negress placed work-baskets and embroidery. I was able to watch them at my leisure.

Miss Angelina, although scarcely twenty, looked twenty-five. She was tall and slender, and had dark eyes and hair. Her demeanour, although somewhat stiff, was not wanting in grace. The features of the learned young woman were irreproachably regular, and gave a severe, even cold look to her countenance.

Her dress, more elegant than coquettish, showed the extreme care she bestowed on her person. In short, with her clear complexion, her handsome mouth, black eyes, fine teeth, and long hands, Miss Angelina was a perfect type of her most refined countrywomen.

Like her governess, Miss Arabella Dumont had dark hair and eyes, but her expression, instead of being commanding and imperious, was gentle and lovable. She was of middle height, graceful in every movement, and distinguished by that languid nonchalance which in hot climates is one of the charms of Creole women. Her dress, less strictly faultless and less prim than that of her governess, appeared to me of the best taste. The young girl's complexion was pallid, her hands and feet were those of a child, and her face was as animated when she was listening as when she spoke; she was, in fact, a French woman.

About five o'clock I was summoned to go to the general by his valet, a young mulatto, about fifteen years old. My host, still in his riding-boots and spurs, had just gone the round of his plantation.

"I had pity on you to-day," said he to me; "but to-morrow you must go with me, and not be afraid of showing your admiration. You probably know that one's own plot of ground is always the best; thus, my cotton is far superior to my neighbours', although each of them maintains the contrary."

We went over the garden, I should say the park, for it extended over several acres. Fine walnut trees were growing side by side with their European brothers, somewhat stunted by the hot climate. It was a whim of my host's to have trees of both hemispheres growing together around his house, where apple trees, pear trees, and apricots were overshadowed by fine mangoes.

"I get pears, peaches, and apricots, which would certainly be despised at Paris," said the general; "but they are better than none at all."

During dinner Miss Angelina, who took the place of mistress of the house, led the conversation on to American politics, just then replete with important questions. I tried at first to put in a word, but soon prudently contented myself with listening. Miss Angelina spoke well, and the general had not always the best of the argument. I was—a spectacle as curious as it was instructive for me—in presence of two compatriots talking of their country; but I doubt if Poland is separated from Russia by deeper feelings of dissension than those which divide North America from the South. There is an antagonism of race, language, religion, and education; the Yankee and the Creole seem destined to hate each other.

We went out on to the terrace to take coffee, and there I was presented to five or six neighbours, who had come to call on the general. The conversation was at first on the price of sugar, cotton, brandy, and slaves; and then every one was silent to listen to Miss Angelina discussing a medical topic with a German doctor. From the topography of the human body the young lady, by I know not what sudden transition, brought us to the topography of the sky, where the beautiful constellation of the Southern Cross was now visible. The visitors, the general especially, seemed charmed to see me listening so intently to their learned countrywoman. They thought I was astonished, when, in reality, I was simply surprised to hear a young girl talking on all subjects with the self-possession of an old professor; and I looked with pleasure at Miss Arabella, who, inattentive and smiling, was playing with a kitten.

The next day, before dinner time, I had been all over the Méssangère estate, and had duly admired my host's cows, horses, and cotton plantations. What most interested me were the slaves' cabins. Thanks to the master's generosity, each cabin was furnished with a bedstead, a chest of drawers, and a table; and the occupants, men and women, had a small garden and a yard, the products of which belonged to them. My host's kindness and humanity were manifest, and his little colony, wisely ordered and managed, was a pleasure to see. Certainly the comfort enjoyed by the negroes at Méssangère did not reconcile me to slavery; but I promised, if ever I was obliged to resign my liberty, I would choose no other master than General Dumont.

The Sunday following my arrival, there was a grand dinner given in my honour. All the afternoon carriages arrived, bringing about thirty guests. All were of French origin, and spoke the language of their mother country.

Miss Angelina soon left the ladies, and began talking business and politics with the gentlemen. Miss Arabella led her younger friends on to the terrace, from whence we could hear their joyous bursts of laughter.

"There is no use in my having Miss Angelina as governess to my daughter; it is already too late to reform the young sapling."

"Was not Miss Arabella educated at New York?"

"Yes; at a French school. Arabella knows how to sew, embroider, draw, and play on the piano, but she knows nothing whatever of the serious things of life."

"I think you are unjust, general."

"No, I am practical. In sending my daughter to a French school in New York, I committed an error, which I shall always regret."

"Miss Arabella is witty, learned, and modest; what more can you wish for?"

"Can she be compared to Miss Angelina?"

"No. I place her far above that pedantic doctress, who has nothing of her sex save her dress."

"And beauty."

"That depends upon taste."

"You are unjust in your turn, or rather, you are reasoning in this matter with your French prejudices. The woman is equal to the man, and the time has come to expect something more of her than love of frivolities."

"We are of the same opinion, general. Women should be instructed; but it is going beyond the mark, to teach young girls certain sciences before they are twenty years old. Your slave chastiser . . . ."

"Would you like to discuss the subject of 'education of women' with her?"

"No," cried I; "I prefer to declare myself defeated beforehand."

The dinner-bell sounded, and I offered my arm to the learned young lady, who undoubtedly had heard my speech.

She looked at me ironically for a moment, and appeared to hesitate. Her large black eyes shone, her rosy lips, half parted, displayed her white teeth: she was really very beautiful. At last she took my arm.

"Do you know," said she, "that an ancient law of my country, which I do not think is repealed, allows the woman who has leaned on a man's arm, to claim that man as her husband?"

I made an involuntary movement backward. The young lady held me.

"Mr. Martin," said she, addressing an old gentleman who was following us, "I ask you to be witness that this gentleman has offered me his arm."

CHAPTER III.

Molière and the education of women—New Orleans—Scarcity of filtered water—The *Cincinnati* and the *Jackson*—Ball on board—A guest without knowing it—Conclusion.

I WAS somewhat embarrassed. Miss Angelina had evidently only joked when she cited a law which in any case could not extend to foreigners, and I had allowed myself to commit a deplorable breach of gallantry.

"Did I frighten you?" resumed the young girl, with a disdainful smile. "Be assured, sir, that if I cared about being married, I should not have recourse either to force or subterfuge."

"You are too beautiful," I replied, with a low bow, "for admirers ever to be wanting. Who would not be happy to be honoured with your hand?"

"You for one," replied the young lady; "for I have noticed

that I have not the gift of pleasing you. Do not excuse yourself; it is reciprocal. You belong to a nation I do not like, particularly on account of its prejudices with regard to the education of women. One of your classical authors—whom you consider as the first comedian in the world, as though Shakespeare had never existed—pretends, or something very much like it, that my sex knows enough when it knows how to sew on a button."

"Molière wrote two centuries ago, before the invention of railroads, the electric telegraph, and free women," I replied. "But you are mistaken, Miss Angelina, in thinking that he only accorded women the right of sewing on buttons; he would have them good, wise, and devoted. He even wishes them to be learned, so long as they do not appear to be so."

"He wanted servants, sir; and that is, in fact, what they obtain in your beautiful France better than anywhere else."

We took our seats at table, and fortunately I was not placed next Miss Angelina, which cut short the bitter-sweet conversation between us.

During dinner the young American lady speechified with her ordinary self-possession, which, undoubtedly on account of our national prejudices, appeared to me more displeasing than ever. With us young girls are perhaps too timid, too modest, if modesty can be considered as a fault. The Americans, I must say with regret, have certainly gone too far in the opposite direction. I must also add that Miss Angelina had for her part passed the boundary in all points of view.

It was decidedly not the learning that I found fault with in my fair antagonist, but the constant showing off of her own powers. I am in no way opposed to women becoming electors and eligible; nevertheless, I have never been able to accustom myself to discuss political or social questions with young girls, who are necessarily inexperienced in these serious subjects, and consequently talk nonsense at random. At New Orleans education is almost the same as in France; one scarcely ever sees a girl without her mother, and on this point, I have some difficulty in explaining the admiration which some Creole ladies evince for their northern sisters. Simplicity and amiability are certainly worth more than scientific dryness, and a woman is incontestably more graceful when she gathers a bouquet, than when discussing the merits of a candidate for the presidential chair.

Ten days after my arrival I reluctantly took leave of my host. War between the North and South seemed every day more imminent; and, in order not to risk being taken prisoner between the two parties, I was obliged to hasten my visit to New Orleans, and from thence make for New York.

I left Méssangerè without having regained Miss Angelina's good graces, who to the last hour took every opportunity of showing the pity with which my old-fashioned ideas inspired her. As to the general and his daughter, I have the warmest friendship for them and a very happy recollection of their kindness to me whilst under their roof.

"Are you reconciled to slavery?" said my host to me, as he saw me to the carriage.

"No," replied I, pressing his hand; "but I am reconciled to masters such as you."

I kissed Miss Arabella's hand, bowed low to Miss Angelina, and entered the carriage which was to take me back to the ancient capital of Louisiana, taking with me the general's promise that he would come and dine with me before I left for Washington.

On the way I talked freely with the negro who was driving me, and I asked him if he were happy in his condition of life.

"Very happy," he replied; "the master is good."

"Do you never want to travel?"

"I often travel with the master."

"I mean to travel alone?"

"I could not if I wanted to," replied he, showing his white teeth with a broad grin; "my old woman keeps the money."

"Are you rich, then?"

"Enough to pay for a ransom if I wanted one," said the negro, drawing himself up.

"And why do you not want to be free?" I asked with surprise.

"Because the master is kind; and if I was once free I should have to leave him and look for another."

"But you would be free."

"What good would that do me? I should only like to be free if I had enough money to live without doing anything. I have a good master and will keep to him."

This way of looking at things is common enough among the negroes; but not so with the mulattos, who, livelier, more intelligent, and proud of their mixed blood, dream of liberty even at the price of misery.

It was noon when I reached the hotel where I was to stay. I dismissed my negro with a douceur which called forth numerous thanks, and an hour later I was wandering at random through the town.

New Orleans, built on the left bank of the Mississippi, was ceded to the United States, in 1803, by Napoleon, who despaired of being able to defend Louisiana against the English. Except the cathedral, the old town did not appear to me to possess any other remarkable building than its market, built after the model of the Athenian propylæum, which astonishes rather than excites admiration. The streets, cut at right-angles, have the monotonous regularity usual in most of the Spanish towns of America. The only part which particularly attracted my attention was the French quarter, not on account of its cleanliness and order, but simply because the French language was exclusively spoken there.

Going down a street which led to the Mississippi, I was surprised to see a ship sailing, as it were, above the town. I could not account for this singular phenomenon until I drew nearer. New Orleans is protected from the overflowing of the river upon whose bank it is built by immense dykes, and when the tide is high it is on a level with the roofs of some houses.

In the centre of the city where shops, more of Spanish than French or American character, are crowded together, people of all nations and all colours may be seen slowly wending their way, overpowered by the burning atmosphere. One must speak at least three languages in order to be perfectly at home

NEW ORLEANS.

in New Orleans; one is as often addressed in Spanish as in French or English, without counting the Creole patois, and the jargon of the negroes, which to be understood requires a long time to accustom the ear to it.

Following the direction of a cigar merchant, I went to one of the best bath establishments in the town. The slave who filled the office of bath-man, had skin almost as white as my own, and slavery seems still more odious when its victims are men in almost all respects like Europeans. Thus it was at the hotel were I stayed—the maid-servants were quadroons whose African origin required the practised eye of the Creole to discern. The young girls were slaves, and I must confess seemed none the less lively on that account.

My white negro—I mean to say my bath-man—filled my bath with a yellowish liquid.

"What is that?" I asked, with surprise.

"Water," replied he.

"Water!—that thick yellow liquid, as frothy as beer?"

"There is no other in New Orleans."

"Have you no filtered water?"

"Yes, sir, you have a decanter full."

"I want my bath full."

The white negro looked at me with an air of consternation, raised his hands, let them fall, and then began to laugh.

After a short explanation, I learnt that at New Orleans filtered water is only used for drinking; and I was tempted to ask, as did Diogenes, "Where is one to wash, then, on coming out of this?"

In the evening I went to the opera to hear a young singer for whom the papers of the town predicted the most brilliant future. After the performance, I had the honour of taking an ice side by side with the artiste who was to become the Marquise de Caux; then Mademoiselle Adelina Patti, a simple *débutante*.

After having taken my walks along the quay for four days, been present shudderingly at several slave auctions, and dipped five times in the yellow water of the Mississippi, I began to find these pleasures monotonous. I had no silken goods, wines, nor spirits to sell, and I did not want to buy either tobacco, cotton, or sugar, so that I was completely out of my place in this large town, the most remarkable monument of which is in reality a mountain of oyster-shells heaped up near the harbour.

Is this innumerable quantity of oyster-shells to be used in commerce, or have the inhabitants of New Orleans from generation to generation taken an oath to put all the shells of the oysters they have eaten in the same place? This was a problem I could not explain. The absence of filtered water, and the abundance of oyster-shells, are two of my most curious memories of New Orleans, for which I must beg pardon of the heroic city.

One morning, faithful to his promise, General Dumont noisily burst into my room.

"Well," said he to me, "and what do you think of our ancient capital?"

"It is a rather fine town, very rich and very commercial, but the manners and customs are too much like those of my own country to interest me greatly."

"Have you been over the American quarter?"

"Certainly; and the brick houses very much resemble those I have seen in England."

"Have you visited the villas in the suburbs?"

"Yes, although the muddy state of the roads is much against any approach to the houses in that direction. I noticed that all the villas were surmounted by lightning conductors, and provided with immense tanks for rain-water, which makes them look like Alembics."

"You are not kind to our large city, the rival of New York; but you have friends here, have you not?"

"None, except one or two acquaintances who are always not at home when I have called."

"Would you like me to introduce you to one or two of my friends?"

"No, thank you, general. I have made up my mind to leave here, and to-morrow I shall take a berth on the first steamboat going up the Mississippi."

After breakfast, I went out with the general. He took me to several houses, where I received most pressing invitations; but I had decided to set out on my journey again, and the general insisted on going with me to the steamboat agency.

"I came with the intention of proposing a pleasure-party: fortunately, your resolution does not oblige me to change my plans in the least. I . . . . No, I will tell you later on."

An hour later, in exchange for fifty dollars, I was in possession of a ticket giving me the right to a cabin on board the *Jackson*, going to Nashville, on the Ohio.

"Be ready to-morrow afternoon at four o'clock," said the general to me; "I will come for you with my daughter and Miss Angelina. We will go part of the journey with you."

I warmly thanked the general for his kindness; and the following day, towards five o'clock, we went on board a steamer on the stern of which was written in large letters, *Cincinnati*.

"But I have to go on board the *Jackson*," said I to the general.

"The *Jackson* has delayed its departure twelve hours; and the *Cincinnati*, which belongs to the same company, is equally well fitted up."

"Must I not change my ticket?"

"It is useless. Leave it to me."

Just as we set foot on board the *Cincinnati*, a band on deck began playing. The ship was adorned with flags, and a numerous crowd thronged the quay to watch its departure. My portmanteau was disposed of in a comfortable cabin, and I followed my guide into a magnificent saloon, where I found Miss Arabella and Miss Angelina.

The general seemed in high spirits, and was continually exchanging bows and compliments with the passengers of the *Cincinnati*, who seemed to be all friends. I had heard a good deal of the luxury of the steamers which ply the Mississippi and its affluents, but the reality far surpassed anything I had dreamt of. Everywhere carpets and gildings such as are rarely found in the most luxuriously furnished houses. The grand saloon was indeed a marvel of sumptuousness.

I had been cautioned against American roughness, and I was

M

surprised to see all my travelling companions bowing and talking to each other like old acquaintances. The finely dressed ladies seemed equally sociable; in the saloon as well as on deck they accosted each other freely and cordially. The general introduced me from time to time to a passenger; they shook my hands with energetic warmth, and the orchestra continued to fill the air with harmonious sounds.

A loud whistle sounded, the captain's voice was heard giving orders, the crew bustled about, and the wheels of the engine, placed on deck instead of being hidden away in the depths of the ship, were set in motion. A quarter of an hour later, New Orleans disappeared from sight, and we were steaming away at full speed.

I sat on the upper deck with the general, and the attentive waiters brought us the thousand and one bitter drinks of which the Americans are so fond. Every one was speaking of the probable war, and each declared that when the time came he would take up arms in defence of his rights. These were no vain words. The Southerners have acted heroically in the long struggle with their Northern brothers, and have always had my sympathy.

Night came on gradually; the steamer's speed was diminished. A splendid moonlight lit up the country, which was still low-lying, and somewhat monotonous. A bell announced dinner, and at seven o'clock precisely I sat down next to Miss Arabella before a bountifully spread table. The ladies, having changed their costumes, now appeared in evening dress.

Never in my life had I been present at a dinner of more than a hundred guests where reigned so much gaiety, cordiality, and good taste. I could not avoid, from time to time, expressing my surprise to Miss Arabella.

"We are among fellow country-people," said the young girl, who smiled at my remarks; "and we all know each other, more or less."

"I should never have thought that in a public place on board a steamer, ladies were obliged to wear evening dress for dinner."

NEGROES CLAD IN THE TRADITIONAL COSTUME OF FIGARO.

"It is a custom which you will find in all the large hotels in New York."

"And that orchestra—very good, upon my word—does it accompany the ship to her destination?"

"I am not sure. But you often have more music than you care for on board our ships."

After dinner the ladies disappeared, and the gentlemen went on deck to smoke.

"Do you mean to go back to the saloon?" said the general to me.

"Yes, certainly; I want to spend the evening with Miss Arabella."

"Then go down and put on a black coat and white tie."

"Is evening dress strictly necessary?"

"Absolutely," said the general. "There were a few frock-coats allowed at dinner, but they will not be permitted in the saloon."

"Then you are not free to do as you like on board your steamers?"

"Never on the first day. You will be free to-morrow."

I went towards the 'tween decks, wondering in which of my trunks I ought to look for my dress-coat.

I was surprised to see the saloon already cleared of the tables, and several ladies sitting there. I took the outside gallery to get back to my cabin, and came upon a large room where negroes, clad in the traditional costume of Figaro, assisted by ladies'-maids, were dressing the hair of three or four fine ladies, and ornamenting them with flowers. I had walked by accident into a hair-dressing saloon, from which I made a hasty retreat.

"There is a ball on board," thought I.

I was not mistaken, for just at that moment the orchestra struck up a waltz. When I left my cabin the dancing had begun.

"Are we going to lead this pleasant life as far as Nashville?" I asked of the general, on rejoining him.

"You, perhaps," replied he; "but as for me, I hope to be back at Méssangère to-morrow."

What I saw astonished me somewhat; there were only nice-looking women, and well-bred gentlemen, and the diamonds that I saw sparkling, looked very much like real. I did not know that all Americans were millionaires.

The dancing was kept up till four in the morning, and going up on deck once, I saw that the ship was lying at anchor. About ten o'clock the general called me, and told me to get my portmanteau strapped. We then went on deck, where I found Miss Arabella and her governess.

"Upon my word!" cried I, "that sailor is carrying off one of my trunks."

"Yes," said the general to me, "you are going to change cabins; do not disturb yourself."

An expression of such wondering surprise was depicted on my face, that the general, his daughter, and some of my new friends who were standing near us, began to laugh.

I then learnt what I should have guessed on first setting foot on board the *Cincinnati*. A rich merchant of New Orleans had hired the steamer for the occasion of the annual ball, to which he invited all his friends, and through the general I had been admitted among the chosen few; at last I understood my old friend's reticence.

The *Jackson* appeared on the horizon; I bade my host, and then Miss Arabella, a last farewell. When I looked round for Miss Angelina, I saw her in the boat which was to take me to the *Jackson*.

"She is going with you," said the general to me. "I was obliged to choose between her and Manon, and I have decided to keep Manon."

A quarter of an hour later, the *Cincinnati* disappeared behind a bend of the river, and I took up my quarters in my new cabin.

On board the *Jackson*, as on the *Cincinnati*, there was a buffet, a hair-dressing saloon, and an orchestra. Unfortunately I did not find there either the style or the agreeable manners of the companions I had just left.

At Nashville I heard of the attack of Fort Sumter. War was openly declared between the North and South. I learnt this news from Miss Angelina; she spoke to me for the first time since our departure, and was leaning on the arm of a gentleman, who, more gallant than I, did not fear to expose himself to the law which could make him the husband of the beautiful and learned young American lady.

"Before a month has passed," said she, pointing to the great plains which the steamer was leaving behind her, "the soldiers of the North will cover that beautiful country with their blue uniforms, and the pride of the Creoles will be brought low. New Orleans, now boasting of her commerce, of her semi-tropical situation, and of her pretended invincibility, will be conquered, and forced to implore grace of New York, whose rival she calls herself."

"Are you not counting your chickens before they are hatched?" said I, eagerly. "The Creoles are brave and resolute, and they have justice on their side."

"We have strength."

"That is rather a questionable argument."

"Do you sympathize with the South?" said the young girl, disdainfully.

"I do not deny that such is the case," I replied calmly. "I like those who like me, especially those who admire my own country. Now, the Northern States disparage France. During the war which gave Venice to Italy, during the gigantic struggle which covered the neighbourhood of Sebastopol with bloodshed, there was not an insult which the New York papers did not shower on the French, on their army, and on their generals. This is why I am indignant with my countrymen for praising America. They see it, and that is their excuse, through the views of M. de Tocqueville's book, a work forty years old, and no longer correct."

My words were imprudent; fortunately we were surrounded by Southerners, the majority of whom shared my opinion. Miss Angelina shrugged her shoulders contemptuously, gratified me with an ironical grimace, and then unceremoniously turned her back upon me. I knew what a scientific arsenal my fair enemy had at her disposal, and I was obliged to confess that her silence, which seemed to leave me the victory, was in reality nothing but ill-concealed contempt for my insignificant self. Certainly I admire as much as any one the material progress realized by the great republic in less than half a century; but as a true friend of liberty, I deplore its moral and political corruptions; they surpass all that can be imagined. The republic of Washington, which was equal to Rome in its respect for laws, is already nothing more than a copy of the lower empire. Will it turn aside from this road which, sooner or later, will give it over into the hands of some low despot? I sincerely hope it may.

Two years ago I learnt with regret that General Dumont had been killed during the War of the Secession. The North, out of policy, and not humanity, as is generally thought, gave liberty to the slaves: may it be none the less blessed for so doing! Miss Arabella would have been ruined, but when the war was ended, her father's servants returned to her. She is married, and Méssangère is still in a flourishing condition. As to Miss Angelina, she is a professor of medicine in a western town, and takes great interest in theology.

THE HORSE-TAMER.

The mouse-coloured horse—Yankees and Texians—An accident—Alone!—
Don José—The wild horse—A terrible night.

TEXAS, although thinly populated, forms at the present day one of the principal states of the great American republic; it is an extensive flat, healthy, and fertile country, abundantly watered by rivers with considerable affluents. The rivers Del Norte, Las Nieves, La Trinidad, and then the San Jacinto, the Brazos, the San Antonio, and the Sabina, offer natural roads of communication—roads which will sooner or later make Texas a privileged country, and perhaps the finest jewel of the American crown.

Although Francis Lassalle, in the year 1684, tried to found settlements in Texas—an attempt which attracted the attention of the Spaniards—this magnificent country remained for a long time abandoned. At the cession of Louisiana, by France, to the United States, the young republic, already encroaching, laid claim to Texas. In 1819, she nominally renounced her pretensions by the treaty of Washington. But two years later, Colonel Austin, having obtained permission to found an Anglo-American colony, under the name of Fredonia, settled on the banks of the Colorado, and there built the capital of Texas. This first attempt at colonization was the beginning of the movement which, by bringing emigrants of European origin to Texas, ended in a proclamation of independence in 1835.

Mexico, on her separation from Spain, having annexed Texas to her province of Coahuila, attempted to maintain her rights by force of arms. Samuel Houston, president of Texas, defeated the Mexican army, commanded by Santa Ana, on the banks of the San Jacinto. In 1845, the United States having admitted Texas into their confederation, a war ensued with the Mexicans, who, after invading their former province, were driven from it. Santa Ana, defeated in several encounters, saw the enemy penetrate into Mexico, by which they lost not only Texas, but the wilds of New Mexico and California.

Two years after this war, that is to say, in 1849, I crossed the Del Norte opposite to the Presidio Grande—a settlement founded by the Spaniards about the year 1610. I intended to go to the Rio de las Nueces, and then up that river as far as Castroville. In order to accomplish this journey, I was obliged to cross virgin countries, forests of oak, cyprus, and magnolias, and above all, vast plains where immense troops of wild horses ranged the country at freedom. The few inhabitants of the country, men of mixed blood, Mexicans by origin and manners, heartily detest their new masters, and in their ignorance easily class all white men under the name of Yankees. Now at this period every Yankee was considered a traitor, and further still, as a heretic, of whom it was a good thing to free the land, whenever an opportunity presented itself.

Notwithstanding the warnings I received, I persisted in my intention of crossing the plains, and I bought, for eight pounds, a strong-looking mouse-coloured pony. I wanted a guide, and my host—a Swiss, who had established himself for many years on the banks of the Rio Grande—decided that for such a journey as I was about to undertake, I should want a safe and experienced man, such as Manuel Oroños, for instance. This Manuel Oroños, a Mexican half-breed, and a horse-tamer by profession, enjoyed an indisputable reputation for horsemanship. He knew Texas well, and no better guide could be found. For two years he had lived a secluded life. He was accused of having taken part with the Americans in the late war; and one of his countrymen having dared to tell him so to his face, was at once stabbed. That is how the story ran at Presidio Grande, but my host did not believe a word of it. Besides, even if it were true, Manuel Oroños was none the less a skilful guide.

Two days later, Manuel Oroños was introduced to me. He was a man of forty, tall and robust, with strong, heavy features. I explained to him my intention of crossing the plains. After reflecting for some time—.

"Very well," said he, suddenly. "When do you wish to start?"

"To-morrow, if possible."

"Be it so, señor."

At break of day, a horseman, in a long scarlet cloak, and straw hat with large flaps at the sides, riding a magnificent horse, with a saddle ornamented with silver, knocked at my host's door with the loaded handle of his riding-whip. I was already busy harnessing my famous mouse-coloured horse, and I went out to meet Manuel Oroños, who, from the richness of his costume and the beauty of his steed, would unmistakably pass for the master. He bowed politely to me, alighted, and eyed my horse *en connoisseur*. Presently he smiled.

"Do you really think you will be able to cross the savannahs on that wretched quadruped?" asked he.

"That wretched quadruped!" cried I, indignantly. "My horse has none of the traditional leanness of Don Quixote's steed; he is well made, good tempered, and if his coat were not such a singular colour...."

"That animal has no stamina, señor—I am certain of that, and only hope that he may not break down with you half-way. But will you take my advice? Let us put off the journey till to-morrow; exchange your horse for another, no matter which, and you will gain by it."

I defended my steed against my guide's criticism, more perhaps out of self-pride than conviction. I would not confess that I had been deceived.

"Such as he is," said I at last, "this horse will quite well carry me from here to the Rio de las Nueces, will he not?"

"Perhaps. Anyway, with God's help, you may do it."

I sprang into the saddle; then, having bid farewell to my host, I used my spur. My steed bounded forward, and set off at a pace which seemed to contradict my guide's gloomy prognostics. Leaving the far-off summits of the Sierra de Guadalupe to our right, we went through the wide street of Presidio Grande, and a few hours later we were riding through a magnolia wood.

Twenty-four hours after starting, we came upon an immense savannah, dotted here and there with clumps of mimosa trees. The heat soon became overpowering. We were, however, obliged to continue our way just the same, for, according to my guide, we had three halting-places to pass before we should be able to find any water. My mouse-coloured horse, which I had as yet only had occasion to praise, now began to lag, and obliged me often to use the spur. All at once the poor beast suddenly stopped short, tottered on its legs, and lay down gently on the ground. Fortunately, foreseeing what would happen, I had taken my feet out of the stirrups. I unsaddled the poor animal as quickly as possible, but it drew its last breath before I could finish the unstrapping.

I then looked at my guide, with bewilderment easy to be conceived; he pulled his thin moustache energetically. We were forty leagues from our starting-point, and sixty from the place we wanted to reach. The situation left much to be desired.

"What am I to do?" cried I.

"My horse could carry both of us very well," replied Manuel Oroños; " but, thus burdened, we shall be obliged to make very short stages, and shall have no pleasant time of it."

"And what about my luggage?" cried I, pointing to a small portmanteau fastened to the saddle, and which, besides a change of clothes, contained my notes and sketches.

"You must leave it as well as your saddle."

This proposition was decidedly not to my taste.

"Take my portmanteau," said I to the guide. "I am not afraid of fatigue. I will follow you on foot."

"Under this sun? You cannot think of it, señor."

"I am a good walker, and if we walk till night . . . ."

"Do you think for one moment," cried the Texian, "that you could walk sixty leagues in this desert?"

"Sixty leagues? No; for we shall turn back, and this time

I will get you to buy me a horse. But tell me, is there no village nearer than Presidio?"

Instead of replying, Manuel looked at the horizon, and again pulled his moustache. I repeated my question.

"There is the Diamond *rancho* about six leagues to the south of us," replied he at last.

"That is a lucky name!" cried I. "Be quick; show me the way."

"Your honour has not an idea of the difficulties you will find in walking," resumed the guide. "First of all, the ground is uneven, the grass is high, and before an hour's time you would be so dreadfully bitten by insects, that your legs and feet would be of no use to you."

"What would you propose, then? I suppose we cannot camp here and wait for help?"

"If your honour had the courage to remain here alone for a few hours, and would trust me with a little gold, I could go to Diamond *rancho*, and bring back another horse."

It was now my turn to be silent. It needed some little reflection, before deciding to remain alone in the midst of a savannah. After all, Manuel was to be relied on, and I had only one fear, which I told him, and it was that he would have great difficulty in finding me in the immense plain, where I should remain lost.

"If you do not move from here," replied my guide, "I promise you I will be here before night."

"Go, then," said I, "and come back quickly."

Without further explanation, Manuel bowed to me, and spurred on his horse. I followed with my eyes for some time, until the mimosas gradually hid him from view, and I was left alone at noon, in the midst of almost absolute silence.

My first care was to cut the grass, arrange it in long bundles, and make myself a shelter. I thus succeeded in improvising a kind of tent, under which I could stretch myself in shelter. The day was spent in defending myself against swarms of insects. The most tiresome were the *pinolillos*, whose venomous bite I had known, to my cost, in former travels in hot countries. How many times I envied the vultures their wings when I saw those bold robbers flying through the cloudless sky. At times the silence around me became so oppressive, I was obliged to whistle or strike the ground with my riding-whip to make a noise.

Just as the sun was nearing the horizon, a light breeze sprang up, and I was able to leave my shelter. About five or six yards from the spot where I had been resting was a hillock, where I resolved to take my stand. From the top of this slight eminence, which overlooked the plain and seemed to have been made by man, I should be able to see my guide in the distance. A fire lighted on the summit would be a signal to him, and enable him to find me sooner.

I flattered myself that this was a very good idea. From the hillock I was able to see the place where my poor horse was lying, and also the trace left by Manuel in the long grass. I gathered sufficient branches to feed my fire, and night found me warming myself before a bright flame, the crackling of which enlivened and reassured me. Two or three times my attention was aroused; I thought I heard the sound of barking in the distance, but hearing nothing the next moment, I attributed the sound to my fancy.

Hours went by, and my guide did not come. This camping in the open plain was not the least curious incident in my adventurous life. If Manuel did not return, what would become of me? I asked myself this terrible question from time to time, and a shudder ran through my body. But one only abandons an enemy in the desert, and Manuel was not my enemy.

Suddenly the galloping of a horse was heard, at first in the distance, and then more distinctly. I got up, shouted, and ran some distance in front of my bivouac. To my great surprise, instead of my guide I saw a horseman with a rifle at his side, who looked at me with curiosity equal to my own. I seized my revolver.

"Friend or foe?" I cried.

"Whichever you like, señor; for my part, I have no evil intentions against you. One word only: are you a Yankee?"

"No, I am a Frenchman, and consequently a friend of the Texians, whatever party they may uphold."

"Well said, señor, and I believe you."

The new-comer then hung his rifle to his saddle-bow and drew near my fire. I imitated his confidence by putting down my revolver, and I briefly told him my misadventure.

"Manuel Oroños!" cried he, when I mentioned my companion's name. "Is Manuel Oroños your guide?"

"Yes," replied I. "He is at present at the Diamond *rancho*, in search of another horse for me."

"He will return as he went, señor. The Diamond *rancho* has been abandoned for almost six months."

I soon learnt with surprise that the horseman lived at less than a mile from the place where I was, and that the barking which I had heard was not imaginary.

"Is not Oroños aware of this circumstance?" I asked.

"Oh yes, perfectly; but there is a death-feud between us, and he does not care to meet me."

These words threw me into great perplexity. Oroños could not now be long in making his appearance, and if he came up unexpectedly, I should most probably be the unwilling witness of some fierce struggle.

"Good evening," said I to the horseman. "My guide will probably not return until to-morrow; I am going to sleep in the mean time."

"By my worthy patron St. Joseph! señor," cried the horseman, "will you not do me the honour of sleeping beneath my roof?"

"No," I replied, "although I thank you for your offer. You have just told me that there is blood between you and my guide, and I am particularly anxious that you should not meet."

"I swear, señor," replied the horseman, "that you and Manuel will be in safety under my roof. Hospitality comes before vengeance. I shall tell him so, for I expect him."

The horseman at once alighted, tethered his horse, and quietly sat down by my side. Ten minutes passed, and at last Oroños appeared. He grew slightly pale on seeing my companion.

"Good day," said the latter, rising.

"Good day, José," replied my guide. "Were you waiting for me?"

"Yes, to invite you to accompany this traveller to my roof. You know I mean what I say, Manuel."

Manuel bowed his head without replying, and soon following the horseman, we came to a large building with a turf roof. On the threshold two young women were bruising maize, by the flickering light of a fire. After having given us some supper, Don José took us to a small shed built against the house, and there he left us to sleep, wishing us good-night.

"What tragical event has happened between you and our host?" I then asked Manuel.

"Four years ago," replied my guide, "in a horse-race I gained a prize which José's brother competed for with me. He became furious, and shot my horse; whereupon I struck him across the chest with a club, from which he died. José and his brother were at that time on the side of the Americans; I was, and am still, for Mexico, and our quarrel was thought to have arisen from political reasons."

"Are you afraid of vengeance?"

"Yes," replied my guide; "but not this evening. Anyway, I shall keep on my guard. Let us sleep; I am quite exhausted with fatigue."

I stretched myself on the mat which had been placed on the ground, and Manuel followed my example. A quarter of an hour later, when he thought I was asleep, I saw him get up quietly, and go away. I looked after him. Instead of going towards the house, as I had feared, my guide went in the direction of the plain. Evidently he had not much faith in Don José's promises, and wished to put himself in safety. The hours went on, and I fell asleep.

When I awoke, the ardent rays of the sun were already burning the great plains, and there were light mists floating in the air. I found my portmanteau and my horse's harness before the door of the *rancho*, and standing round a young horse were Don José, Manuel, and two servants. Manuel was examining the horse carefully, and I learnt that it was the one my host wished to sell me.

"Is it a wild horse?" I asked, seeing the way in which he was fettered.

"Wild? no," replied the seller. "He has the red mark on his thigh, which proves that he has been thoroughly broken in; only he has lived free on the plains for a year, and will be a little restive until he is reminded of obedience. Is he not a fine animal, Manuel?"

"Yes," said Manuel, "there is a good look about the creature; but he must be ridden to know what he is worth."

"Certainly," replied Don José.

Two Indians, who were breaking in a colt, were at once called. Before us stretched a savannah, the grass of which had been burnt away for some distance; a precaution generally taken by *rancheros*, as much to rid themselves of harmful insects as to have tenderer grass for their cattle.

"Will you not show the animal off yourself?" asked Don José of Manuel.

"Yes," answered my guide, shortly.

To my great surprise, the two Indians led the horse to an enormous branch covered with foliage, which they fastened to the long tail of the trembling creature. Meanwhile Manuel stripped himself naked to the waist. He passed a horsehair rope through the mouth of the *potro*—a name given to young horses—which, with a slip-knot, served as bridle and bit at the same time.

The Indians hung on to this curb, holding the horse, which, frightened and angry, lowered his head and pawed the ground restively.

"Stay," cried I, seeing my guide ready to spring on to the animal's back; "what I want is a quiet, tractable animal. What would be the use of a wild horse like that to me?"

"Before an hour's time, señor," replied Don José, "Manuel, who has not his equal in the country for breaking in wild horses, will bring back his pupil as pliant as the backbone of a tiger."

I turned to Manuel, and he said abruptly—

"All right; we will talk about it presently."

He immediately sprang on to the *potro*, which curveted, gave a prolonged neigh, and shook his head to free himself of the two Indians who kept him prisoner, lifting them from the ground as he did so.

"Let go," cried Manuel.

Just as the Indians were obeying this order, Don José, with a rapid movement, cut the cord which tied the branch to the horse's tail. The animal, feeling itself free, made one or two swerving steps, and then darted forward like an arrow.

"What a treacherous act!" I cried, advancing towards Don José; "it may perhaps be the cause of that man's death!"

"I have an old account to settle with Manuel, señor," quietly replied my host. "Take my advice; don't interfere in the matter."

Borne away by his steed, Manuel had disappeared. The Indians and the half-castes, as much surprised as myself, looked at their master without saying a word.

"I have put my vengeance in God's hands, and He will decide," said Don José, loftily.

For an hour I walked over the plain, looking continually in the direction where I had seen my guide disappear. Carried away by the mad pace of his steed, the horse-breaker, dashed against the trunk of a tree, was now perhaps lying on the immense savannah. At last, taking possession of the unhappy man's horse, I saddled it with the full intention of going in search of him.

"Where are you going?" asked Don José.

"I am going to try and find your victim," said I, indignantly.

"My victim! Of course you are at liberty to speak and do as you like; nevertheless, if you believe me, the best thing you can do would be to resume your journey peacefully. You are going to the Rio de Nueces, are you not? One of my Indians will serve you as guide; I place him at your disposal."

I was about to set out, when an exclamation from one of the Indians made me look towards my left, and it was with a

"LET GO!" CRIED MANUEL.

"I THOUGHT I HEARD THE CRACKING OF BRANCHES."

feeling of inexpressible relief that I saw Manuel returning to us full speed. At less than five hundred yards from me, he suddenly checked the foaming horse, made him walk, turned him to the right and to the left; and at last, after another gallop, he stopped short at my side.

"He is a good animal," said he. "You can buy him. He is worth thirty piastres. Pay, and let us start."

Astounded by this incredible coolness, I stood open-mouthed. Manuel rapidly dressed himself and saddled my horse, which, almost exhausted, no longer offered any resistance. Half an hour later, Don José having received his thirty piastres without any remark, Manuel persuaded me to mount his horse, and he took mine.

"Good day, José!" cried my guide. "You have played me a trick I shall not forget; so *au revoir*."

"*Au revoir*," replied José mechanically, and, riveted to the spot where he stood, he watched us out of sight.

Directly the *rancho* had disappeared behind the mimosas, I drew near Manuel.

"This good beast deceived his master's hopes," said he, stroking the *potro's* neck, "and your acquisition is good. Before three days you will be able to mount my pupil without any danger."

I wanted to question my guide, and speak to him about Don José; but he was silent, pulled his moustache, and rode on in front. When night fell, the horse-breaker, after having carefully examined the ground, made several circuits and finally halted. The horses were tethered. He led me further on, and we settled down among the cacti and mimosa trees.

After a frugal supper, Manuel placed his fire-arms within reach, stretched himself on the ground, and fell asleep. More agitated than he by the events of the morning, although they had ended happily, I did not get to sleep till much later. In the middle of the night, I thought I heard the crackling of branches; I got up quickly, and saw my guide still slumbering peacefully. I lay down, but it was some time before I again fell asleep.

N

It was daylight when I opened my eyes, and what was my surprise on seeing Don José and one of his Indians quietly saddling my horse. I turned quickly to the place where Manuel Oroños was lying. He was still sleeping. Surprised at his long sleep, I went up to him, and then stood aghast. Before me lay the unhappy man, white and livid, a gaping wound on his breast, sleeping an eternal slumber. He had been assassinated during the night.

"It is your work!" I cried, advancing towards Don José.

"It is my work, by the hand of Ametl," replied he, pointing to the Indian. "It was high time to pay an old debt. Thus perish," added he, with energy, "all those who delivered Texas to the Yankees."

It was a singular thing, the two antagonists bore the same accusation against each other.

Don José took the poor horse-breaker's place, and the corpse was left to the birds of prey. For three days the assassin served as my guide, and his company caused me a certain uneasiness, especially in the evening, when I was obliged to lie down side by side with my terrible conductor.

As soon as we were within sight of the Rio de las Nueces Don José left me, without taking any compensation for his trouble. I related my adventure at the first house, where I was hospitably received, and instead of being indignant, my hosts seemed to think the incident quite natural. Two days later I again told the story to some American planters.

"We shall never have any peace," said one of them, "until the country is rid of these Spanish half-castes; and it will not be long before it is, if they begin killing each other."

The law of virgin countries is that of the strongest; is it not so sometimes even in civilized lands?

TENOCHTITLAN.

Arrival of the Spaniards at Mexico—The palaces of Montézuma—The modern town—The National Palace—The theatres—Itinerant merchants —Society.

It was on the 20th of March, 1852, about four o'clock in the afternoon, when, mounted on a sturdy mule, I had a first glimpse of the capital of Mexico. The sky was a magnificent deep azure, and the somewhat scanty verdure of the central plateau bright with vernal tints. A number of vultures were hovering over the ancient city of the Aztecs, that town of Tenochtitlan which, founded in 1327, taken and sacked by the Spaniards and their allies in 1521, was almost immediately rebuilt, as it now stands.

I had just crossed the *Terre tempérée,* and I must confess the dwarfed trees which I saw here and there gave me a very unfavourable idea of the valley of Mexico, which, nevertheless, passes for being very fertile. Fertile! Well, be it so, especially towards the west; but, in order to call it fertile, one must forget for a moment the vast tropical forests just crossed, the coffee plantations of Jalapa, the orange woods of Orizava—in a word, the verdant country sloping from the great Cordilleras.

To tell the truth, the impression I had was anything but pleasing on perceiving the city, which for more than two centuries was considered as the finest and most opulent city of the New World. But before saying anything of the modern town, let us speak of the great city described by Cortez, Torquemada, Bernard Diaz del Castillo, Clavigero, Herrera, and finally by M. l'Abbé Brasseur de Bourbourg. One can see that historians are not wanting of the ancient capital of the Mexicatls, or Aztecs, which, for a long time unrivalled, is now surpassed in splendour, population, and riches by many cities of the United States.

Built partly on piles, in the midst of lakes, Mexico is often called by the Spaniards the *Venice of the New World*. At the time of the conquest, it was intersected, at right angles, by a number of canals, bordered on either side by paths for foot-passengers. These canals, wide and deep, were incessantly covered with boats, and at certain distances spanned by bridges, fixed or movable, according to the necessity of the position. In fact, Mexico then possessed only four roads of any importance, which, starting from the four doors of the temple of Huitzilopochtli—the god of war—were the means of communication between the city and the country. These causeways, built on piles, were paved with admirably cemented flag-stones, wide enough to allow of ten men passing abreast.

At that time Mexico contained no less than sixty thousand households. The commodious and spacious dwellings of the nobility and merchant aristocracy, situated in the centre of the city, stood on terraces varying in height. These houses, built of lava—*tetzontli*—had only one story above the ground-floor; a court surrounded with porticoes, and adorned with a fountain placed in the centre. Some of the richer occupants had gardens.

The lower quarters of the city, inhabited by the poor, were comprised of houses built of *adobes*, or sun-dried bricks. On account of the public health, these houses had been built on a layer of stone several yards deep, to protect them from inundations.

At the time of the arrival of the Spaniards, no capital could boast of being better regulated than Mexico. No one, except the soldiers of the emperor's body-guard, was allowed to carry arms in the public roads. At night, brasiers in the streets, carefully attended to, lighted the city until daybreak. A vigilant body of police kept the canals constantly dredged, the streets swept, and the public squares watered. Everywhere in this model city

MEXICO.

the water, winding through numerous pipes, abundantly supplied each house.

Besides the principal temple dedicated to the god of war, and enclosing seventy-eight sanctuaries, Mexico contained more than four hundred buildings erected in honour of its divinities. That which added further to the splendour of this great city were the numerous palaces built by Montézuma and his ancestors. The ordinary residence of the emperor, built of rose-coloured pumice-stone, had twenty gates opening on to as many squares, and in the centre of the building were three vast courtyards ornamented with fountains. Marble, porphyry, and alabaster were everywhere to be seen, under the form of columns, flag-stones, and steps. Rich carpets and mats of the finest texture covered the floors. There were more than a hundred rooms, and as many bath-rooms, without counting the armouries, in this sumptuous palace, where gold, silver, and feathers rivalled the marble of the porticoes in brilliancy. "The roof of this palace was so extensive," said a gentleman in the suite of Cortez, "that more than thirty horsemen would have been able to joust on the terraces it formed, as easily as in the large square of a town. In the interior, vessels filled with perfume were continually burning, and the daily service, according to Torquemada, occupied no less than three thousand persons.

A building not less remarkable than that of which I have just spoken, was the palace destined for the rearing of birds, whose feathers, carefully collected and prepared, were used in making those pictures now so rare, that only fragments of them are to be found in museums. Extensive gardens were enclosed within the building, where tanks supplied with salt or fresh water, according to the nature of the birds, were placed near them.

Not far from here was the imperial menagerie. The fauna of Mexico, birds, quadrupeds, reptiles, fish, had been collected in this palace, and enclosed in gardens, cages, or tanks. One of the rooms of the building was appropriated to the lame, club-footed, dwarfs—in short, every species of deformity that afflicts the human race.

We will now return to my subject after this digression.

After contemplating for a moment the great city stretching before me, its numerous spires reminding me of Spanish towns, I with some difficulty persuaded my mule to pass through a monumental gateway, bearing the name of *Garita de Puebla*, leading into a long, wide street. Scantily clad half-breeds, both male and female, sitting on the pavement, or squatting in front of their doors, watched me pass with a dogged expression on their faces. As I got further into the city, it became gradually transformed. The houses were higher and more elegant, the streets more crowded with people, and the shops better fitted up; besides this, the costumes of the people I met were more in European style. At last, after having crossed the cathedral square, and ventured into the famous street of the Plateros, I found myself riding in the midst of carriages and carts, and among gentlemen wearing frock-coats, silk hats, and kid gloves. To my great annoyance, my terrible steed would stop short from time to time and begin to bray. At last, about six o'clock in the evening, I entered the courtyard of a large hotel. At seven o'clock a waiter, in a blue cloth jacket, white apron, and serviette under his arm, brought me a bill of fare, and awaited my orders. I could almost have believed myself in Paris.

The next morning, according to my custom, I set out to wander through the streets of the city, and this time on foot. I was favourably impressed after this first excursion. Mexico is decidedly a fine city, well-built, well-situated, with the elegance of civilization curiously contrasting with the singularities of the savage world. But what has become of its former police? As to cleanliness, Mexico cannot be compared either to London or Paris; nevertheless, it is certainly better ordered than New York and the Havannah cities, where edileship leaves much to be desired!

And again what have become—and I am not the first to ask the question—of the canals, the palaces, the temples, and the gardens, descriptions of which left us by early historians, especially by Cortez, seem like pages taken from the *Thousand*

and One Nights? The traveller seeks in vain for traces of the past in the modern city. Urged by deplorable religious zeal, the conquerors, it is said, destroyed all the marble and jasper monuments consecrated by the Aztecs to the worship of their gods, the principal of which enclosed more than three thousand statues. Without having the slightest claims to being an archæologist, I venture to express my opinion that the Spaniards singularly exaggerated the wonders of the world they had just discovered. However great their ardour of destruction may have been, some vestiges of the past, separated from us by scarcely three centuries, would still exist. Now in this great city, with its streets cut at right angles, not a fragment belonging to the Aztec city is to be found. Everything is modern, and built in the Moorish or Italian style, which the Spaniards introduced into every country where they set footing.

The finest and most extensive buildings of modern Mexico are decidedly the convents, of which there are not less than twenty-two. The riches of these communities, for so long proverbial, are at the present day much diminished. The gold, silver, and precious stones which adorned the smallest shrine, have gradually become the spoil of the revolutionists. Some pictures of rare artistic value, and a few books curious on account of their antiquity, are now almost the only treasures preserved by the monks, whom a recent law has expelled from Mexico.

The National Palace, of which the Mexicans are very proud, has scarcely anything remarkable about it except its proportions. It is an immense kind of barracks, serving as residence to the president of the republic and its different ministers. The *Diputacion*, or Mansion House, is a large, square stone building, where the offices of the administration of the city are to be found, and, curious assemblage, the municipal prison and the Exchange.

Mexico possesses five or six theatres, all of modern construction, perfectly regulated, and luxuriously fitted up. Old Spanish plays, and especially French dramas, form the greater part of the representations; nevertheless, a company of Italian singers, generally well selected, attract the preference of the higher classes in Mexican society. The national amusements of the Mexicans are bull-fights, and perhaps also marionette shows.

When intelligent excavations have brought to light the objects which the Chichimecs and the Toltecs amused themselves with burying in caves, the National Museum will become one of the most curious in the New World. At the present day it is nothing but an incoherent heap of heterogeneous collections: insects, birds, and quadrupeds are mingled with archæological objects found in the valley. Mexico must have years of peace to regain anything like her ancient splendour. Devastated by civil war, this unfortunate country sees her frontiers continually ravaged by powerful neighbours. The Mexican, like many other nations, alas! wears herself out in seeking in vain for the best form of government.

Like all great cities, the capital of Mexico has its itinerant merchants, with their singular costumes and cries. From break of day, Indian coal-men traverse the streets, calling to purchasers in a droning, mournful voice. Behind them come butter-men, announcing the price of their goods, their guttural voices alternating with that of the butcher, who, driving before him a mule laden with joints of meat, sells his merchandise without allowing a choice of pieces, and with superb disdain of the most elementary rules of cleanliness. In their steps follow the rag-and-bone merchants, whose trade consists in exchanging fruit or spices for rags and bones, cinders, tallow, and crusts of bread. Last of all are the haberdashers, and the pork-butchers, who, with lighted stoves on their heads, splash the passers-by with grease in which their sausages are frying. Walking in a file are brush, straw-mat, barley-sugar, and sherbet vendors. Everything you can think of is sold in the streets of Mexico: remnants of stuff, spurs, hats, jewellery, even false money. These good people, in their picturesque dresses, enliven the streets with their incessant cries, and take up their positions on the pavement, to the dire discomfort of foot-passengers.

The Calle de los Plateros is the principal commercial street.

Here millinery, jewellery, and drapery shops, all in imitation of European style, are crowded together. One scarcely meets any one in this part of the city who is not dressed in the latest Parisian fashion. As one gets nearer the suburbs, blouses are seen instead of overcoats, caps replace hats, shawls mantles, and shoes boots. Quite on the outskirts of the city, a simple pair of bathing-drawers for the men, and a short petticoat for the women, was the only attire generally worn. From this point of view, Mexico is certainly the most singular city in the world. That downright democrat, the Indian, props his bamboo cabin against the walls of a palace, and struts proudly in his semi-nudity among the elegant young dandies, who, although affecting to despise him, are nevertheless of the same race, and his countrymen.

The highest society of Mexico is polished, engaging, hospitable. It follows as closely as possible French customs. The women of Mexico, for centuries renowned for the beauty of their eyes, the smallness of their hands and feet, and the wealth of their hair, are still worthy in some respects of the reputation of their ancestors. They are reproached for indolence. How can it be otherwise, in a country where the height of good manners forbids them ever to go on foot?

THE PEARL FOREST.

CHAPTER I.

Isidro—Don Anastasio Véga—The Pearl Forest—The Hermit's Cave—The ambush.

To the east of Orizava stretches a vast plain, overshadowed by a mountain covered with ancient forests. This mountain, a branch of the great Cordilleras, runs from east to west, and bears the name of the *Pearl Mountain*. It is only passable by abrupt, steep paths, winding through the forest of the same name. But beyond this, one has a glimpse of picturesque, fertile valleys, a veritable Eden, where all the productions of the tropics, cacti, cocoa-nut, orange, lemon, and coffee trees crowd together in profuse luxuriance. At the time of the possession of Mexico by Spain, these valleys were well cultivated; but at the present day they are abandoned, and are gradually returning to their former wild state. Gigantic trees entwine their branches across the high roads, creepers block the paths, and cypresses wave their sombre boughs over the ruins of habitations destroyed by fire.

On the 5th of January, 1830, nine years after the final proclamation of the independence of Mexico, two Indians, who, from their orange-coloured skin, the regularity of their features, and the fine proportions of their figures, might have been recognized as descendants of the ancient Totonac race, were laboriously climbing the last slopes of the Pearl Mountain. They were dressed in sleeveless woollen shirts, cotton breeches, wide straw hats, and wore sandals on their feet. Two large travelling-bags, strapped on their shoulders, visibly impeded their progress. It is always difficult to guess the age of an Indian, for the men of that race have the privilege of preserving their teeth to extreme old age, and their hair does not turn grey until very late. Nevertheless, from his walk, less elastic and free than his companion's, although his limbs were more robust, it might be supposed that the one taking the lead was much the elder.

"Father," said the second, in the Aztec tongue, "I do not hear the master."

His companion at once stood still, breathed heavily, and then listened. The atmosphere was calm, the forest quiet; not a sound, save the buzzing of insects, disturbed the reigning silence.

"They are coming, Isidro," replied he. "Listen!"

Isidro made a sign of assent, and the two continued their way. Before long, about a hundred steps below them, appeared a horseman, dressed as a Spaniard, and, a remarkable thing in a Mexican, he wore the Andalusian hat. Whilst guiding his steed, the horseman continually turned towards a woman, who, enveloped from head to waist in a thin shawl, guided the spirited pony she rode with a firm hand.

"Take care, Lola," said the horseman. "A false step up this hill would be very dangerous."

"You make yourself too uneasy, father," replied the young girl. "You forget that I have been a horsewoman ever since I was a little child, and that we have made more than one excursion together like this in the Sierra de Léon."

"The roads were better, Lola."

"You like to say that, father, because it was in your own country."

"Be it so. Any way, you were well used to the horse you rode. Here we are shut in between two walls of rocks. Be careful."

"Really, father, if we are to travel along roads like this for two days, as you have told me, you must be less doubtful of my skill, or you will make yourself ill with anxiety."

Just then the two travellers rejoined the Indians, who were resting, leaning their burdens against the rocks.

"If my memory does not deceive me, José," said the horseman, speaking to the elder of his two guides, "we shall be out of this forest in twenty minutes, and on the top of the mountain in half an hour."

"You are right, master; but the worst part still remains for us to cross. The last earthquake caused a landslip, and destroyed part of the old path. Come along," continued the Indian, speaking to his companion; "we will rest further up."

The four travellers resumed their arduous ascent, and soon came upon fallen heaps of rock, held together on the hill-side by trunks of trees.

"Master," said José, "the time has come for you to alight. Isidro will lead the señora's horse, and I will attend to yours."

Don Anastasio Véga—such was the Spaniard's name—at once alighted. He was a man of about forty-five, with a bronzed skin, serious countenance, and stern features. He was short, strongly built, and, judging from his powerful limbs, of no uncommon strength. He assisted his daughter to alight, and Lola, throwing back the scarf, showed a delicate oval face, animated with large, brilliant, intelligent eyes. Scarcely had she alighted, than she ran towards a rock to gather a flower, which she at once placed in her hair.

"Ah, coquette!" cried Don Anastasio.

Lola blushed, not because of her father's remark, but from the artless admiration with which Isidro was regarding her. At the risk of breaking the beautiful flower with which she had just adorned herself, the young girl quickly pulled the scarf over her head, and took Don Anastasio's arm, whilst Isidro, seizing hold of the pony's bridle, led him on in front. José and his son climbed the almost perpendicular slope with surprising agility, considering the burdens they carried on their shoulders. Taking advantage of a gap in the wall of rock, the two Indians obliged the horses to walk over blocks of sandstone, where their hoofs had hardly anything to cling to. This difficult passage was fortunately very short, but when Don Anastasio and his daughter had crossed it, they looked back with surprise, and could scarcely believe that their steeds had been able to get over such a difficult pass. The travellers then left the last trees of the forest behind them, and found themselves on a barren soil, strewn with large blocks of stone, less dangerous, but more difficult to climb. At last they reached the top of the mountain. Lola had bravely surmounted all obstacles, but she was now almost breathless. She took a few steps forward on the crest of the hill, and then turning to her father, who had followed her, uttered a cry of admiration.

From the height at which she stood, the young girl saw at her feet part of the forest she had just crossed, and further on the valley bordered by a lesser chain of the Sierra de Songolica, enclosing the city of Orizava.

"Oh, father, how beautiful it is!" cried Lola, delightedly.

The Spaniard put his arms round her, and clasped her to his breast.

"That is just what your mother said when I brought her here for the first time," said he. "Ah, dear child, what memories it awakens!"

Don Anastasio bent his head and stood for some time lost in thought, and his daughter respected his silence. After having freed themselves of their burdens, the two Indians unbridled and fettered the horses, to let them graze. Without deigning to look for a shelter, José and his son sat down on the ground; then, taking some maize cakes and dried fruit from a bag, they began to eat with good appetites. Rousing himself at last from his reverie, Don Anastasio led his daughter towards a tree recently struck down by lightning, and over which creepers were already twining in flowery garlands. There, sheltered from the sun's rays, the father and daughter in their turn took some food from their saddle-pockets and ate with as good appetite as their guides.

Whilst they lunched, the travellers were able to survey the magnificent panorama before them at their leisure.

"Father," said Lola, pointing towards Orizava, with its spires standing out against the blue sky, "is that the city where I was born?"

"Yes, my child; and if the sun were not so dazzling, I could even show you our old home."

"Is it imagination, father, or is my memory awakening? It seems to me that I can remember these plains and mountains, these gigantic trees and wonderful flowers, and that city lying between the hills—in fact, all the landscape I can now see."

"You were just five years old, Lola, when we left this country, and since then I have so often talked to you about Mexico, that it is not strange you think you recognize it all. Alas! I have seen that plain stretching before us covered with smoke, and strewn with the corpses of my brave countrymen."

"Do not think about it, father."

"I wish I could not, my child; but how can I forget the past? I knew this country, when it was happy under the paternal rule of the King of Spain; then I saw his children, his sons, revolt against their mother country, and ravage by fire and sword everything belonging to Spain. I saw my lands devastated, and myself exiled by those whom I had protected."

"Once more, father, do not think of the past. The ports of Mexico are now re-opened to the Spanish; to-morrow we shall be on your old estate."

"In the midst of ruins."

"Which you will rebuild by work and energy. My mother was a Mexican; I was born here. Do you mean to consider me also as an enemy?"

"You have Spanish blood in your veins, Lola," eagerly replied Don Anastasio.

"And I am proud of it. But we have other things to think about. Do you not want to regain the fortune which the war snatched from us? To work, father! It is not the time to despair or grieve, just as we are at the end of our long journey. Is not the meeting with José and his son a lucky omen? For them, you are always the good master, on whose land they were born; and no doubt your other old servants will come round you. The Indians like you, we know."

"It is fourteen years, Lola, since I was obliged to leave this country."

"Do you tell me the time to remind me that I shall soon be nineteen?" asked the young girl gaily.

"No; but to make you understand that more than one of my old friends and servants are dead."

"We have to do with the living, father. According to José, and from what you learnt at Orizava, it is a half-breed, named Rendon, who has taken possession of your lands."

"Yes—Salvador Rendon, a child I have often taken on my knee."

"He will restore your possessions."

"That is just what I am not sure about."

"You can go to law; you are on the right side."

"Can there be any justice in a country which has disowned its rightful king, and which has no settled government yet?"

"I know nothing about that, father," replied Lola, laughing; "what I know is that I love you, and that I am happy anywhere with you. If you do not succeed in regaining this fortune which would enable me to ride in a carriage, well, then, I shall go on foot as before."

"Who would have thought," resumed Don Anastasio, "that the miserable revolt in the village of Dolorès, in 1810, would end, in 1821, in the separation of Mexico from Spain! Who would have thought that Iturbide, the friend of my childhood, would become emperor, and would perish beneath the bullets of those whom he had restored to so-called liberty! Finally, who would have thought that I should see again this country, which I believed I had left for ever!"

"Who would have thought, father," cried Lola, "that I should see you so sad just as you are within sight of your journey's end, and I on the verge of possessing the carriage you have so often promised me?"

"Little goose! Are you only mocking at my affection for you?"

"I am not foolish, father; the proof that I am, on the contrary, very sensible, is that I hold to my carriage. Do you not think that I should know how to recline on the cushions as gracefully as the governor's wife? You have often told me that when once you have got back your property, you will be rich enough for me to marry a prince, as they do in fairy tales. Only, father, you would be obliged to return to Europe, for there are no princes to be found now in this beautiful country."

Don Anastasio, like a true Spaniard, maintained a seriousness which not even his daughter's gaiety could disturb; and she began to gather the bright-coloured orchids growing in wild profusion. In making her collection, Lola approached the two Indians. Old José had stretched himself on the ground and was sleeping, whilst his son, leaning with his elbow against a rock, like a fine copper-coloured statue, watched the young girl as she flitted about.

"Is it not time to be starting, Isidro?" asked the Spaniard of his guide.

Isidro got up and lightly touched his father's arm, who at once aroused himself.

"Master wants to start," said the young Indian.

The horses were soon bridled. Lola and her father mounted, and the two Indians, having resumed their burdens, crossed the narrow summit of the mountain. Reaching the other side, the little caravan followed a path less uneven than the first, but perhaps more perilous on account of the slope. As they went further on, the trees grew closer together, the ground became moist, and the daylight could hardly penetrate the shade. A dull noise was heard, proceeding from a torrent flowing through the bottom of the narrow ravine which the travellers' had to cross.

Having reached that spot, a halt was made to take refreshment and rest. The place was picturesque and wild. Gigantic trees everywhere, but not a bird enlivened the foliage with its song. The sun could only enter these depths for a few minutes, and yet that rapid passage of its rays was enough to maintain life there. Lola was lost in silent admiration as she listened to the roar of the torrent, awakening a thousand echoes with its noise, and making a continual roar like thunder in this primitive corner of the world.

It took more than an hour to get out of the ravine and into the sunlight again. Every one had been silent during this ride. The first sunbeam that darted its golden arrows across the path, brought back the smiles to Lola's face. She urged on her horse and breathed more freely. Flowers soon were seen growing by the roadside, and the far-off roar of the torrent died away into a vague murmur.

It was five o'clock in the afternoon, and the slanting rays gave warning of a speedy sunset.

"It will be dark in half an hour, master," said José. "Let us push on, if you want to reach the Hermit's Cave."

"Yes, let us go faster, that is easily said," cried Lola. "For my own part, I should like nothing better than a good gallop; but I do not see the possibility of getting one."

"Let us press on," said Don Anastasio; "the nights are bitterly cold on these heights, and the Hermit's Cave is the only place where we can find shelter."

"The Hermit's Cave—what is that, father?"

"A hollow made in the side of the mountain we are crossing, where an old monk used to live. He must be dead now."

"He is dead," said José; "he was assassinated."

"Assassinated! Good Heaven, and by whom?" cried Don Anastasio.

"No one knows. His body was found at the bottom of the ravine, pierced with bullets, and half devoured by vultures."

"Was this crime committed during the revolt?"

"No; two years later, when there was no fighting going on."

"And has the murderer never been discovered?"

"Never."

"He was a holy man," resumed the Spaniard, crossing himself. "He was my friend, and at the time of my prosperity I helped more than one poor man whom he sent to me for assistance."

Saddened by his reflections, Don Anastasio again fell into his usual passive humour. Wishing to arouse him from his reverie, his daughter urged on her indefatigable horse; and the more her father remonstrated with her for her imprudence, the

O

more the pretty Lola laughed at the obstacles, and even seemed to enjoy them.

By a last effort, the travellers reached the crest of the mountain, where they hoped to find a shelter, and were passing between the huge blocks of granite which periodical earthquakes precipitate into the ravine. José was walking in front, his son following him at a short distance; then came Don Anastasio and Lola. Suddenly two or three pistol-shots were heard. The old Indian, who at this moment was climbing a rock, turned round and fell on his face. Isidro, throwing down his burden, sprang into the bushes, and Don Anastasio's horse was shot under him. This scene passed like a flash of lightning before Lola's eyes; for her horse, rearing and turning round, set off at a mad gallop down the slope, which it had had such difficulty in climbing.

CHAPTER II.

The flight—A deliverer—A walk in the forest—Old José—An unexpected meeting—The bandits' retreat.

LOLA was an excellent horsewoman, but she tried in vain to rein in her steed; the noble animal, frightened and excited, was quite insensible to the bit. At each of his bounds it seemed as though the rider must be dashed on the rocks, or crushed against the trunk of a tree.

"Father!" she cried, in a tone of anguish; then she shut her eyes.

All at once the horse neighed low and piteously, and slackened its speed; it trembled and shook all over, then suddenly stood still, and the young girl had hardly time to jump off its back, when the poor beast, wounded in the chest by a bullet, fell down as though struck by lightning. Lola stood for a moment quite overwhelmed by this new difficulty; then, thinking she heard the sound of footsteps above her, she

"PRETTY LOLA LAUGHED AT ALL OBSTACLES."

instinctively sprang into the thicket, and walked on for some time, scarcely knowing whither she went, but going towards the bottom of the ravine. Night came on suddenly, without any twilight. Lola stopped to listen—she heard some one calling—and again she walked on. At last, not being able to see where to stop, she collected her thoughts and remembered her father.

"Foolish creature that I am!" cried she. "I am leaving him."

She tried to call out, but her throat was parched and she could utter no sound. After discovering where she was, the courageous young girl walked resolutely towards the place where she had seen old José fall; but soon she could neither see nor hear anything.

"I must find my father," said she, with the energy of despair.

And she again began to walk, stumbling against some obstacle at every step, or getting her feet entangled in the trailing creepers. Not being able to move a step further, lost in a forest inhabited by wild beasts, and fearing lest her father should have been killed, the poor girl sank on her knees and prayed.

More than an hour passed. Lola, shivering and sitting at the foot of a tree, kept her eyes shut, while anxious thoughts were passing through her brain. She again saw old José stretched on the path, Don Anastasio's horse falling under him, and it seemed to her as though she were still being carried away by the mad speed of her own horse. How was it that they had been attacked in this solitary place? Who was it that had laid in ambush for them?

The air was so still that not a leaf moved; but instead of reassuring, the profound silence scared her, by making her more keenly sensible of her loneliness. The darkness gradually decreased; a dim light penetrated the forest.

"Can it be daylight?" said the young girl to herself, for the minutes had seemed to her as long as years.

She raised her eyes and soon saw that it was the moon's pale beams. Dawn was still far off.

She tried to find her way back to the path. New fears now

assailed her, in the dim, uncertain light; trees, bushes, and rocks took fantastic and appalling shapes; but summoning up her courage and good sense, Lola succeeded in quieting her terror. She wanted to go to her father and share his fate, whether he were a prisoner or dead. After walking for a quarter of an hour, she gave a sigh of satisfaction on finding herself in the narrow path she had followed several hours ago.

Then walking on, taking care to make no noise, she slowly climbed the steep mountain-slope. Fortunately, through her father's advice, her boots were strong, and her delicate feet did not suffer much from the rough ground. Suddenly she stood still. She thought she heard some one move in the thicket; she had several times had the same idea, but now she was not deceived. She hid herself behind a tree and waited.

The footsteps drew nearer. Lola, again seized with terror, left the path and fled into the woods, violently pushing aside the branches without reflecting that the noise would attract the attention she wished to avoid. In fact, she soon knew that she was being followed, and even imagined that she heard some one calling her, just as she had become helplessly entangled in the brambles.

"Oh, God!" she murmured, "have pity upon me."

Not being able to move, she held her breath, and then saw a shadow glide among the trees, lean forward, stand still, then advance cautiously.

"Doña Lola, is that you?" said a muffled voice.

The young girl did not reply. She tried to distinguish the face of the speaker, who, on his part, was carefully examining all around him, and would certainly have discovered the fugitive had not chance placed her under the shadow of a tree. Lola followed every movement of her supposed enemy, and now saw him go slowly and noiselessly away. She again heard herself called; and attempting to answer the call, she made a quick movement and freed herself from one of the brambles which held her prisoner. The flexible branch, set at liberty, sprang back, making a slight noise, and the stranger, who was almost out of sight, immediately stood still. After having listened, he again advanced in the direction of the young girl. The moonbeams fell upon his face, and Lola at once recognized her young companion, the Indian Isidro.

"Come to me!" she cried.

In a moment the Indian was by her side. Lola unconsciously clung to her guide as though she were afraid he would go away again.

"Oh, save me!" she murmured; and, thoroughly exhausted, she sank down on the ground and burst into tears.

"Are you hurt?" asked Isidro.

"No, but I am frightened!" said Lola at last.

"Do not be uneasy. They think they are quite sure of finding you, and will not look for you till to-morrow morning."

"Who will not look for me?"

"The bandits."

"And what of my father?" cried Lola, hastily springing up.

"He is alive," replied the Indian eagerly.

A flash of joy shone from the young girl's eyes, and her features relaxed.

"Where is he?" asked she, with more composure.

"He is a prisoner."

"And your father also?"

"My father is dead," said Isidro; "they killed him."

Lola looked at her companion. His head was bowed, and two large tears ran down his cheeks. She took his hand.

Isidro shuddered, and quickly freeing himself from her clasp, said—

"I am only your servant."

"Your father was my father's friend, Isidro."

"I am only your servant," repeated the Indian.

He was silent a moment, and then, in a voice full of energy, he continued—

"My father is dead! but his blood shall be upon the heads of his murderers, that I swear!"

The young girl had knelt down and was praying.

"Arise," said Isidro to her, "and follow me."

"Where are you going to take me?"

" To Orizava."

" I want to go to my father."

" The bandits have taken him prisoner. Did you not understand me ? "

" These men can have no grudge against me. It is my duty to share my father's fate; let us go."

Isidro shook his head.

" They want your possessions," he said.

" I am ready to give them up in exchange for my father's liberty."

" I am not going to put the dove in the eagle's nest ; no, my father's son will never do that," replied Isidro.

" What are your intentions, then ? "

" I have told you. I want to take you to the city, place you in safety, and then return to save your father and avenge mine, or perish."

Lola reflected for a moment.

" Whatever you undertake I will go with you," said she, firmly. " Do not shake your head. I am courageous."

" The forest is large, the roads are rough, and there will be bloodshed," said Isidro.

" Let us go," resumed Lola. " I have made up my mind."

" One moment of weakness may cost you your liberty, and me my life," said the Indian, slowly, as though weighing his words.

" Let us think of your father and mine, Isidro. Once more I tell you, I shall not be weak."

The Indian placed his hand on his chest, and simply said—
" Follow me."

He went back to the path, seemed to reflect, then, penetrating the underwood, he broke the branches to make an opening for his companion.

" Wait for me," he said, suddenly. He disappeared noiselessly, and came back, carrying an enormous stone. Then they continued their way, Isidro breaking the branches, and stripping the creepers of their leaves, as though from sheer amusement. All at once he left the wood, and Lola thought she saw a plain stretching before her; she was in reality on the edge of an abyss. Isidro stood still.

"Give me your scarf," said he, holding out his hand for it.

Without any remark the young girl gave it to him. Leaning over the perpendicular ravine, the Indian let the light fabric flutter to the bottom; then taking the large stone he had brought, he sent it after the scarf. They could hear the stone rolling and bounding for some time, then the noise died insensibly away.

"The bandits will come in search of you at daybreak," said Isidro. "Since you will not go to the city, I want them to think you have fallen down this abyss."

"Cannot the bottom of it be seen?"

"No; the rocks hang over. It would take several hours' difficult walking to get down to the torrent."

Returning by the way marked by breaking the slender branches, Isidro brought his companion back to the path. She followed in silence, admiring her guide's sagacity. She felt full of confidence in this unlooked-for protector, whom she had only known for a week, and hardly spoken to before.

Sadly and sorrowfully poor Lola again climbed the road which but a few hours before Don Anastasio had watched her ascend with so much uneasiness. On passing her little steed, so full of fire in the morning, now lying motionless where it had fallen, she turned her head aside. Isidro now began to walk very quickly. She sometimes saw him disappear under the shadow of the trees, and could then hardly stifle a momentary fear. Two or three times, feeling almost out of breath, she was on the point of calling to the Indian; but having promised not to show any weakness, she was determined to keep her word.

All at once she saw her guide kneeling on the ground, and the reason of this rapid walk was explained. Isidro was holding his father's lifeless body in his arms; he was speaking in a low tone in a tongue Lola did not understand. She thought he was praying; and joining her hands, she also fell upon her knees.

"Oh! father," said Isidro, "thou wouldst willingly have lived longer; thou didst love the flowers and the sunshine; and yet there thou art, lying in eternal sleep. The wicked men struck thee down by surprise; they have deprived thee of a gift, given thee by God, a gift no man can restore to thee. Father, thine ear hath become deaf, but thy spirit hovers around me, and listens to my words. Thou art gone into the great spirit-land, where my mother, she whom thou lovedst, hath waited for thee."

Isidro was silent. One would have said he was expecting a reply.

"Father," continued he, "I will punish thy murderers. Thou wilt help and guide me, as thou always hast done. I swear to thee, thy body shall rest in consecrated ground. Wait for me. I shall come back again."

The Indian rose, and saw Lola praying.

"Thank you," said he. "He loved your father; he was good. Hush!" murmured he, seeing that she was about to speak.

Lola held her breath, whilst Isidro, leaning forward with bent head, listened attentively.

"Ah!" cried he, "it is one of our enemies, and we have no fire-arms."

Although Lola was also listening, she could hear nothing but the far-off murmur of the torrent. Carefully parting the foliage, Isidro made a sign to his companion to follow him into the thicket. There, hidden behind a tree, he could see the path, on which the moon was shining. Several minutes passed, and Lola gradually distinguished the sound of a horse's hoofs. All at once the animal stood still and neighed; it was most likely passing by old José's corpse. But the measured tread was again heard, and Lola saw a man on horseback about twenty feet below her.

He advanced cautiously, and was intent on guiding his horse. He wore a wide-brimmed hat, and as protection against the cold, he was wrapped up to his eyes in the woollen covering or *sarapé* which the Mexicans always wear over their shoulders. The horseman passed near the two fugitives without being aware of their presence.

"Let us go on now," said Isidro.

"THE BANDITS SURROUNDED AN IMMENSE FIRE."

"Are we to follow that man, then?" asked the young girl.

"Yes, if we can."

"Do you know him?"

"I think I recognized him, but I am not sure. He ought not to be here."

They followed the horseman for twenty minutes, sometimes getting near enough to see him appear and disappear along the moon-lit road. The moon was suddenly hidden behind a cloud, and the forest was plunged in deep gloom. The rider slackened his pace, but in spite of the darkness Isidro walked steadily on; not so with Lola, who, whilst hurrying on to keep beside her guide, often stumbled, or struck herself against the trunks of the trees. She gradually fell behind; and seeing this, Isidro hastily walked back to her.

"Courage," said he; "we are almost there."

The horseman suddenly stood still, as though hesitating which direction he ought to take.

Isidro listened attentively. When the horse went on again, the Indian uttered another exclamation.

"I was not deceived," said he; "that man is your cruelest enemy, and I know now where to find your father."

They were again obliged to enter the thicket, where the darkness made the walking doubly painful to Lola; for the brambles caught her clothes, and the creepers slashed her face, every step she took. Accustomed to such excursions, Isidro walked on as though his sight could pierce the darkness. Raising her eyes by chance, Lola saw the tops of the trees illumined with a red light.

"Is it daybreak?" asked she.

"No," replied her guide, in a low voice; "it is the bandits' encampment."

Taking double precaution not to stir the foliage, and now watching every step his companion took, the Indian led her within twenty yards of their enemies' encampment.

The men, four in number, were grouped round an immense fire, believing themselves safe in this solitude. They had ransacked Don Anastasio's portmanteau; for one of them was dressed in his clothes, and another had his hat on. Lola looked for her father, and not seeing him, gave an involuntary start.

"Have they killed him?" she asked in a hurried whisper, seizing Isidro's arm.

The Indian understood who it was his companion meant, and shook his head.

"Where is he?"

Without speaking, Isidro drew the young girl out of the shade in which they were hidden, and showed her Don Anastasio lying gagged on the ground.

At that sight, Lola separated the foliage, and made a few steps forward; but an arm of iron instantly held her back. Fortunately, the bandits were talking loudly; nevertheless, one of them turned his head in the direction of the rustling branches; but hearing nothing further, he again joined in the conversation.

A whistle was heard. The four men at once sprang up.

"The master!" said they.

And soon, wrapped in his woollen covering, the young girl saw the man who had passed them on horseback.

"Upon my soul!" cried he, "you have done a smart piece of work. Did they fight for it?"

"Like madmen, señor," audaciously replied the eldest of the bandits, "and we were obliged to use our pistols."

"Cowardly liar!" muttered Isidro.

"Were any of you wounded?" asked the horseman.

"No, señor; nothing but a few scratches."

"Where is the girl, Toribio?"

Toribio took off his cap, scratched his head, and looked embarrassed.

"The poor little thing is wandering in the forest," said he at last.

"Curse you! did you let her escape?"

"Her horse ran away, señor, and we could not follow her until we had got rid of her companions. Night came on, and she has most likely hidden herself behind some rock; but do what she may, she cannot go far; she will soon fall into our hands."

"Why on earth did you not search for her?"

"It was quite dark, señor, and it would only have been loss of time! We came back here to the rendezvous, bringing all the game we could lay hands on."

Saying this, the bandit who answered to the name of Toribio pointed to Don Anastasio.

The horseman stood thoughtful for a moment.

"What has become of old José's son?" he asked.

"He must be dead in some corner of the wood, for he was wounded."

"I did not want any one killed," resumed the horseman; "and you must have been fools not to have taken them easily, for they had no arms. I only wish I had been with you; but it was prudent for me to be seen in the town whilst you were at your little game. Trouble for nothing, thanks to your stupidity! Take your men off a little, Toribio, and bring me your prisoner."

The bandits obeyed the order, grumbling to themselves at being sent away from the fire. Toribio hastened to untie Don Anastasio's legs, and helped him to get up; but the Spaniard's limbs were so stiff he could scarcely stand, and Lola was horrified at seeing his mouth covered with a gag.

"My father!—save my father!" said she to her companion.

"Patience," said Isidro. "We can only save him by keeping free ourselves."

The tears flowed down the young girl's face.

"Oh that I were a man! that I had a pistol!" thought she.

Her attention was soon captivated by the scene which was passing before her eyes. At the horseman's order, Toribio took the gag out of Don Anastasio's mouth. The Spaniard's piercing eyes could now examine the man whom he heard addressed as master, and who, after laying aside his *sarapé*, sat down on the trunk of a tree, close to the fire.

Lola also watched the stranger who held her father's life between his hands. He seemed to be about thirty years old. His regular features, black curly hair, and olive complexion, showed him to be a man of mixed blood, a half-breed.

"Where is my daughter?" suddenly asked Don Anastasio. "For your mother's sake, young man, tell me what has become of my child!"

"She lives," replied the horseman.

"God be praised! I wish to see her."

"It is not my intention to separate you from her," resumed the horseman; "and it depends upon you whether she is restored to you at once or not."

"What do you want of me? Speak."

The stranger took off his hat and stood in front of his prisoner.

"Do you recognize me?" he asked of him.

"I think I do," said the Spaniard. "You are Salvador Rendon, are you not?"

"Upon my honour! you have a good memory, señor. Yes, I am Salvador, and you can undoubtedly guess what I want of you."

"I shall know better when you tell me."

"The lands which belonged to you have been given me as recompense for services which I rendered the cause of independence; and you will find them in a prosperous condition, for I have managed them wisely."

"I shall know how to recompense you well for your service," replied Don Anastasio.

"In what way?"

"I am waiting for you to tell me yourself what your wishes are."

The bandit took a few steps and stood quite close to the prisoner.

"A month ago," said he, "when I heard of your arrival at Vera Cruz, I thought, and not without reason, that a deadly struggle would ensue between you and me; for I did not feel in the humour to restore to you the lands which I thought I had firmly in possession, and I know you would not think of giving them up to me. I went to Orizava to watch your movements, to know what your intentions were, and there I saw your daughter. We can soon come to terms, Don Anastasio. Give me Doña Lola for my wife, and all will be peacefully settled between us."

"Never!" cried the Spaniard, energetically.

"You are too hasty," said Salvador. "My offer requires a little time to think over; besides, I expected this refusal, and took my precautions. You are in my power, and so is your daughter. I have determined that she shall be my wife."

"I will yield you all my possessions for her ransom and mine," replied Don Anastasio. "Give me back my child, and I swear I will go back to Spain with her."

"Not so," said the young man. "Were you once out of my hands, you would go to law, and Salvador would run the risk of again becoming what he once was—a poor half-breed, whom you would treat as your servant. Give me your daughter. I am now a steady man, and every one will be satisfied with our reconciliation. You will not? Be it so. Your daughter will not refuse me, for your sake."

"What do you rely upon doing?" cried Don Anastasio.

"I intend to offer her my hand in exchange for her father's life. I had no other object in getting you into my possession."

The Spaniard's eyes glared like an angry lion's. He twisted his arms in a vain attempt to break his fetters, and feeling the uselessness of his efforts, he bowed his head sadly. At a sign from Salvador, they stretched him on a heap of dry leaves a little distance from the fire.

"You can think over this matter now, and we will resume our conversation to-morrow," said the half-breed.

Then, without taking further notice of Don Anastasio, Salvador went back to talk with Toribio and his companions. These men, of mixed blood like himself, had served in the guerilla formed by the young man during the War of Independence. They were all his tenants since his former master's possessions had fallen into his hands; he could therefore perfectly rely upon them.

At last each of the bandits rolled himself in his blanket, and Toribio alone kept watch.

"Come," said Isidro to his companion.

The young girl seemed to awaken from a dream.

"No," said she.

"We must take a little rest; we shall want strength to act to-morrow."

"I want to save my father."

"His life is in no danger just now. Come."

Lola stood motionless.

"Do you wish to become the wife of Salvador, a murderer?"

"I want to save my father."

"I promise you solemnly I will save him or perish," said the Indian in a low tone; "but follow me."

Lola at last obeyed. Guided by Isidro, she climbed a kind of flight of steps in the rocks which seemed to her interminable. She felt overpowered with fatigue, and notwithstanding her great anxiety, her eyes closed, and she tottered in her walk, although Isidro often took her hand to guide her through difficult places. which the darkness made still more perilous.

"Rest yourself here," said the Indian, standing still.

Lola sank down on the grass, not knowing where she was, so dark was the night. Overcome by fatigue, she soon fell into a deep sleep. Isidro stayed beside her for some time: he seemed to be gazing on her through the darkness. Suddenly he got up and went away. After taking about ten steps he stopped to listen, and heard nothing but the measured breathing of the young girl.

"God of heaven!" cried he, lifting his arms to the sky, "I leave her in Thy keeping."

Then entering the forest, he walked on with a rapid step.

CHAPTER III.

The nocturnal walk – Indian and half-breed—Méthal—The Hermit's Ravine.

NOTWITHSTANDING the fatigue which weighed him down, Isidro had undertaken a long walk. He must have help or fire-arms, to be able to fight with the men to whom his father had fallen victim, and who, not content with keeping Don Anastasio prisoner, were intent upon getting possession of Lola. The Indian at first thought of going to Orizava, but he calculated that it would take more than twenty-four hours to reach the town and return; and what might not happen during that time! And then at Orizava who would listen to him when he asked for help? He belonged to a despised race; but something must be done, and that quickly.

Unfortunately, the nearest dwelling-place to the bandits' encampment was precisely Don Anastasio's property, now occupied by half-breeds, old war-comrades of Salvador, who, if they did not assist in their former captain's designs, would not be disposed to act against them.

"Father, father!" repeated the Indian, "direct me what to do. Now that thou canst see everything, thou wilt not allow the wicked to triumph!"

All at once Isidro remembered that at about three leagues from the place where he was, on the other side of the mountain, there lived a family of his own race, who had been his father's friends. He immediately resolved to go and ask this farmer's help. As he set out, a new anxiety troubled him. Ought he to tell Lola of his absence? The idea of remaining alone and unprotected might frighten the poor child. She would want to go with her protector, and her strength would perhaps foil her courage. Isidro thought that exhaustion would make her sleep long, so that he would have time to return before she awoke, and she would thus be spared cruel anxiety and painful fatigue. Having made up his mind to act according to the dictates of his reason, he set out resolutely.

The Indian walked on towards his countryman's dwelling, as directly as the ground would allow, with that assurance which custom and the knowledge of the place where one has been brought up gives. Notwithstanding his diligence, the brave man took more than two hours reaching the farm. Day was beginning to break when he reached the outskirts of the forest, and came upon a small savannah covered with a mist, which was soon tinged with rosy sunlight.

The birds broke forth with their joyous songs, as though hailing the apparition of dawn. Isidro had stopped for a moment to make sure of his road, and then again continued his rapid walk. The mist cleared off, and a picturesque cabin, situated on a hillock a few hundred feet off, was to be seen; but the Indian, surprised at hearing no sound, advanced with precaution.

He reached the rose-bush hedge which in this country often grows near the cottages of the natives, without seeing any signs of human beings. He called. No voice answered him. Isidro then entered the open door of the humble dwelling. The fire was still burning on the hearth, but the inhabitants were absent.

The Indian sat down and looked disconsolately around him. It was a bitter deception. His eyes wandered for some time over the woody heights in front of him; willingly would he have pierced their depths. The sun was gilding the trees; the flowers, wet with dew, slowly raised their drooping heads; the birds chased each other from shrub to shrub, and the great vultures of the Cordilleras, flapping their powerful wings, soared higher and higher in the heavens. The smiling indifference of nature, contrasting with the grief which overwhelmed him, troubled the gentle, simple spirit of Isidro.

What was to be done? Go to Huatusco, the nearest village? What precious hours would be lost, especially now when the bandits would most certainly be setting to work; now when Lola, awakened by the daylight, would find herself alone and think she was abandoned! Entering the inner room of the cabin, Isidro searched everywhere for some kind of fire-arms, but found none. Near the fireplace he saw a long hunting-knife, seized it, and put it into his belt. He also took a gourd and some maize cakes; then casting a last glance over the savannah to assure himself that it was deserted, he set out once again.

This time the Indian took a beaten path, which enabled him to make more speed. For more than an hour he climbed and descended the sides of the ravines, and then he suddenly came upon a half-cultivated field where a dozen cows were grazing.

The Indian skirted the forest, then slackening his pace, he went in the direction of a cabin built of wood. Near the threshold a woman, kneeling before a large stone, was bruising maize; not far from her sat an Indian, looking at the cattle grazing, and apparently tending them.

The plaintive bark of two lean greyhounds warned the inhabitants of the cabin of a stranger's approach. The man and woman both got up to see who was the early guest who had come to visit them. Isidro, with lowered brow, and no word of greeting, passed close by the husband and wife, walked towards the door of the rustic dwelling, and entered the outer room, where the Indian and his wife at once followed him.

The young man had sat down near the hearth; he had separated the three stones which formed it, and was scattering the fire-brands and the cinders. His hosts followed the new-comer's movements with troubled looks, wondering what ill news they were to learn; for Isidro's action was a presage of mourning.

The woman had a son absent. She falteringly mentioned his name. Isidro shook his head negatively, and said—

"My father is dead, and I am an orphan."

There was a long silence.

"Thy father was my friend, and his son shall be my son," said the Indian at last. "Rest awhile, for thou art weary. Presently thou shalt tell us where is thy father's grave, and we will carry him the game which he loved; and till a priest can bless the ground where he lies, we will plant flowers there."

"My father has no grave," continued Isidro; "his body lies on the bare ground in the Pearl Forest."

"His foot was nimble and his eye clear," said the Indian; "how was it he fell into the abyss?"

"He has been murdered."

The Indian and his wife crossed themselves.

"By whom?" asked they together.

"By him whom the white people call Salvador Rendon."

"What dost thou want of me, Isidro?" quickly asked the Indian.

P

"That thou wilt help me to avenge my father, and give him burial. My cause is a just one."

The Indian sat down.

"Speak; I am listening to thee," said he.

Then, laying aside the grave and lengthy formulas which Indians make use of in solemn moments, Isidro briefly recounted the treacherous attack, the death of his father, the capture of Don Anastasio, and Lola's flight. His hearers listened with deep attention, and he had hardly ended his story, when his host, hastily unhooking an old gun hanging from the beams of the cabin, and girding on a leather cartridge-belt, stood before him, saying—

"I am ready."

"Stay," cried the Indian woman, "and reflect a little. Salvador Rendon is a half-breed, and thou art only an Indian; Salvador Rendon is powerful, and thou art poor."

"Are those reasons, wife, for leaving my friend without burial?"

"No. If needs be, I would help with my own hands to bury him; but I would not see thee shed blood."

"I am not a child," replied the Indian, "to use a gun like a plaything. I shall not attack, I shall defend myself. It is but a good action, wife, to try and save a young girl out of wicked men's hands."

"Go, then," replied the woman submissively, "and do not forget that I shall watch for thee till thou art come back."

Then covering her head with her cotton scarf, she busied herself in putting the hearth-stones together again.

Isidro was already out of the cabin.

"My father's spirit shall protect the days of Méthal," cried he. "Méthal is a true friend."

Then he went towards the forest, followed by his companion.

The sun was far above the horizon, when the two Indians, although they had walked without stopping, reached the rocky enclosure, in a corner of which Isidro had hidden Lola. The young man hurried on Méthal, thinking of the anguish of Don Anastasio's daughter, who, without water or food, must be wandering about with fright in the solitude; and he now regretted that he had not told her of his project.

Suddenly he stood still.

"It is here," said he to his companion. "Wait for me."

He went slowly forward, looking anxiously around him, in the hope of seeing his young mistress. The place was deserted. Isidro entered the rocky enclosure, and came out again almost immediately.

"Ah!" cried he, "we have come too late; the dove has flown."

Two tears fell down the young man's bronzed cheeks, and crossing his hands on his breast, he stood motionless for some time, vaguely looking towards the horizon.

"Arouse yourself," said Méthal to him; "the time is passing."

"True," replied Isidro. "Come."

He led his companion towards the forest, and both of them began to examine the ground. Isidro saw that, notwithstanding his precautions to hide their nocturnal walk, the bandits could still trace their footsteps, and discover the young girl's hiding-place.

"She is in their hands," said he, with despair.

"Dost thou know the place where they hide themselves?" said Méthal.

"They camped yesterday near the Three Oaks."

"Let us go on," said the Indian, resolutely.

After a moment's reflection, Isidro bent his steps towards the place where, on the preceding evening, the bandits had taken up their quarters. He soon found himself near the rock behind which, with Lola, he had been able to watch Toribio and Salvador. He exchanged a few words in a low voice with Méthal; the old Indian gave a sign of approbation, and knelt down in the position of a hunter, on the look-out for game.

Isidro crawled noiselessly towards the bivouac, then stood up suddenly and called to his companion, who at once ran up to him. The bandits were gone, and profound silence reigned in the place which a few hours before resounded with their coarse laughter. The Indians described a large circle round the fire, which was still smoking—looking for a trace which might show them the direction taken by the outlaws. The footsteps all ended on the path, which greatly increased the perplexity of the two friends. They resolved to return to the place where Isidro had hidden Lola; and having reached the enclosure where the young girl had passed the night, Isidro again called her, and, as before, the echo alone answered him. Still keeping on, the two explorers reached the crest of the mountain, and looked down upon the tops of the trees in the forest. Overcome by fatigue and heat, Isidro could no longer stand. At his companion's entreaty, he sat down, drank a few drops of water, then leant against the trunk of a tree, and fell into a deep sleep. Respecting his companion's rest, Méthal again began scrupulous investigations alone. He traced the light prints of the young girl's footsteps, and these tracks having led him to the forest, he suddenly recognized the footmarks of several pedestrians. The Indian gave a low, satisfied whistle, entered the wood, and soon convinced that he had discovered the track, he hastened back to his companion.

Isidro was still sleeping, and Méthal, thinking rightly that they would have several hours' walking before they could find the bandits, judged it prudent not to awaken his friend; and stretching himself on the ground, he also fell asleep.

It was almost five o'clock in the afternoon, when Isidro, opening his eyes, measured the height of the sun and sprang up with a bound.

"Up, up!" cried he to Méthal. "And God forgive us for having forgotten that our unhappy friends count the hours waiting for us!"

"The time has not been lost," replied Méthal; "it has restored thy strength, and I know now what path we must follow."

"Speak quickly."

Méthal led his friend to the rocks, then brought him towards the forest, and the sagacity of the two Indians told them that, on awaking, Lola must have left her refuge to go into the forest.

There the footsteps of a man mingled with hers; but there was no trace of violence. The young girl must have voluntarily accompanied the man whom she had met. Méthal and Isidro followed the footprints step by step. Before long they saw that a man on horseback would not have been able to climb the ridges, nor descend the perpendicular slopes, followed by the bandits, and they concluded that Salvador had not accompanied them.

Night came on. Isidro, always in advance, ran rather than walked, tearing his face and hands with the branches that barred his way.

"Stop," cried Méthal, suddenly; "we are on the wrong track."

The young man turned back.

"Ah!" said he, "one would say that God was abandoning us."

"The stag is fleet of foot; nevertheless it is caught," resumed his brave companion.

Thanks to Méthal's self-possession, the track was found again, and for half an hour the two explorers were able to follow it; but soon the darkness became so thick, that they were obliged to stop.

Isidro, leaning against the trunk of a tree, had closed his eyes and was reflecting. Sometimes he started and leant forward to listen; he seemed to hear Lola's voice in the distance calling him in a piteous tone. Once the illusion was so strong, that he hurriedly seized Méthal's arm.

"Did you not hear anything?" he asked.

"Nothing," replied Métahl, "except the noise of the torrent, and the plaintive cry of the night-birds."

Isidro was again silent. Suddenly, notwithstanding his fatigue, he clung to the tree, and making use of his hands and feet with the agility of men of his race, he soon disappeared in the branches, where presently there was a great flapping of wings from the numerous birds which he had scared from their roosting-place. When the Indian came down again his eyes shone with feverish gladness.

"They are there," said he, stretching his hand towards the west. "Méthal, my father is watching us."

"He will avenge himself," answered Méthal, raising his gun above his head; "he is waiting for you to tell him where he must strike."

Walking this time slowly and cautiously, Isidro again led the way. From time to time low growls were heard, cries of hungry tigers in search of prey; but these were not enemies of a nature to frighten the two Indians. Suddenly Méthal seized Isidro's arm, led him a little to the left, and showed him a feeble ray glimmering through the foliage. The young man's breast heaved, and he uttered a deep sigh of relief.

"They are there," repeated Méthal, " camping on the border of the Hermit's Ravine."

"May the spirit of the holy man aid us! Let us go on."

Then crawling silently along like two serpents, the Indians gradually approached the new encampment chosen by the bandits. The sound of voices reached them, when a piercing cry, uttered by a woman, made Isidro bound forward. Standing up, Méthal saw Lola struggling in Salvador's arms. The impassive Indian shouldered his gun, aimed it cautiously, and the report of fire-arms awoke the echoes of the Pearl Forest.

CHAPTER IV.

The venture—An unfortunate meeting—Salvador Rendon—The right of the strongest—Pray for him.

IT was broad daylight when Lola, still greatly fatigued, opened her eyes. She looked around her, and was surprised to find herself lying in tall grass in a rocky enclosure. Isidro's name fell from her lips, but no voice answered her, and she was scared by a large eagle which flew off the peak of a rock, beating its long wings over her head.

Supposing that Isidro was only a short distance off, Lola

followed the granite wall, and found the opening through which she must have passed the evening before. Hardly had she made three steps, when she discovered she was on a bare mountain crest, with the tops of the trees in the Pearl Forest lying like a sea of verdure at her feet.

The young girl again called, and receiving no answer, her heart beat violently. She walked rapidly towards the outskirts of the forest, trying to find the path she had followed with Isidro. She would not believe that the Indian had forsaken her; so, gradually recovering her courage, she tried to retrace her steps, and soon perceived that she had lost her way.

For more than an hour the poor girl wandered about the forest, walking round and round, and invariably finding herself back at the place she started from. Lola taxed her memory in vain; she could not remember whether the sun was on her left or her right when she left her hiding-place. She dared not call out except at rare intervals, for dismal sounds, the cries of wild beasts or birds of prey, often answered her.

At last, thinking that the slope must bring her to the top of the mountain, Lola began to climb it energetically. When she reached the summit it was covered with trees, so that she could see nothing. Exhausted, suffering from hunger and thirst, she was obliged to sit down for a moment to rest herself. The young girl resolved to follow the summit she had reached, however rough the ground might be, until she came to some opening in the trees, by which she would be able to find out where she was.

What bitter sadness and anguish weighed down poor Lola's spirit, a stranger till now to any care save the light vexations of childhood! She had never left her father's side before, and now she was alone, lost in a forest, pursued by murderers, who held her father prisoner. Everything appeared so extraordinary, so fearfully unnatural to the poor child, that she continually repeated—

"I must be dreaming! I shall awake."

Alas! this nightmare was but too real, and more than one proof still awaited the unfortunate young girl.

She had been sitting down for a quarter of an hour, strengthening her resolutions with earnest prayer, when she thought she heard the sound of voices. She got up and listened, but the noise died away. She had just sat down again, when she heard the crackling of broken branches.

"Isidro!" cried she, involuntarily.

There was a moment's silence, then Lola listening intently, knew that some one was coming towards her. Her first movement was to fly; but feeling her strength spent, she resolved to face the danger, and stood still.

Several minutes passed. The new-comer was advancing cautiously. Lola's heart beat loudly; she was hoping to see Isidro. The foliage parted, and showed her the face of Toribio.

The bandit stood still for a moment, evidently surprised at this meeting, then he sprang forward quickly towards the young girl.

"'Pon my soul!" cried he, with a coarse laugh, "here's a Godsend!"

"Take care," said Lola to him—for he had taken hold of her arm—"I am the daughter of Don Anastasio Véga."

"I know it, my beauty; and if I had any doubt about it your eyes would tell me, for there are none like them in all the country. So you are here, my dear. Well, upon my word, I thought you were at the bottom of the precipice."

"Take me to my father, señor."

"Presently, my pretty one. Do not tremble; I am not going to harm you. Are you alone?" asked he, looking distrustfully around him.

"I am alone," replied Lola.

"By Heaven! you must have had a sorry time of it since yesterday. You should not have fled from us; we are not your enemies. How did you manage to get up here?"

"I walked up," replied Lola.

Toribio shook his head and seemed to reflect; then placing two fingers between his lips, he gave a long, shrill whistle, and a similar sound answered in the distance.

"Let us go on," said the bandit. "But have you strength enough? You are very pale; lean on me."

Lola drew back with such visible repugnance, that Toribio cried—

"Oh, oh! I tell you, you need not be afraid. I am so much your friend, that I would defend your life if necessary. Come along. If the walk is too much for you, lean on me. I bear you no ill-will."

"Is your chief with you?" asked Lola.

"My chief?" cried the bandit, with surprise, looking at the young girl. "Who told you that I had a chief?"

Not knowing how to answer, Lola walked on in front.

"This way, this way," said Toribio, pointing to the left, and, with another whistle, he added: "What a prize!"

Lola walked on rapidly, absorbed by the one thought of seeing her father again. A few minutes brought them to the encampment. At the sight of Lola, the bandits uttered exclamations of surprise, and congratulated Toribio. Lola looked for her father. She saw him, bound with cords, sitting on the grass, with his head bowed. She flew towards him, and embraced him, whilst tears rolled down the Spaniard's bronzed cheeks, and he was unable to speak.

"Ah, my poor child," said he at last, "what peril my ambition has brought upon thee! And how will the just God deliver us from this danger!"

The fetters chafed the prisoner's limbs; but it was in vain that Lola begged Toribio to loosen the knots.

"No, no," said the bandit; "we do not want any fighting, and the only way to avoid it is to keep the enemy bound, or kill him."

A large joint of meat was roasting before a roaring fire. After having feasted themselves, the bandits allowed Lola to help her father, and take something to eat herself.

"Be sure," said Toribio to the young girl, "that you do not try to loosen the prisoner's cords, or you will oblige me to discharge my pistol between his eyes, and I am not fond of killing where there is no need for it."

The bandits stretched themselves on the ground to take their afternoon nap, all except Toribio, who would allow no one else the care of watching the prisoners. The unhappy father and child were allowed to talk to each other. What harm could that do? The young girl spoke in an undertone of her meeting with Isidro, and then of the Indian's disappearance.

"He is doing his best, be sure of that," said Don Anastasio, with a look of gladness. "I am a judge of men's characters, and I know Isidro will never desert us."

"What are we to do in the mean time?" asked Lola.

"Alas!" replied Don Anastasio, twisting his bound arms, "I cannot advise, nor help you. Listen," added he, in a low tone; "try to seize one of those knives the first opportunity you got, and . . . ."

"Bad advice," quietly remarked Toribio, whose keen ear had caught the prisoner's last words. "You will oblige me to make use of my pistol; and I tell you once more, I do not care to shoot when there is no need for it. Besides, no one here wants your father's life or yours. Be patient; you will soon be free."

Toribio aroused his comrades, and the party resumed their march. Lola guided her father along the narrow path which the brigands had taken, whilst Toribio walked behind them, his gun on his shoulder. They stopped for a quarter of an hour to refresh themselves from a spring gushing from the mountain's side. They had been walking for about three hours, when they reached the border of a perpendicular ravine, and it was beginning to get dark.

"Halt!" cried Toribio.

His companions, promptly obeying his orders, immediately set out in search of dry wood, and before long an immense fire lit up the trunks of the ancient pines—the only trees growing in this wild spot.

Don Anastasio gazed around him, sometimes shutting his eyes, as though trying to collect his thoughts.

"If my memory does not deceive me," said the Spaniard to his daughter, "we are only a short distance from my old house."

Night is coming on; you are free, and I will then tell you which direction to take. You must try to put these butchers off their guard."

"I will not leave you, father!"

"You must, my child. Better you should wander in the woods, at the mercy of the wild beasts, than that you should remain in the power of Salvador."

"I know what he wants of us, and I am ready to give him my life to save yours."

"I will not hear of that, Lola. My life is nothing; your happiness is everything, and I will not let you become the wife of a man you can never love. Yes," added the Spaniard, fiercely knitting his brows, "I would rather know you were dead than see you unhappy."

"But, father, I assure you I can never be unhappy, as long as you are living near me. Don Salvador is a Christian, after all; he will never think of separating us."

"Do not talk like that," said Don Anastasio, bitterly. "You become the companion of this brigand!"

"We are at his mercy," said Lola, sadly.

"Let us pray," said the Spaniard. "God is just, and I trust in Him."

The shades of night gradually closed over the forest. Don Anastasio listened intently to every sound; he hoped that Isidro would come unexpectedly to deliver them. Lola shared her father's hopes; but still so many hours had passed since the Indian had disappeared, that she had anxious misgivings lest some harm might have befallen him. They were waiting for Salvador. Toribio had told them so more than once, and the prisoners longed, and yet dreaded, to see the man upon whom depended their liberty and their life.

The moon had shed her silvery light over the tree-tops in the forest for some time, when at last a prolonged whistle was heard. The brigands at once sprang to their feet. Toribio answered the signal, plunged into the forest, and soon reappeared, preceded by Salvador. The young man wore the same costume as on the preceding evening. He strode rapidly up to Lola.

"I hope, señora, that my servants have behaved politely towards you?"

"Señor," replied the young girl, "I entreat you to give orders that my father may be freed from his fetters."

"Now as ever," said Salvador, "your desires shall be my commands. One word, however," added he: "I ought to tell you that my reason, in having recourse to violence, was to get possession of you."

Lola blushed.

"I know," said she, "what you require of me, and I am ready to make any sacrifice in exchange for my father's liberty."

"That is the way to speak, although the word *sacrifice* is somewhat harsh," replied Salvador. "But perhaps you are not aware that I have asked your hand of Don Anastasio?"

"My father and I are ready to give up all our rights to the property you now occupy. We only ask one thing in exchange—the liberty of returning to our country."

"You do my gallantry little honour," replied Salvador. "Those possessions, which you seem to think are uppermost in my mind, I am willing to share with you, if you will consent to be my wife."

Lola leant against her father, whilst he fiercely exclaimed—"Never!"

"You speak too quickly," said Salvador, frowning. "You always seem to forget that you are in my power, and that your life depends upon one of my gestures."

"Strike, then!" cried the Spaniard; "take my life, since it is powerless to defend my child."

Lola placed herself between Salvador and her father, her face deadly pale.

"Señor," said she, with an effort, "here is my hand; it is for you now to keep your promise."

"Be still!" cried Don Anastasio.

The Spaniard made new efforts to burst his cords, till his hands were bleeding and he fell back exhausted. The unhappy father admired the sacrifice his daughter would have made for him, but nevertheless refused to accept it. What! was this pure, loving child, this noble creature whose heart and mind he had helped to form, was she to become the wife of a robber, of a murderer! The prisoner bowed his head, and his breast heaved with tearless sobs.

"Here is my hand," repeated Lola.

"Upon my soul! this is something like, at last," cried Salvador, for a moment abashed by the young girl's dignity and surprised at seeing his desires so quickly realized. "Holloa! you fellows there!" cried he to his companions; "three cheers in honour of your mistress."

As he spoke he took Lola's hand and drew her towards him. She tried to free herself.

"Señor," said she, "my father is still a prisoner."

"Patience, señora; everything in good time. 'Pon my honour! that pale face, those brilliant eyes, and rumpled curls, only add to your beauty."

"Leave me alone!" said Lola, with a tone of annoyance. "I am not your wife yet, señor."

"Who can prevent you, then, from being mine? Hang it all! Toribio, we made a mistake in sending that sermonizing old hermit to hell; he would have been able to bless our union on the spot."

On hearing this cynical confession of a sacrilegious crime, Lola recoiled with horror, and almost succeeded in freeing her hand from Salvador's grasp.

"For the love of your mother, señor," cried she, "leave me alone; have a little respect for me."

"Who dare be disrespectful to you?" resumed the brigand. "We must have a priest to unite us, just to ease your conscience. Don't be alarmed; the thing shall be done to-morrow. Meanwhile, what power on earth can prevent you becoming my wife? Do you think, then, that I shall say 'no' before the altar?"

As he spoke, Salvador wound his arms round the young girl. She uttered a frightened cry, and as she struggled in his grasp, tried to get near the precipice. At that moment a shot was heard, and Salvador, turning round slowly, fell with his face to the ground, and lay there motionless. Méthal had aimed well.

At the same moment Isidro, armed with the long knife, sprang out of the thicket. He stumbled against Don Anastasio, cut the cords with which the Spaniard was bound, and rushed up to Salvador just as the latter fell forward on his face. Having seized a pistol, Toribio discharged it at the Indian; but before the brigand could fire a second shot, he was knocked down and pinioned to the ground by the terrible cutlass. Another shot was heard, and a third brigand fell.

Directly Don Anastasio was free, he tried to run towards his daughter; but his stiffened limbs prevented him from stirring. He was fired at by one of Toribio's men; then, seeing the fourth pointing his pistol at Lola, the Spaniard sprang on to him and pushed him over the precipice. At that moment Méthal issued from the wood; and having got possession of a pistol, Don Anastasio was about to fire it at the brave Indian.

" Stop! " cried Isidro; " it is a friend."

Scarcely had José's son finished these words, when he fell down beside the tree against which he was leaning. Toribio's ball had entered his breast.

Lola, her father, and Méthal ran up at once to the wounded man. His eyes were closed, his teeth clenched, and his ears deaf to their words of pity. Picking up a gourd, Don Anastasio bathed his forehead, and tried to make him drink.

" Isidro! Isidro! " repeated Lola, continually.

The Indian opened his eyes and gazed intently on the young girl.

" Fly," said he, suddenly, " fly! Oh, Méthal, thou wilt bury me beside my father! "

" You will live," said Lola, raising his head and resting it on her knee.

" Fly! " repeated he.

" Our enemies are no longer to be feared, through your help, Isidro."

" Is that true? " he asked.

" It is true," replied Méthal and Don Anastasio together.

A smile played over Isidro's pale lips; he quickly raised himself, and then of his own accord placed his head on Lola's knees, and seemed to be going to sleep. In a low voice Méthal told of his companion's forced marches and dreadful anxiety.

"Brave heart!" said Don Anastasio. "Grant, merciful Father, that he may live!" added the Spaniard, raising his eyes to heaven.

"No," said Isidro, suddenly opening his eyes; "better far that I should die."

He asked for water. Don Anastasio and Méthal hastened to fill the gourd. Isidro again spoke in such a feeble voice that Lola was obliged to lean forward to hear him.

"I am happy here," said he; "very happy." He was silent for a moment, and then continued.

"The birds sing, the sun shines. I see over yonder the great blue sky. It is there where the spirits go, there where my father and mother are waiting for me. Before many minutes eternal slumber will have closed my eyelids; but my spirit will not want these poor eyes. Live happily, señora, and think sometimes of poor Isidro; he had nothing but his life to give you, and he has given it."

"You will live, Isidro; you will live with my father, and me."

"I would rather die .... I should have too much to suffer ...."

These last words were pronounced so low that Lola could hardly hear them. Two tears fell from her eyes on to Isidro's brow, as he again lay motionless. Méthal came up, and called his friend by name.

"Who calls me?" asked the young man; and half raising himself, he added, "I am coming, father; I am coming."

Then he fell back on the ground and expired.

A few days later, Don Anastasio took possession of his lands, and appointed Méthal his steward.

Crossing the Pearl Mountain one day, I came by chance upon a white marble cross. A rose-bush, the Indian's favourite shrub, entwined itself round the cross, and covered it at all seasons with its sweet-scented flowers. The monument bore no inscription. I questioned my guide about it.

"Isidro and his father lie here. Dona Lola Véga had this cross erected."

"Why? Who was this Isidro?"

My guide looked at me with surprise; then, being convinced of my ignorance, he told me of the young Indian's tragic end.

"Doña Lola," added he, finishing his story, "refused to marry for a long time. She died a year ago, and it is of her son, Don Isidro Lopez, that we are going to ask hospitality this evening."

THE TUXPANGO CASCADE.

The sick child—The Escamela river—The fox—The cascade—A tiger.

To the right of the road leading up from Cordova to Orizava, through the Cordilleras, stretches a forest whose gigantic trees seem to defy the pioneer's axe. During my stay at Mexico, I amused myself with catching insects on the outskirts of this virgin forest, and it was here that I collected most of the hymenoptera which I gave to the Museum of Natural History at Paris. One day, having entered the forest further up than usual, I unexpectedly met with an Indian and his wife. The man was very plain; but his companion, about fifteen years old, had not yet been disfigured nor deformed by the rough work which falls to women of her race. She was carrying a little child in a cotton shawl tied across her chest.

"May God chase the serpents from thy path!" said the Indian, greeting me.

"And may He scatter thine with roses!" replied I, according to the usual formula.

The Indian woman said nothing, but her large eyes examined me attentively.

"I know him," said she to her husband, pointing unceremoniously to me with her finger. "He is the *tictil* (doctor)."

"Are you sure, wife?"

"Yes, I am quite sure."

The woman walked up to me, and rapidly untying the knots

of her cotton shawl, uncovered her child, who was crying, and held it out to me, saying, in a supplicating voice—

"He is ill. Cure him."

I sat down at the foot of a tree, took the little one on my knees, and after having examined it, and questioned the young mother, I advised her to use some simple remedy, the only medicine attainable by the Indians. I was overwhelmed with thanks and blessings from the young couple, when I said that the child could, and would, get better. After having taken some food, which quieted its cries for the moment, the little invalid was again wrapped in the shawl, and put back upon its mother's shoulder.

"Where does this path lead to?" I asked of the husband.

"To Tuxpango," replied he.

"Do you live at that village?"

"No; my cabin is near the fall."

"What fall?"

"The fall of the Escamela river."

"Then does not the Escamela follow this level?"

"Yes; but in front of Tuxpango it falls from the top of a mountain into the plains below."

The inhabitants of Mexico, either from carelessness, or use, are so indifferent to the beauties of their country, that I had never heard anything before of the Tuxpango Cascade. I questioned the Indian minutely, and the description he gave me excited my curiosity.

Indians generally measure distances by the time it takes them to go from one place to another; thus I asked my new friend how many hours it would take to reach his cabin.

"Not more than one hour," he replied.

"Would you like me to go with you?"

The Indian looked at his wife as though to consult her. These poor people live in distrust of everything. I was armed, and my companion carried no weapon, not even the short dagger, without which scarcely any one would venture in these woods.

"Do as you like," he at last replied.

"Let us go on, then. When we once get out of the forest, we

shall find the plant which can cure your child, and I will show your wife how she is to use it. Carry my gun," I added.

The Indian took hold of the gun I held out to him, examined it, and placed it on his shoulder.

"If we see any game, may I fire?" he asked of me.

"Certainly; and then you will give me some dinner."

"If you cure my child," said the young mother, in her gentle voice, "all that is in the cabin shall be yours."

The Indian took the lead, I followed him, and his wife brought up the rear.

We walked for more than half an hour through the forest, without meeting with anything except a fox.

"Shoot!" cried I to the Indian, who had shouldered his gun. He shook his head with contempt.

"It is not good to eat."

"I want its skin."

It was too late. The animal had disappeared. A hundred feet further on an armadillo crossed the path, and was cleanly shot. My guide at once skinned the animal, which when cooked has very much the flavour of sucking-pig.

We took more than an hour and a half in reaching the cabin, and I suspected the Indian of having brought me by the longest way in the hope of meeting with more game. Directly we left the forest I heard a dull roar; it was the noise of the cascade, still a quarter of a league distant.

My host's dwelling-place, built of bamboo, covered with cocoa-nut matting, stood in the centre of a little garden full of lettuces, a kind of spinach called *acelgas*, potatoes, and cayenne pepper plants. A pig, some lean dogs, half a dozen hens, and as many turkeys, came out to meet us, and followed us familiarly into the only room of the cabin. I first of all busied myself with preparing a soothing drink for the little invalid; then, still allowing the Indian to carry my gun, I followed him in the direction of the cascade, whilst his wife occupied herself with roasting the armadillo, which was to form the principal dish at our dinner.

We walked rapidly downhill for twenty minutes, lost from

sight between castor-oil plants and gigantic thistles. An unexpected opening in the bushes allowed me to get a glimpse of the fertile oblong valley of Tuxpango. The large farmhouse bearing this name was on my left, standing out perfectly white against the background of verdure. On my right hand were immense sugar-cane plantations, through which long files of mules were passing backwards and forwards. We again entered the woods, and the noise of our footsteps put to flight a fine black adder, which we were unable to catch.

This encounter reminded me that it was in the valley of Tuxpango that the largest serpent ever known was caught. The reptile measured no less than eleven yards, and in the last century was the principal object in the Madrid museum, where, perhaps, it may still be seen.

I thought that we had descended directly into the valley, but was surprised to find myself at the bottom of a ravine. Instead of crossing the steep bank facing us, my guide followed a narrow stream of chalky water.

On the banks of this stream I picked up petrified branches, leaves, and fruit at almost every step, and I lost more than an hour in examining these natural curiosities, whilst my guide went in pursuit of wild-fowl.

At last we again continued our walk in the direction of the cascade, and the roar became more and more deafening. My Indian understood what he was about. He led me unexpectedly before the cascade, that is to say, in front of a sheet of water about six yards wide, which precipitated itself into the valley from a height of more than three hundred feet, a height double that of the Niagara Falls.

Certainly the volume of the two bodies of water cannot be compared; but the Tuxpango Cascade would attract more than one tourist were it not situated in the heart of a wild country at more than two thousand leagues from London and Paris. We were obliged to descend still further, in order to see the water dash forth, then flow swiftly among the rocks heaped at the bottom of the ravine from century to century, and I ventured on a damp stony path covered with yellow and red moss.

"THE TIGER SEEMED TO BE CONTEMPLATING THE FALL."

Suddenly my guide seized hold of my arm.

"What is it?" I asked, turning round with surprise.

"Hush!" said he. "Look!"

I looked towards the spot he pointed to, and saw a tiger crouching on a rock, and apparently contemplating the fall attentively. Undoubtedly appreciating the spectacle before him, the splendid animal yawned, and carelessly stretched himself out on the rock, which served him as a pedestal.

I turned round to claim my gun. My companion had disappeared noiselessly. I was going to call him, but I stopped myself in time. A gesture, a cry, would have attracted the enormous creature's attention to me, and I was defenceless. I looked around me in search of a shelter, and a somewhat keen feeling of uneasiness made my heart beat quicker than usual.

For a moment I thought of climbing a tree. Unfortunately, the enemy I dreaded was more nimble than I at that exercise. I saw him suddenly prick up his ears, lash his sides with his long tail, and slowly turn his head to the right. He crouched like a dog on the watch, then bounded towards the forest. At the same moment a shot was fired. I heard the sound of broken branches, and wondered anxiously whether my guide had paid for his temerity with his life, and whether I had not to expect an attack upon myself.

Ten minutes, which seemed to me a century in duration, passed. I was hoping every moment to see my guide appear, and, on the other hand, I dreaded meeting the terrible animal on my way. The slightest movement of the foliage made me shudder with fright, and I cursed the fatal good-nature which had left me without a weapon. In such circumstances immobility adds to the torture of suspense; thus I made up my mind, with a thousand precautions, eye and ear on the watch, to get down to the basin into which the river fell.

This object attained, I quickly climbed on to one of the rocks surrounded by water, from whence I thought I might brave the enemy. I was hardly stationed there, when the Indian made his appearance.

"Have you had good sport?" I cried.

"No," replied he, in a tone of disappointment. "Your gun contained nothing but small shot."

"Then has the tiger made its escape?"

"Yes; but it will not leave these parts."

"Why not?"

"Because it is just the time now when the goat-keepers bring their flocks into the valley, and the tigers know that."

"Are you not afraid that your game is lying in wait to spring on us unexpectedly?"

"Tigers are only brave with a coward."

"A coward? That is exactly what I am," I resumed, smiling; "and I have no desire to serve as a repast for your neighbour."

The Indian looked at me for a moment, as though he doubted the sincerity of my words.

"A hunted tiger is not in the least to be feared," said he. "He only becomes so when he is wounded; and this one's skin is whole."

Reassured by my guide's calmness, I began to interest myself with the cascade. Imagine a perpendicular mountain, from the top of which falls a river, several feet wide, in a single body. Half-way down the fall the water comes in contact with an enormous jutting rock, which divides it into a thousand little foaming threads, then allows it to fall into a basin half filled by the detached pieces of earth. Filtering through the *débris*, the water disappears for a moment, and then is seen again a hundred feet further on, flowing calmly and limpidly along.

I stood for a long time contemplating this magnificent spectacle, incased in the most picturesque scenery. The white foam of the little river, falling with mathematical regularity, sometimes even appearing motionless, stands out against the background of verdure. The rock over which the first column of water dashes, has for thousands of years resisted the formidable, ceaseless shock; but it must certainly one day give way and roll into the valley. One trembles involuntarily at the thought.

I was so thoroughly captivated by the magnificent scenery

before my eyes, that I forgot all about the tiger and my Indian, when a shot, fired quite close to me, made me start. This time my anxiety was of short duration, for my guide reappeared between the rocks, carrying a magnificent otter over his shoulder. I then learnt, with much surprise, that the waters of the little river abound with fish, at a short distance from the place where they execute their perilous leap.

The sun was almost touching the hill-tops; his rays gilded the cascade, and allowed me to admire it under a new aspect. My guide interrupted my reverie by saying—

"We must be starting. Night is coming on."

I followed him. Just as we were about to enter the wood, I cast a last look at the fall. It was a side view, and I could see at a single glance the immense arc described by the column of water. The sun soon tinged the valley with a rosy light; then the twilight deepened, rapidly effacing the beautiful tints flickering over the water. Half an hour later, I was eating a portion of the armadillo, killed by my host and cooked by his wife, whilst their little child slept peacefully in a cradle adorned with banana leaves in lieu of drapery.

During the short evening, the conversation naturally turned on the subject of Mexican tigers, or jaguars. I learnt that these fine carnivorous animals formerly infested the valley of Tuxpango. Good year or bad, there were always a dozen killed at the time when the goat-keepers returned to Mistèque, or the province of Aajaca. I expressed my regret that my host had missed the fine animal he had fired at; its skin I should have been glad to have possessed.

When my hosts were about to retire for the night, I stretched myself on a heap of dry leaves arranged for me, for I had declined to make use of the matting which served my hosts as beds. The little child was still sleeping peacefully, and its mother already thought it cured.

"I like thee," said she, artlessly, kissing my hands. "Thou art good: thou dost not despise the Indians."

"I am a Christian," I answered, "and the Indians are my brethren."

At nine o'clock in the evening we were all sleeping profoundly. Not *all*. I was aroused by the dogs, the pigs, and the inhabitants of the poultry-yard, who came grouping round me. Towards the middle of the night I awoke with a start. It seemed to me that some noise, which I could not account for, had disturbed my sleep. The atmosphere was calm; the sky brilliant with stars; not a leaf stirred, and the roar of the waterfall was perfectly audible in the silence. I quietly lay down again, when I thought I heard a distant gun-shot. The dogs gave a low growl; but they soon went to sleep again, and I followed their example.

When I opened my eyes at break of day, I was not a little surprised to see my host fastening a magnificent tiger-skin on the ground, by means of wooden pegs.

"Have you been hunting, then, during the night?" I asked him, getting up.

"Yes," replied he, "and your gun is a good one."

"Did you kill that fine creature near the waterfall?"

"I shot him in the valley, near a goat-park."

"Will you sell me the skin?"

"It is for you."

"What price do you want, then, for it?"

"It is for you," said the Indian, "on condition that you will stay with us to-day, and continue to cure our child."

The young mother anxiously listened for my reply. She clapped her hands with joy when she heard me declare that I would accept the condition.

"You ought to have awakened me," said I to the Indian. "I would have gone with you."

"White men have no patience," he answered. "I have spent a week on the look-out; and, besides, the night was cold."

"And did you kill the animal the first shot?"

"To be sure of killing a tiger, and not losing the prey, one must fire close to it."

And in fact it is by lying in ambush, and firing close, that the Indians kill their tigers.

I spent three days at the cabin, which gave the child time to get well, and the tiger's skin time to dry. In short, I carried home with me after my excursions the memory of one of Nature's most marvellous works. If I dared, I would advise my readers, even those who have seen the Niagara, to pay the Tuxpango Cascade a visit. There are spectacles as grand; but there is not one more curious.

THE SERPENT-CHARMER.

The curado—Chépé Solana—The huaco plant—The trial—Fears calmed.

In my rambles one day I came by chance to Acula, an Indian village, situated about ten miles from Tacotalpam; and finding myself on unexplored ground, I began to make a collection of hymenoptera. My first search was very successful; and delighted at seeing my collection so rapidly enriched with bees and hornets still unknown in Europe, I determined to make a short stay at the village.

One morning, on peeling the bark off a gigantic tree which had fallen down with old age, the Indian who acted as my guide came upon a nest of rattlesnakes. It was of no use crying to my companion to sheath his hunting-knife; he ruthlessly hacked to pieces a whole colony of these rare and magnificent *ophidians*.

"Why did you want to save these reptiles?" said he to me: "is it not the duty of a Christian to kill them when he can?— You wanted to keep their rattles, did you not? Well, I took good care not to spoil them."

"I wanted especially to have two or three of these reptiles alive," replied I. "Do you know any way of getting possession of them?"

"No; I am not a *curado*."

"What does that mean?"

"That I am not proof against a snake's bite."

"You are not different from any one else in that respect."

"You are mistaken. If Chépé Solano had been here, he

would have got hold of this swarm of serpents without one of them trying to bite him."

"Is Chépé Solano a snake-charmer, then?"

"No; he is only a *curado*, that is all."

"And how does one become a *curado*?"

"By drinking an infusion of *huaco* prepared in a certain manner."

"Is this preparation a secret, then?"

"Yes. Chépé Solano got it from his grandfather."

"Will he not consent to tell it any one?"

"Yes; but he asks too much money."

"Can you introduce me to Chépé Solano?"

"Certainly. He lives next-door to me, and is godfather to one of my children."

"Did you say that he could handle snakes without any danger?"

"I have seen him do it."

"And how much does he want for his secret?"

"Forty piastres."

"That is not dear," I said, "if the remedy is really efficacious. Let us return to the village. You shall bring Chépé Solano to me, and I will pay for you as well as myself if you get him to reveal his secret to us."

The Indian seized my hand and kissed it in token of gratitude; it was evidently one of his ambitions to become a *curado*. In this country, where one risks treading on a venomous reptile at every step, and where there are annually three or four victims to the bites of rattlesnakes, to be invulnerable is naturally a privilege desired above everything.

The same evening my Indian brought Chépé Solano to me. He was a little old man with cunning features and quick eyes. He dealt in quack medicines, and gained a good livelihood by the exercise of this profession.

"Do you know what I want you for?" said I to him.

"Yes; only will you have the courage and the patience to undergo the necessary ordeal?"

"In what does the ordeal consist?"

"You must lie down for a week, and then drink a pint of *huaco* juice morning and night."

"And after that?"

"Your body will have a nauseous smell for six months."

"What then?"

"The day the odour leaves you you will be able to handle any reptiles without any danger; they will respect you."

"Very good; but what guarantee is there for my becoming a real *curado* at the end of six months?"

"My example."

"Can you handle reptiles?"

"You shall see me do it whenever you please."

"And how much will the beverage cost me?"

"Sixty piastres for you, and forty for my neighbour."

The neighbour who had squatted himself on the ground, sprang up hastily, and looked at me anxiously, dreading lest the large sum—twenty pounds—should make me change my mind. I reassured him, and then it was agreed that the following day we should go serpent-hunting with Chépé. Directly I was convinced of the *curado's* invulnerability I was to place a hundred piastres in his hand, and the secret of the preparation of the *huaco* juice would be revealed to me.

When Chépé came out of the hut which I was living in, he was surrounded by at least twenty people. They already knew that my guide was going to become a *curado*, and every one congratulated him on his good fortune.

I was aware that *huaco*, an aromatic plant of the *eupatorium* species, is considered by the Indians as a sovereign specific against the bites of venomous serpents. *Huaco* is also very much employed in Mexico as a medicine for yellow fever, and it has been vaunted in Europe as a specific against cholera. In fact, it is an excellent sudorific, which is its principal property. As to its being able to make any one invulnerable to a serpent's bite, this was a virtue I hardly credited; but I was very glad to have an opportunity of seeing in what way an Indian, pretending to be a *curado*, succeeded in handling venomous snakes with impunity and deceiving his audience.

The following morning at eight o'clock, I saw Chépé coming towards my hut, followed by my guide. We started in the direction of some marshy land, where swarms of snakes were to be found. Evidently Chépé did not often give his countrymen the pleasure of admiring his invulnerability, for a dozen men, and as many women, set out after us. We were just going to enter the forest, when an Indian cried out—

"A yellow snake!"

And there indeed, near a palm tree, lay a magnificent snake, about a yard long, with a fine gold-coloured skin. Every one kept at a distance, for the yellow snake was as much dreaded as the rattlesnake.

Chépé went up to the reptile, seized it in the middle of its body, and raised it above his head.

Cries of terror and admiration fell from all lips at the sight of the reptile winding itself round the Indian's copper-coloured arm.

I went up to Chépé, and, to the general amazement, seized the snake in my turn. I had known it for a long while; it is as harmless as the common European snake.

"My good fellow," said I to the Indian, in an undertone, "you will not gain my hundred piastres by handling such harmless creatures as these."

He gave me a stealthy look, and entered the wood.

After having walked for ten minutes, we found ourselves in a thick underwood. Here and there lay trees crumbling away with old age, their decayed trunks completely hollowed out. Suddenly Chépé uttered an exclamation; a black snake, a yard and a half long, was twining itself round his body. The Indian held out the frightful reptile to me; but this time, although knowing it was to be feared only on account of its strength, I instinctively drew back. The Indians uttered a cry of satisfaction, and with a rapid movement Chépé made two pieces of the snake, which covered him with blood.

"Are you convinced?" said he to me.

"Not yet," I replied. "You have some knowledge of snakes, and this one you have just cut in two is as harmless as the yellow snake. You promised me you would handle a rattlesnake."

"Find one," said the Indian, in a disdainful tone.

And he sat down on the trunk of a tree, enjoying the admiration of his countrymen.

Fortunately, the lookers-on who had followed us were as desirous as I was to see the *curado* struggling with a rattlesnake; thus I was saved the trouble of looking for one myself. A shrill noise was suddenly heard under a flap of loose bark.

"Here it is!" cried they.

Chépé Solano turned visibly pale, notwithstanding his dark complexion, and he went very slowly towards the trunk they had pointed out to him. It was an exciting moment, for the bite of a rattlesnake is fatal. With a slightly trembling hand, Chépé slowly raised the piece of bark, and I noticed that he did it in a way to allow of the snakes making their escape; but in spite of his precautions, one of the snakes glided on to the imprudent man's hand, and he fell down, crying out—

"I am killed!"

I hastened up to him to cauterize the wound. Unfortunately, the blood with which the black adder had covered the poor wretch, prevented me from discovering the spot. I called for water, and all the gourds were immediately emptied over Chépé's arm; who, by a miracle, had escaped the fang of his terrible enemy. He gradually recovered his self-possession, and began to talk in a language I did not understand.

I kept myself in the background, not wishing to appear to make fun of the *curado's* discomfiture. I declared myself satisfied, and told him I would speak with him on the subject later on. He went away, followed by the sight-seers, and I resumed my search for insects with my guide.

"Do you still believe in the invulnerability of *curados*?" I asked him.

"Certainly," he replied. "Did you not hear what Chépé told us?"

"I heard, but I did not understand."

"Well, the invulnerability lasts ten years exactly. Now

"I AM DEAD!"

Chépé forgot that at nine o'clock it was ten years since he had taken the *huaco;* that was how he was able to handle the yellow and the black snakes without any danger; but the time of invulnerability had just expired when he wanted to take up the rattlesnake."

Every one in Mexico has seen the Indian *curados* handle venomous snakes gratis. I have often laid down a hundred piastres to enjoy this spectacle, and have always won my money back, which proves that among savages, as well as among civilized beings, there are credulous people and clever conjurors.

THE DEAD CITY.

CHAPTER I.

Bishop's River—Indian cooking—Eulalio and Célestin—The king of vultures—A newly married couple—Wedding-feasts—The cotton plants—Wild turkeys—An escort of alligators.

On the 20th of July, 1860, beneath a blue sky, with a gentle breeze from the Gulf of Mexico faintly rustling through the foliage of the trees, I was led with great pomp by three of my friends down to the boat which I had hired from the head fisherman in Cosamaloapam, with the intention of exploring the partly unknown course of the Obispo.

The Rio Obispo (Bishop's River) mingles its bluish waters with the usually muddy stream of the Papaloapam, at the village of Amatlan. No one in Mexico knew the exact source of this fine stream; they knew vaguely that it passed through lakes, plains, and forests, but no one could say precisely where it came from. During my stay in Mexico, I often hunted along the picturesque banks of the Obispo, watching for tapirs or otters, and always puzzled by the enigma of its calmly flowing waters, down which a palm or an ebony tree would sometimes float. A river without a source? This idea pursued me, and sometimes even disturbed my sleep. My insatiable curiosity could not rest.

I had more than once consulted the old Spanish authors on the subject of this mysterious river, especially the learned Franciscan monk, Juan de Torquemada; but the good man says no more about it than does his compiler, the Jesuit Clavigero.

The old geographical maps of Mexico do not even condescend to mark the Obispo. As to modern maps, the most exact boldly insert its name, Rio de l'Obispo to the right of a little serpentine line, which rejoins that of the Papaloapam, below Tlacotalpam. These maps know just a little less about the matter than I do. It is above, and not below Tlacotalpam, that the Obispo falls into the Papaloapam; but this fact, which I can guarantee, throws no light whatever on the place where it takes its rise.

I questioned an old *Vaquero*, that is to say, one of the centaurs, who are continually scouring the immense savannahs where herds of wild bulls pasture. He was considered an intrepid, conscientious man, and his master's lands extended partly along the left bank of the Obispo. He informed me that he had followed this bank for a whole day, making his way through the brambles, and that, contrary to other water-courses, this one grew wider in proportion as it was further from its mouth, which appeared to me somewhat paradoxical.

I also questioned an Indian of the village of Acula, who was supposed to be a sorcerer, and pretended to cure his countrymen's sickness by means of plants gathered on the banks of this mysterious river. At first the Indian replied evasively, whilst he gave me to understand that he had long known all about it, but that reasons of a particular kind prevented him telling what he knew. I showed him a piastre, which only provoked a smile. Two piastres made him quite serious again. I was obliged to go as far as five to get the better of his scruples. I then learnt that the Rio Obispo, which is a purely Spanish name, passes through forests, plains, and savannahs, a fact which I rather doubted. I learnt besides, that it took its rise in the Sierra Oajaca, and that it issued from a cavern with massive silver sides, and that whole blocks of this precious metal were washed down its course. These details, added to the description of a diamond rock more dazzling than the sun, made me regret my twenty shillings; but there was no retracting from the bargain.

Finally, I made up my mind to question an old fisherman,

who had lived for a quarter of a century on the banks of the Obispo, where it joins the Papaloapam. Don Bernardo invited me to dinner, when I partook of two or three dishes, the composition of which I dared not inquire into. In one of them there was certainly turpentine and onions, unfortunately there was not enough onion, and the turpentine had been too freely used. At dessert, I was obliged to crunch some ant's eggs, a sweetmeat I do not recommend to any one. Whilst taking our coffee, reclining luxuriously on a bull's hide which served him as a hammock, Don Bernardo told me that fifteen years before this time he had ascended the river for a day and a half, that it was bordered all along its course by dense forests, and that on the second day of his exploration he had landed near a hut inhabited by an Indian from Amatlan. This man, who was about forty, had committed a murder in the village, and escaped justice by taking refuge in this solitary place with his wife and sons.

This information was valuable, although it threw little light on the real whereabouts of the source. Seized with an ambitious impulse, I formed the project of going myself to the discovery, and of at last informing the natives, who cared very little about the matter, from whence came the blue water, the transparency of which they admired and found so much superior to the chalky water of the Papaloapam.

As it was a perilous excursion, I was obliged to look out for a travelling companion upon whom I could rely. I tempted a French mechanic, an enthusiastic treasure-searcher, by telling him of the cave with the silver walls, the existence of which the Indian sorcerer had revealed to me for the sum of five piastres. My first words seemed to convince M. Vignon that this statement was very plausible; it flattered his favourite dream of finding the lost riches of the Aztec emperor Monteuczoma. Thus he begged me to allow him to accompany me, asking as sole recompense the quarter of the treasure which we could not fail to discover, and of which I generously agreed to give him the half. This, therefore, was the reason of my friends conducting me with great parade down to the boat which, through a thousand windings, was to take me to the unknown source of the Obispo.

My little craft, made all in one piece out of the trunk of a cedar tree, measured about five yards from stem to stern and scarcely a yard in width. Its flat bottom, gliding on the water instead of cutting through it, greatly reduced its speed. I had stored it with dried meat, maize-cakes, oil, vinegar, wine, brandy, lead, and powder. My companion had taken care to provide himself with a mosquito-net, hammers and chisels to detach the blocks of silver from the cavern, without counting a dozen sacks intended to hold the precious metal.

We had two rowers; Célestin, an old French sailor, who had left his ship stationed at Vera-Cruz, and the Mexican mulatto Eulalio, his inseparable companion. Our voyage of discovery had assumed great importance in the eyes of the inhabitants of Cosamaloapam, thanks to our two boatmen. A number of men and women crowded the banks of the river at the time of our embarkation. The children plunged into the water, and swam round our boat like fishes. All my men being on board, I sprang into one end of the boat. Eulalio, with a long boat-hook in his hand, occupied the other. I raised my hat and vigorously pushed off the bank. Our craft launched out in the middle of the stream, turned round, and was soon carried along by the current. The huts seemed to fly past us. A sudden bend hid the little village from view, and in less than an hour from our departure, we landed at the mouth of the Obispo, in front of Don Bernardo's cabin.

Hundreds of black vultures were hovering through the cloudless sunny sky. These were of the *cultur atratus* species so common in Mexico, and which custom still more than law protects against all aggression, as a just recompense for the service they render in freeing the towns from the dirt accumulated in houses, and the carcases of animals, which without them would infest the streets. A *sarcoramphus papa*, or king of vultures, as the Mexicans generally call it, took wing a few steps from us. From its hooked beak, surmounted with a yellow caruncle, the use of which naturalists have not yet been able to explain, hung a strip of meat it had just stolen whilst it was drying in the sun. Its cheeks, variegated with yellow, blue, and violet, encased in a collarette of feathers of a pearl-grey colour, resembled the wings of a butterfly. It flew swiftly upwards, making a whizzing sound through the air with the strokes of its powerful wings, and then, crossing the river, disappeared.

"There is a good omen for you," said Eulalio: "he who meets a condor sees his dearest wish fulfilled."

I looked at the river, at once thinking of its source; M. Vignon turned towards his pile of sacks; whilst Célestin seized his gourd full of brandy, crying—

"Let us be quick and empty it, since it ought to be always full."

Don Bernardo lived with his wife and two daughters, and I was surprised to see no one appear at the door of the cabin, although a dense line of smoke was escaping from the roof. Three or four lean dogs came barking round us, and a small tame seal dragged itself with difficulty over the sand, trying to imitate its terrestrial companions by grunting. On reaching the little house, I saw three or four earthen pots over the fire, and two old Indian women busy skimming them. I then learnt that my friend the fisherman was celebrating his daughter's wedding, that the young couple had received the nuptial benediction the same morning before daylight, according to the Mexican custom, and that they were expected to return every moment. I was about to embark again, rather vexed at not being able to get a few last words of information as to the route we were about to take, when the sounds of merriment were heard, and five or six canoes came alongside the bank near our boat.

Don Bernardo's daughter was a rather pretty girl; she was scarcely sixteen, but would have passed for twenty in Europe, where nature is less precocious than in the tropics. The young bride had a tall, slight figure, her skin was faintly tinged with a copper-coloured hue, and, like all her countrywomen, she had long black hair, large eyes, beautiful teeth, and small hands. She was enveloped in a blue striped cotton shawl, which she took off on landing, and appeared dressed in a simple low bodice and long petticoat trimmed with three rows of flounces. Her hair, plaited in thick tresses, was brought over her forehead in the form of a coronet, and fastened by a semi-circular comb, and one or two red pomegranate blossoms. From her ears hung pieces of unpolished coral, simply threaded, and alternating with small gold coins. She wore white shoes, and could hardly bend her fingers, laden with heavy rings.

Don Bernardo was radiant, adorned in his holiday clothes; that is, in a white shirt, blue breeches, tied at the waist by a belt of red Chinese crape, and magnificent yellow shoes. His son-in-law, dressed in more modern style, wore white trousers, with a short linen jacket, and had contented himself with black shoes. With the usual Mexican hospitality, we were at once invited to the wedding-feast, which was to take place about noon; and this invitation we were obliged to accept, in order not to violate the most elementary laws of Mexican politeness.

The bride, assisted by her sister, offered to each guest some sugar-cane brandy instead of absinthe, or bitters. Célestin and Eulalio, delighted at the good luck that had befallen them, asked for a good measure. As for me, Don Bernardo's daughters served me all the more generously with the fiery liquid in proportion as they wished to do me honour. If I had been imprudent enough to drink the dose of *chinguirito* which was gracefully offered me, I should have been intoxicated before I had finished. I pretended to have a coughing fit, which obliged me to turn away, and shaking the gourd that served as a wine-glass, I managed to spill a good part of its contents on the ground. Having succeeded in emptying it by occasional tilts, I returned it to one of the beautiful Hebes. Vignon, less honoured than myself, had only a reasonable dose, and found himself obliged to drink it.

They then sat down to table, that is, every one squatted as well as he could on the furs spread out under a large sapote tree. A kind of tomato soup was first of all handed round; then appeared the famous turkey, with piquant sauce, the national Mexican dish, called *molé*. Woe betide the novice who, tempted by the fine appearance of the gold-coloured sauce, and by the evident relish with which the natives feast themselves on it, partakes of this dish without being prepared for it by a long apprenticeship. After the first mouthful he swears that he will never touch another morsel of it, and with streaming eyes, swollen lips, and mouth open, he breathes fiercely to try and calm the self-inflicted torments of the frightful burn. After a time one gets used to this fiery food, and even finds it a stimulant to the appetite in a climate where thirst rivals hunger; and more than one European, after staying for some years in Mexico, becomes as fond of the celebrated *molé* as any Creole is.

When dessert came, and sherry was flowing freely, I was obliged to keep an eye upon my two rowers; but I was rather behindhand with them. The heat was overpowering, and the generous Spanish wine had sent half of the guests to sleep, with Eulalio among the number. It was about four o'clock when, deaf to all remonstrances, and energetically seconded by Vignon, I succeeded in getting our men back to the boat. Still Célestin, who had already sung one or two French songs to our astounded hosts, wanted to go back and dance when he heard the sound of guitars.

Scarcely was Eulalio in the boat when he lay down full length at the bottom, and I obliged Célestin to follow his example; then, taking possession of the oars, I succeeded somewhat awkwardly in unmooring our boat. Unfortunately, Vignon was not more skilful in the art of boating than myself, and we had to struggle against the current without making much progress, our boat describing a series of zigzags as fantastic as though it also had been assisting at the wedding-feast.

All at once, when we had lost sight of Don Bernardo's cabin for more than an hour, there was a sound of guitars to our right, and on a bank we were just about to pass, we saw a group of the wedding guests. Ten minutes' walking had brought them to this place, which, through the winding of the river, we had taken almost an hour to reach. The married couple, arm in arm, looked smilingly towards us, and two young girls sitting near them waved their scarfs, whilst the guitar players scraped away furiously on the bass cords of their instruments. Eulalio having raised his head, and begun to talk of

"THE MARRIED COUPLE, ARM IN ARM."

landing, I hastily steered the boat towards the bank opposite that which the picturesque group occupied. With a spring which almost capsized us, the mulatto jumped into the water, and was soon followed by Célestin. For the moment I was seriously angry, and I obliged the two swimmers to get back into the boat. They took up the oars, and, refreshed by their immersion, pulled away vigorously.

It was a day lost; but in the desert time is largely dispensed with, and I quickly became reconciled to this annoyance. We passed through the midst of magnificent forests. The difference of level between the ground and the river was barely a yard, the banks more often than not being perpendicular. Creepers. hanging down from the tops of the trees, swept the surface of the water, and served as a shelter for the beautiful kingfishers with their short but powerful wings.

At sunset we found ourselves passing near a cotton-field, and we made up our minds to camp there. Mexican pioneers employ fire when they want to clear the land; thus the ground was strewn with charred trunks, from which green shoots were springing, so fertile and hardy is vegetation in this burning climate.

Having moored our boat safely, we made a fire at about a hundred feet from the river, in order to avoid the insects which already began to annoy us. Night fell rapidly, the sounds died insensibly away, even the breeze subsided, and the paroquets, those merciless chatterers, were silent. Two macaws, perched in a neighbouring tree, and undoubtedly frightened by our fire. uttered a cry of distress from time to time, which was answered by the gobbling of a band of wild turkeys roosting in the middle of the forest. We meant to get up early and shoot one or two of the beautiful birds imported into France by the Jesuits, and seen for the first time on a French table at the wedding-feast of Charles IX. in 1570.

The wild turkey, or *meleagris*, has a greenish brown plumage with golden tints. It has been successfully acclimatized in all latitudes, and everywhere its flesh is esteemed. The turkey loses the brilliancy of its plumage in its tamed state, as much in its native country as in Europe; but as compensation, its flesh is more succulent. The Indians who rear these fine birds about their cabins, call it *totalé*, a name which they also give to cowards.

Towards nine o'clock we were stretched on the ground, sleeping profoundly. I awakened my companions long before daybreak, and the rising sun found us more than three miles from the place where we had camped, struggling with a swarm of microscopic flies, and followed by a dozen hideous-muzzled alligators.

CHAPTER II.

A virgin forest—Alligators—A rough alarm—Wild bulls—A victim—Paroquets and cardinals—An Indian family—Flies—The lake.

ALL trace of human life had disappeared; ancient forest trees interlaced their lofty branches overhead; clusters of creepers were flung in garlands from one bank to the other, forming cool retreats for the feathered songsters; grenadillos, or passion-flowers, wound and climbed round the trunks of the trees, their blue, red, and yellow flowers producing a fruit very much resembling red Easter eggs, filled with sweet transparent pulp. By the side of these beautiful creepers were the dragon plants, a species of which, with drilled leaves, passes among the Indians as a specific against the bites of venomous serpents, and is commonly called *adder's-wood*. The begonias, with their panicle-shaped flowers, promised us a wholesome seasoning for any game we might bring down, especially the brilliant begonia which owes its family name to Dr. Bégon, and the leaves of which, as much from their appearance as their acid flavour, greatly resemble sorrel.

Among the trees passing before us, I admired the green feathery plumes of the royal palms, the *ceibas* with their enormous trunks, and seeds enveloped in a fine down used for making cushions; the mimosas with their odorous flowers and knotty trunks, and amongst them fine specimens of sensitive plants; *ingas, melastomes,* balsams, and among others the *élémifère* or candle-tree. But what botanist could enumerate the marvellous plants crowding before our delighted eyes?

If in imagination the reader adds to the spectacle of this luxuriant vegetation, the air filled with brilliantly coloured butterflies, dragon-flies, coleopteras, and dipterals, and the sun shining upon their feathery or gauze wings, making all this corolla of velvet or satin, golden and ruby-coloured, he will yet have but a faint idea of the splendours of the virgin world near a water-course in these unknown regions, which, once seen, are never to be forgotten.

Here and there, sometimes to the left and sometimes to the right, were large open glades where hundreds of alligators, with widely opened jaws, were basking in the sun. A sickening musky odour warned us beforehand of these encounters, and we rowed as quickly as possible to get out of the tainted air. As for the monsters, some of them near the bank turned round slowly, and glided indolently into the water, to come and prowl round our boat. Most of them looked as though they were petrified, and did not even deign to shut their yawning jaws, so that we were able to admire at our ease the formidable teeth with which nature has provided these hideous reptiles. We had on an average five or six of these creatures always in sight; they sometimes followed us with only their eyes above the water. Our white flesh tempted them, so said Eulalio. In short, the Rio de l'Obispo has nothing of the bishop about it, and if I had the authority of baptizing it again, I should certainly call it the *Alligator River.*

It was a singular fact that the river abounded in fish, which sported familiarly round our boat; nevertheless, the alligators must have made a considerable consumption of them. A kind of carp, with a blue back and pink belly, jumped giddily into our boat; it weighed about four pounds. Célestin immediately took possession of it and put it on one side for our breakfast, which saved us one or two gunshots.

Towards ten o'clock the heat became so unbearable that we were obliged to think of looking for a shelter, and allowing our oarsmen a rest. We landed on the left bank, and having moored our bark, we entered the forest in search of a cool spot where we might rest and grill our fish.

While Célestin and Eulalio were busy making a fire I ventured into the forest, taking care to notch some of the trees as I went along in order to be sure of finding my way back. Vignon helped me in this necessary precaution; for one easily gets lost in these virgin forests, and death from hunger, thirst, and exhaustion, or the teeth of wild animals, is the terrible consequence of such a misadventure. Thus we walked on, our hatchets in our hands, listening attentively to every sound. Under the bark of a *ceibus*, uprooted by a hurricane, I found five or six enormous insects called *longimanus*, on account of the disproportionate length of their front legs, their red shell-like wings being irregularly spotted with black lozenges, like the stones of a mosaic. At the same time I was about to make prisoner of a pretty salamander which I hardly expected to find there, when an inexplicable noise was heard. I crouched with my companion behind the fallen tree, and presently we saw a black and white bull coming along at a sharp pace, with bloodshot eyes, infuriated by a swarm of ox-flies buzzing round his head. On seeing us the animal looked as though it would trample us down; but the trunk in front must have baffled his evil intentions. He dashed his head against the obstacle, gave a prolonged bellow, and continued his mad pace.

The presence of such a guest in the forest revealed the proximity of a savannah, and curiosity led us forward. We had hardly gone a distance of three or four hundred yards, when, to our great surprise, we came upon a wide-beaten road, trodden down by the cattle, and along which all vegetation had been destroyed. Here and there were a few traces of horse's hoofs. What did such a sign mean? Two days later we should have thought of the proximity of a village or an unknown town; but we were still too near Cosamaloapam not to know for certain that all this side of the river was uninhabited.

"THE BULLS FILED PAST US BY HUNDREDS."

Bending forward, we were looking, like Robinson Crusoe, for the trace of human feet on the moist earth, when a noise like that which had just startled us was again heard. We thought it was our new acquaintance returning with hostile intentions, or a band of monkeys making their approach. The noise grew rapidly louder; one would have thought that it was a waterspout devastating the forest in the distance, and we made haste to fly. Passing close by a cluster of creepers, my companion laid hold of their strong tendrils and climbed into the tree which they encircled. I followed his example, for the uproar was getting louder, and drawing nearer. There, breathless and pale, for we were really frightened, we leaned down anxiously over the road, wondering what horrible animal we were going to see. I uttered an exclamation of relief when I saw a herd of bulls, their leader having a tawny hide, marked with a star in front. The wild herd were only on their way to drink, and it was their daily journey from the savannah to the river that had made the beaten track which we had been unable to explain.

We had done well to fly. The bulls filed past us by hundreds, without uttering a sound, and we should have been trampled to death had we been in their way. We got down noiselessly from our place of observation and hurried back to our companions, who were undoubtedly anxious at our long absence. On reaching the fire I saw the fine fish which had smelt so savoury left to turn to cinders; Eulalio and Célestin, our cooks, had disappeared.

We went towards the river; our oarsmen had most likely been frightened by the bulls and taken refuge in the boat.

"Unless they have been eaten by a tiger," said my companion, smiling.

The joke might well have been a reality, for tigers often follow the herds of bulls. But neither Célestin nor Eulalio were of the stamp to let themselves be crushed without saying a word; we should have heard their cries, or the report of their fire-arms, if they had been assailed. Nevertheless, I was troubled for the moment when we reached the bank and found the boat gone.

"We must have mistaken our way," I cried.

"No," replied Vignon; "look."

Looking in the direction indicated, I saw Célestin and Eulalio about a hundred yards off, standing up in the boat, both looking scared, and listening attentively. On seeing us they came hurriedly back.

"Whatever has been going on up there?" cried the mulatto; "one would have thought that all the infernal spirits were let loose."

I told him of our encounter with the bulls, and we had a good laugh over our mutual alarm. The boat was again moored; but just as we were going back to the fire, a strange cry, followed by a mournful bellowing, made us turn round. A young bull, surrounded by alligators, was struggling in the middle of the river, which was dyed with its blood. The same idea of delivering the poor animal from the monsters' jaws, led Vignon and me to fire together. The alligators immediately plunged, but without losing their victim, which disappeared with them. Our balls had skimmed over the butchers' horny hides, and we had spent our powder and shot for nothing.

The unusual noise of our shots had evidently frightened the bulls, for we heard them bellowing and scampering off at a mad gallop. We again returned to the fire, walking slowly back, and on the alert in case of any attack. One or two scouts appeared in the distance, but the sight of them did not trouble us; we knew now how to deal with the enemy. It was no less than an hour before the forest was quiet again, and during this time Eulalio fried some strips of dried meat for our frugal meal, the carp being reduced to a cinder. After having eaten, my companions went to sleep, whilst I amused myself with tormenting a poor sensitive plant by obliging it to fold up its leaves. About three o'clock I awoke my men, and the boat resumed its adventurous course through the midst of the alligators.

A flock of ducks with black and bronzed plumage passed close to us and insured our dinner. We killed three of them, but the last was seized by a crocodile, who snapped it up just as Célestin was leaning over the boat to take it. At sunset, our boat was sheltered in a creek, and we put up the mosquito-net at the foot of a sapotilla tree, from the bark of which oozed a milky gum, very much liked by Mexican women. The night passed without any remarkable incident, and long before dawn we were rowing between two gigantic hedges of flowering shrubs.

At breakfast time, on approaching a glade in the forest, we saw about a hundred paroquets, no bigger than our sparrows. These charming birds meeting with a flock of cardinals of fiery red plumage, a noisy rather than murderous battle ensued. The glade was sown with maize, which explained the presence of these little marauders, and revealed the proximity of the hut of which Don Bernardo had spoken; so, notwithstanding the heat—it was nearly eleven o'clock—we pressed forward.

Not knowing how the Indian who was incontestibly lord of these solitudes would receive us, I kept the boat near the right bank of the river. It was not until one o'clock in the afternoon, on account of the numerous windings of the stream, that we heard a dog give a low howl, which replaces a bark with those animals brought up in the desert. We were overpowered with fatigue, and the sun's rays, reflected from the smooth mirror of the water, almost blinded us.

Two children, about eight and nine years old, with shaven heads and quite naked, stood behind the trunk of a tree, looking at us with open-mouthed surprise. I called them, but they ran away. A young man next appeared, and then an old woman.

"May God protect thee!" cried I to the old lady.

"And may He guide thee!" she replied.

"Wilt thou show us hospitality?"

"I have neither bread nor brandy."

"We only ask for a shelter from the sun."

"How do I know but what you are bad people?"

"We are good Christians," I replied, advancing towards her alone; "but we will go on if thou wilt have it so."

"I am a Christian also," replied the Indian woman. "Be welcome."

They led us behind the principal cabin to a hut with a leafy roof, simply supported by stakes driven into the ground. Five stalwart young men came up to us, soon followed by their wives, and at last by an old Indian, the father of this little colony. We had thought ourselves formidable, but were now obliged to keep on our guard, being by far the fewest; however, we were dealing with honest folks.

After dinner, which had consisted of chickens, with rice and black beans fried in fat, I offered all the guests a bumper of brandy, which at once tied the knot of our friendship. As soon as the sun had gone down, I visited my host's cultivated land. Three of his sons were married, and the family went in turns once a year across the plains to the *Sanctuario*, a little village situated on the right bank of the Papaloapam. There, in exchange for tiger's skins, they got provisions of salt, powder, shot, and all necessary household objects. It must be confessed, I should never have thought for one moment that the calm, good-natured patriarch before me was the murderer whose history I had heard related.

The old man could give me no more information than his sons as to the course of the Obispo river. Not one of the inhabitants of the hut had ventured beyond the great lake which we should reach in less than an hour. During the half-century that she had lived in this place, our hostess told us that ours was the second boat which had dared to venture thus far. In fact, the following day we should be in totally unexplored regions, and one does not enter upon such excursions without some feeling more or less of keen emotion.

In the evening the mosquitos assailed us in such large numbers, and with such fury, that we were obliged to retire as quickly as possible behind the mosquito-net. But the terrible blood-suckers succeeded in getting into this shelter; and taking the advice of our hostess, we burnt the leaves of a pepper-plant under our transparent curtains, to the great injury of our eyes and lungs. Our hosts themselves were obliged to have recourse to this expedient, but they were accustomed to the disagreeable odour which suffocated us. At the time of the rainy season, they have no other recourse than to take refuge under their shelter a little before sunset, in order not to be literally devoured. One knows what the unbearable itching caused by a gnat's sting is: imagine this pain repeated a hundredfold and without intermission, and you will have some idea of one of the terrible tortures endured by travellers in foreign countries, a torture which often intimidates the bravest.

One cannot sleep much under the action of a thousand venomous needle-points; thus we were quite ready to start at daybreak. The sun, red and lustreless, shrouded by a crimson mist, appeared over the tree-tops in front of us, and we knew what overwhelming heat we were to expect. The paroquets, awakening with us, were chattering on all sides, whilst the cardinals, perched on the shrubs like scarlet flowers, uttered their little monotonous cries. I admired a cross-bill with olive-coloured body, brown neck, and eyes surrounded with a circle of golden feathers, which fluttered quite familiarly near me. Grallies flew over our heads on their way to swamps. The air was already burning, and the dry, motionless leaves, when they should have been sparkling with dew, hung lank and withered on the parched-up branches.

Célestin's nose was swollen from the sting of an insect, and his companion, with his eye half closed, could scarcely afford to make fun of him; Vignon and I not being seriously attacked yet, except on the cheeks, which did not add to our appearance. Our hosts would not let us go before we had taken some coffee. These good people could not understand the curiosity which led us to brave perils and unheard of sufferings, and that with an object as futile as the discovery of the source of a river near which we had no intention of living.

"May God protect thee from the fall of a tree!" said our aged hostess to us.

"May God protect thee against the alligators!" said her husband.

"Beware of the tigers," said the eldest son.

"Guard against the flies!" cried the younger women to us.

"Mind the serpents do not bite you!" cried all the children to us in their turn.

We bowed to each of the parting salutations well calculated to induce us to turn back.

The flies, which it seemed strange to see so sociable with each other, are first of all gnats—there are twenty species of these—then the ox-flies and *moyocuiles*, pretty diptera, with gauze wings tinted like mother-of-pearl.

At last we set off, and an hour later came out into the immense lake filled with tortoises and alligators, among which we should be obliged to row in order to find the mouth of the Obispo again.

CHAPTER III.

Lake Vignon—A serious misadventure—The bird of the sun—Discouragement—*La terre tempérée*—The cascade—Excursion on foot—The black tiger—The Dead City.

WITH the exception of the lake of Catemaco, on whose banks I dream of going to live some day, I know nothing more picturesque than the immense lagoon which suddenly opened to our view, and to which I gave the name of my travelling companion. Lake Vignon, capriciously shaped, and surrounded with forests, is an immense sheet of water, fed by the overflow of the Obispo. It is about five or six miles in length, and three or four miles wide. Nearly in the centre is a flat, oblong island, on which the alligators bask themselves in the sun, destroying all vegetation. Further on it seemed to me there was a heap of brown rocks, and thinking to find traces of volcanic eruption there, I steered the boat towards this point. But as we advanced, I saw the rocks sink away, roll one over the other, and disappear into the water without making a single bubble, and then float peacefully along. The dark masses were alligators. Having come within fifty yards of this army of monsters, we resisted the temptation of sending a few shots after them. One impudent fellow, swimming slyly near us, suddenly put his horrible jaws on to the edge of the boat, and just missed snapping off Eulalio's arm.

"He takes thee for a truffle," cried Célestin, raising his oar rapidly, and pushing the reptile back into the water.

The mulatto armed himself with a hatchet, then standing up in the boat, bravely defied the enemy; I ordered them to row, and the boat sped away from the dangerous island.

"It is the first time that an alligator has ever been disrespectful to me," said Eulalio, as seriously as possible; "and I am very sorry I was not able to give him a lesson."

"The Cosamaloapam alligators are civilized," replied Célestin; "they have been to school, whilst these are country boors, whom we shall do well to distrust."

In fact it was agreed that we should watch these monsters more closely than ever, and that we should beware in future of dipping our hands into the water to cool them.

The whole morning passed in looking for the mouth of the river. Every moment we lost ourselves in some canal with no outlet, scaring away pink spoonbills, egrets, ducks, and *anhingas*, whose long necks, when the birds hide their bodies in the grass, resemble the undulations of a serpent. Every quarter of an hour we turned back, to begin our futile work a little further on. We found but one compensation for this loss of time: the trees sheltered us from the sun's scorching rays.

After making a scanty breakfast, and having taken a few hours' rest, we again began our explorations. When the sun had reached the summit of the forest, we were still wandering about at random. Our ardour increased, for we felt an inexplicable repugnance to passing the night on the lake. If chance had led us to the right bank instead of towards the left, a great deal of our trouble would have been spared. Just as we were about to sound the inlets of a large bay, I thought I saw the trunk of a tree floating in the distance. There was a difference of opinion on board on this account; but it was soon acknowledged that I was right. I gave the rowers a bumper of brandy to raise their spirits, and after that we quickly shot across the bay. Suddenly a violent shock nearly capsized us. We had stranded on a mud-bank.

This misadventure put a finishing stroke to our good humour.

To remain on this mud-bank in the middle of the bay, was to condemn ourselves to fearful torture, perhaps to a rough encounter with the alligators, who, when night came on, would be sure to surround us. I got into the water. My companions followed my example, and all four of us pushing the boat, we succeeded in getting it out of the mud. Going cautiously along the side of this mud-level, we were speedily convinced that it reached to the land; and this new deception discouraged my companions.

Two alternatives presented themselves: to go back for a mile or two, or simply land among the palm-trees which rose before us. Suddenly struck with an idea, I steered the boat so as to strand it again, then urged the men to help me in pushing it before us. Thanks to its flat bottom, the boat glided easily along. A quarter of an hour later the bar was crossed, and we rapidly advanced towards the place where we had seen the tree floating. It was with cries of joy that we at last found ourselves between the banks of the Obispo, which we recognized by its bluish waters. In less than an hour, protected by three fires, we were sleeping soundly.

Paroquets flying in couples over our heads, undertook to awaken us the next morning. Before long, the air was alive with wild woodland notes, soft cooings, blithe songs, and plaintive melodies. A flock of wild ducks, with crested heads, alighted about twenty yards from us, whilst a *caurale*—commonly called sunbird—with a brown and grey plumage, striped in curving lines, reminding one of certain night butterflies, settled almost at my feet. Touched by the simple confidence of the graceful bird, I resisted the temptation of enriching my collection at its expense, and I let it look for its food in peace.

I was less magnanimous in dealing with a poor spoonbill. I had long known the delicate flesh of this heron, and its black crest, falling back like a plume, added to the temptation. A long fluttering of wings answered to the gunshot, which rendered me possessor of the spoonbill; but neither the pink flamingoes, nor the curlews, nor the *ardeas*, nor the ducks around us, flew away. A second shot, fired at a pretty water-fowl, commonly called *surgeon-bird*, was hailed with a chorus of hoarse cries. Nevertheless, the herons philosophically continued their fishing, not even deigning to raise their heads, or put down the leg folded away under their plumage.

Just as we were about to continue our way, a deer appeared on the opposite bank. After looking at us for some time, the graceful creature stooped to drink. It would have been useless slaughter to kill it, for we could not keep its flesh. It browsed for a moment, then looking at us again with its large black eyes, went back slowly into the forest. We were more surprised than I can tell at the confidence shown by the inhabitants of the lagoon ; the poor animals had evidently never been hunted, and did not regard us as enemies.

This and the following day were spent in sailing under flowery bowers, through swarms of dragon-flies, butterflies, and brilliantly plumed birds. Nevertheless, I remarked that the tropical plants disappeared in proportion as the vegetable nature became changed. On the sixth day of our voyage it was very evident that the trees of the forests were of quite a different species from those which had bordered the river on our departure. No more creepers or shrubs, no more alligators prowling round our boat. In revenge, clouds of insects, ox-flies and gnats, followed us like a ravenous pack of hounds. Our faces and hands were black and blue, and we could get no sleep. My two oarsmen bitterly complained, wanted to turn back, and incessantly called for brandy, which lessened their sufferings by numbing their senses. But it was a dangerous palliation, and a remedy which I permitted to be used very sparingly ; for when the intoxication was over, the torments were more intense than ever, and complicated with fever.

Vignon, with dreadfully swollen eyelids, could hardly see, and nothing less than the prospect of the incalculable treasures of Montcuczoma could have upheld his courage. He sometimes imparted his enthusiasm to Célestin, by promising him a few million pounds, which made the old sailor profuse in his thanks. As for Eulalio, he was less credulous, and in virtue of the proverb, as true in America as in Europe, that *a bird in the hand is better than two in the bush,* he often asked to be allowed to barter his future treasure for a drop of brandy at once.

The river, now wider than deep, seemed to justify the statement that the Obispo grew wider in proportion as you drew near its source. We could not help feeling enraged with the forest which bordered it, hiding all view from us, and preventing us getting any idea of the way which we had still to traverse before reaching the mountains. Towards the evening of the sixth day, we noticed that the banks became higher, and the aspect of the soil was again changed. Sapotillas, ebony-trees, and pepper-plants, were insensibly replaced by black oaks, larches, and cedars. The ground became undulating, a few hills were in sight, and the heat was less oppressive. In the afternoon of the seventh day, when we were least thinking of it, our boat ran aground at the foot of a cascade.

Nothing could picture our dismay on seeing the water flow from rock to rock with a dull noise, which till then we had thought was the wind swaying the tops of the pine-trees. Our voyage, thus abruptly interrupted, could only be continued under unforeseen conditions for which we were ill prepared. For the first few moments, happy at feeling ourselves at last free from the insects, which had so severely harassed us, we thought of nothing but taking rest. A fire was made about two hundred yards from the cascade, at the foot of a rock covered with moss, and under the shelter of a cedar-tree several hundred years old.

In the evening, following the banks of the river now transformed into a torrent, I climbed the hill, from the summit of which it fell not in one sheet, but by stages. Having reached the top, I saw wooded slopes before me, and the Obispo, calm and tranquil, flowing out of a dark mountain gorge. I turned round, and my eyes wandered over an immense horizon.

The forests stretched in every direction as far as the eye could reach, their black undulating outline seeming to mingle with the horizon in the sun's dazzling rays. To the right was a vague bluish line, faintly indicating the chain of the great Cordilleras. In front of me was a new line of mountains mingling with the clouds, and then the peak of the Orizava with its eternal snow. I looked round me in vain for a trace of humankind. The trees which surrounded me, gigantic, mossy, and straggling, were as old as the world, and more than one, conquered by time, was lying on the ground half hidden under a balmy shroud of flowering ivy.

Vignon came and stood silently beside me. A gentle breeze, rustling the tiny leaves of the cedars, made a mournful sound, and seemed to be complaining to the cascade. A falcon flying overhead uttered a hoarse cry; we saw the swift bird dart over the forest, describe large circles, and then swoop down upon a victim invisible to us. The sight of a gay band of squirrels roused us from our reverie, and helped us to shake off the irresistible sadness which had fallen over us—a sadness full of charm, which I cannot recall even now without a vague melancholy feeling.

Oh, happy hours vanished for ever! is it my youth that I see again through this past which still entrances me, and which I love to recall? Oh, profound terrors of the great woods, majestic silence, intoxicating splendour of light and life! what power is yours, that one forgets the anguish, sufferings, and death, which must be braved to get a glimpse of you; that the eye is unweariedly dazzled by your enchanting grandeur!

The following day we set out, lightly equipped, to reconnoitre. We had taken care to hide our boat under a heap of branches, and it was our intention to follow the course of the torrent as far as the nature of the ground and our resources would allow. Beyond the gorge we found a savannah of high grass, through which the river flowed peacefully. It took us a whole day to cross this valley, and at nightfall our fire was burning brightly at the foot of a hill, on which grew rare species of broom.

At daybreak we were on our road again, climbing bare hillsides and descending valleys encumbered with rocks. Here and there were stunted aloes, mimosas with rare foliage, and yellow dried-up grass. The Obispo, in its foaming, headlong course, was dashing over enormous rocks of granite; the luxuriant vegetation of the preceding days had disappeared, and an arid inhospitable desert, except in the damp soil of the banks of the torrent where ferns grew profusely, rendered our excursion extremely fatiguing.

We determined to shoot small birds to stock our larder, to the great loss of powder and shot, for it requires more than a dozen larks to satisfy the appetites of four famished men. This sport, considering the scarcity of the game, made us lose much time, which we would rather have employed in pushing forward. Our best sport, from a natural history point of view, was that of a *Cassican calybé*, a kind of bird of paradise, a native of New Guinea, and a *cotinga* with carmine plumage. But, without being epicures, we should have much preferred one of the fat, homely-looking turkeys, which had enlivened us two days ago with their loud gobbling, to these gaudily plumed birds.

We were in the heart of the Cordilleras; ascending and descending, rolling down endless slopes, and having no other horizon than that of the mountain-top we had to cross. Sometimes we had to follow the torrent for whole hours through obscure damp gorges. The crocodiles were left behind, but there were swarms of serpents, and although mostly of a harmless kind, we were nevertheless obliged to advance cautiously. Once or twice we were thoroughly disheartened, and it was seriously a question of turning back, for nothing whatever indicated the approach of more varied vegetation, and consequently the return of abundance.

For two days more the torrent itself served as our guide. We had never left its banks except when the nature of the ground obliged us to make long *détours*; but suddenly a palisade of rocks rose before us, over which the Obispo, majestic and magnificent, precipitated itself from a height of more than a hundred and sixty feet, and fell with wild uproar into an immense rocky tunnel.

We held counsel. Vignon, with unswollen eyes, saw the treasures he coveted more clearly than ever, and was for continuing our onward march. This was also my desire. Nevertheless, the insuperable barrier obliged us to reflect well. It might extend so far that our powder store would be exhausted in shooting larks, and what would become of us among these

"BEFORE US SPREAD A VALLEY........"

inhospitable rocks without ammunition or provisions? It is true, an hour's march would bring us into a part abounding with game. I put an end to the discussion by venturing amongst the gigantic piles of rocks which shelved off to my right, and gave us some idea of chaos.

On my way, I amused myself with watching a charming colony of martins, which were flying over our heads with little frightened cries, and hastening back to their nests in the clefts of the high cliff we were trying to scale. Sometimes a kite appeared on the scene, and the martins would hover together, ready to offer battle to the terrible bird of prey skimming over their aërial dwellings with evil designs.

Towards evening, we met with a little black tiger, a kind of wild cat, the flesh of which is supposed to be good to eat. Now was the time to make the experiment. Unfortunately, the animal, although wounded by Eulalio, disappeared from our sight. A little before sunset, our fire was made up near a pine forest; we might meet with squirrels here, and with this hope I ventured among the trees. Climbing the steep slopes, I soon found myself on a plateau covered with heath. A hare darted past me. I followed in pursuit, and the sound of the gunshot which made me possessor of it, drew my companions to the spot.

Going across the plateau I came out of the wood, and climbed a slight eminence; it seemed to me that I could see the top of a square tower in the distance. Greatly surprised, and thinking that it must be an illusion, I went to the edge of the ravine, and stood dumb and motionless with amazement on seeing at the bottom of the valley which I was overlooking, a city built in stone, bathed in the light of the setting sun.

I summoned my companions by rapidly discharging both barrels of my gun. They immediately ran up, thinking that I had encountered some formidable wild beast. Scarcely had they cast a glance below them, when they simultaneously uttered an exclamation of surprise.

Before us opened an oblong arid valley, enclosed by a wall of granite, and through which flowed a brook shaded by stunted shrubs. The brook wound through the ruins, composed of square buildings, most of them windowless, their crumbling terraces disclosing the interiors. About the centre of the town rose a gigantic broken pyramid. The "Dead City," as Eulalio named it, was surrounded by a stone wall, the capricious outline of which we could distinctly make out. The same inflexible straight lines characterized all these singular buildings, even the ornamentation of the square tower which had first attracted my attention.

As far as we could judge, we were lost in one of the windings of a branch of the Sierra d'Oajaca, the route supposed to have been followed by the Toltecs when they emigrated from Mexico to spread themselves over the peninsular of Yucatan and reach the Isthmus of Tehuantepec, where numerous monuments bear witness of their passage. Nothing is more obscure than the history of the primitive people of America. It is known that powerful civilized nations preceded the Aztecs on this ground; but in what order or from whence did the emigrants come? From the north; and nothing more is known about them. Modern American historians have rather complicated than enlightened the matter by hypothesis.

However, of these nations the Toltecs seem to have been the most civilized. In the Aztec tongue the word Toltec has become synonymous with architect, or skilful workman. The Toltecs, essentially agriculturists, imported pepper, cotton, and maize into their adopted country. They knew how to melt certain metals, to cut precious stones, and it is from their astronomical knowledge that the Mexicans have borrowed a calendar where the civil and solar year agree. It was beyond doubt that the ruins we had just discovered were the work of this extraordinary people, whose first known king, Chalchiutlanetzin, reigned in 667 of the Christian era.

I immediately began to look for a road which would take me to the bottom of the valley. But night came rapidly on; the scanty verdure looked like dark shadows, and the stunted trees growing here and there among the ruins, lifted their barely covered branches like skeletons. Suddenly, by a magnificent sunset effect not uncommon in tropical regions, the whole valley was bathed in a crimson light, and appeared as though on fire. For a moment we could distinctly see the pyramid, the tower, and an immense building in the form of a parallelogram which we had designated the temple, then all suddenly vanished. I stood for some time anxiously leaning over the abyss. I seemed to hear distant sounds floating upwards to me, and I almost expected to see a light appear, or to hear a cry, which would reveal the presence of man in these places where he had once lived. I waited in vain, and with my head full of thoughts, fell asleep whilst watching the night-birds hovering mysteriously round our fire.

CHAPTER IV.

The mist—Aërial gardens—An armadillo—The temple—Sculptures and hieroglyphics—The coral snake— The ibis—*Belzebuth* monkeys—The tapirs—A nest of rattlesnakes—Montcuczoma.

LONG before daybreak I was up, impatient and feverish. I accused the sun of being behindhand. I stirred the fire, for a north wind made the air chilly. As on the preceding evening, I listened attentively to every sound, sometimes imagining that I heard a cock crow or a dog bark, a sound revealing the presence of man. I anxiously wondered whether it had not been a dream or caprice of my imagination. But Vignon, Célestin, Eulalio, had also seen the heap of ruins which filled the narrow valley. Besides, the form of the pyramid and that of the tower and the extensive parallelogram were too clearly outlined in my mind for me to believe that I was under the influence of an illusion.

Besides, this was not the first discovery of the kind which I owed to chance. In the month of March, 1861, when crossing with my friend Sumichrast the mountains of Jalapa, which one might have thought had been explored in every corner, we came unexpectedly upon the ruins of an Aztec village. It was now a question of more importance than the village of Jalapa. I could not think without emotion of the treasures which perhaps I was on the eve of discovering, archæological treasures which might throw new light on the obscure history of the first inhabitants of Mexico.

The day broke at last; but by a phenomenon which I might have expected, but which nevertheless caused me much disappointment, the valley was enveloped in a thick mist. Whilst Célestin and Eulalio hastily prepared the coffee, I leant anxiously over the valley, watching for the moment when the veil which hid it from sight should be lifted or dissolve away in dew. Ere long the sun's rays dyed the humid shroud with the rainbow tints of mother-of-pearl. At the same time, great black vultures, seeming to emerge from the fog, flew up, greeting the light with a hoarse cry. We immediately set out in search of an opening by which we could get down into the valley.

Venturing between two rocks, Célestin thought he had found a practicable path; but, to tell the truth, the slope was almost perpendicular, and of a nature to make us hesitate. Had it not been for the mist which partly hid the danger, we should never have dared to take such a road. A series of tumbles made us very cautious, as we risked breaking our necks. At last the mist, "devoured by the sun," according to Eulalio's expression, was instantly dissipated, and the "Dead City," with its tower, its pyramid, and its grey houses, was again to be seen.

At that moment we were passing along a platform, the step of an immense staircase raised by the hand of man. I had often seen a colossal work of this kind, in the neighbourhood of Orizava, in which it was easy to recognize the stratum of one of those aërial gardens spoken of with great admiration by the old Spanish authors. In two or three minutes we reached the foot of the cliff, and it was with no slight emotion that I saw before me a building, the front of which having crumbled away, left the interior exposed to view.

On a closer inspection the building seemed to us more dilapidated than we had supposed the evening before; the distance had only allowed us to make out rough outlines, which had led us to expect less rustic works than those before our eyes.

We passed through a wide gap in the wall of the rampart and entered the town, now gloomy, silent, and blackened by the sun's rays. Behind this wall rose a second fortification of solid stone. Evidently the enemy who ventured to scale the first rampart would fall into the space which separated him from the second—a rather ingenious defence against enemies obliged to fight hand to hand.

A wide street opened before us, down which I sauntered, walking slowly over its irregular pavement. The houses were all of the same height and the same construction. The low, massive walls were composed of roughly hewn blocks of lava or stones, soldered with a cement composed of sand and chalk. The interior consisted of three rooms uniformly arranged. At first we separated, each going where his curiosity led him; but I very soon called back my companions. We were obliged to use some precaution in making our discoveries, and then think prosaically of breakfast.

Later on we had the idea that the ruins might serve as shelter for wild beasts. Although we had heard no roar during the night, the presence of vultures and hawks revealed the existence of living creatures; thus prudence was absolutely necessary. Célestin, who was standing within gunshot of the river, saw a small armadillo, and succeeded in killing it. A dull, prolonged echo followed the report of his gun; one would have said that the valley formerly filled with sound was longing for human noises to trouble its quietude once again

On the heaps of ruins, the aspect of which must have been changed a hundred times by earthquakes, grew stunted shrubs and plants which one finds in places where man has lived—ivies, mallows, thistles, and gilliflowers. We found the soil everywhere very rocky, which accounted for the barrenness of the valley. At the entrance of the great building which we called *The Temple*, stood two colossal figures, in bas-relief, facing each other. That on the right side represented a warrior holding a kind of sceptre in his hand, his head surmounted with a fantastic helmet; the figure on the left hand held a basket full of fruit in its outstretched hands. Although wanting in proportion in some parts, these figures showed, nevertheless, somewhat advanced art. In looking at works of this kind, it must be remembered that the first inhabitants of Mexico were ignorant of the use of iron; they hewed and sculptured the granite with unknown implements.

Near the entrance of the temple, the front of which measured more than two hundred yards, after having passed a heap of *débris*, which encumbered and concealed the principal entrance, we found ourselves at the foot of a flight of steps, composed of large white flagstones. To the right and the left were wide passages with glazed walls, imitating stucco, and ornamented here and there with paintings. A few square pillars, capriciously arranged, and sculptured with bas-reliefs and hieroglyphics, taxed our sagacity. The terrace, up to which the flight of steps led, had crumbled away, and everywhere loosened stones were ready to fall. A formidable earthquake could alone have displaced the massive stonework before us, and this disaster, occurring perhaps a thousand years ago, had driven the inhabitants from the city, through which we were now passing with none to dispute our rights, and which seemed to have been ruined since we looked on it the evening before.

I followed the course of the stream; it led me out of the town, which had a superficial area of barely two square miles. Here I found a narrow gorge terminating in a pine forest. On my return I climbed one of the stages of the pyramid, from whence I could see a succession of wooded hills, closing in the horizon on one side. An ibis, the sacred bird of the Egyptians, alighted at the foot of the tower.

Heaven knows what were the thoughts each gave himself up to during breakfast. Even the impassible Eulalio began to talk, make conjectures, and get bewildered in supposition. Ignoring the past history of his country, the mulatto believed in witchcraft. "A dead city," who ever heard of such a thing? Célestin overwhelmed me with questions which I was unable to answer; besides, I was too much absorbed by the strange spectacle before me to be very communicative. As to Vignon, he talked of nothing but excavations, mines, and trenches, to clear away the rubbish from the whole town; but how were we to undertake such a work with such resources as were at our disposition? There were four of us, and we had but one hammer and chisel between us. My companion chafed at my objections, and according to him I lacked enthusiasm.

We again began our wanderings from right to left, admiring in the distance a piece of sculpture, a tablet, or a frieze enriched with arabesques of a singular character. Some of the immense flagstones, with which the principal streets were paved, were hollowed out with small gutters. I had the idea of cleaning one of these stones, and then rubbing a piece of coal into the grooves. I then saw the design of a warrior raising a naked child above his head, and presenting it to an eagle with outstretched wings. In the corner a palm leaf, terminating in a gigantic P, represented a date; 420, according to the chronology of the Jesuit Clavigero.

I proposed to sound the bed of the stream, which flowed through a gravel soil. We went up as far as the place where the water, foaming and roaring, dashed over the rock and fell into a lozenge-shaped basin. I there picked up a few broken pieces of pottery of no definite shape, and also a small golden bell.

Eulalio made a kind of pickaxe, which Vignon seized with delight; but, to his great disgust, the implement broke with the first blow. It took us three hours to dig a hole a yard square; so we soon gave up this drudgery, which only resulted in fatiguing us beyond measure. The day passed in turning over blocks of stone, wandering at hazard, and scraping off the moss which covered the bas-reliefs. At sunset our archæological treasure-trove amounted to two earthenware jars of different designs.

The next day we thought of concentrating our strength, and working at one point only. Vignon proposed that we should clear away the *débris* from the interior of a house situated near the temple, the front of which, covered with hieroglyphics, seemed to have been the dwelling of the high priest. Our work was fruitless; we only discovered the three stones of an antique fireplace, where a magnificent coral serpent lay coiled up. The reptile, who was not prepared for our visit, raised itself in a threatening attitude, then took advantage of our surprise to glide into a hole, where we left it in peace.

The temple attracted us, but how were we to lift the great blocks of granite before us? We had the folly to attempt, and the wisdom not to persist in, the impossible task. I set out in search of a cemetery, which led us to make a fruitless tour of the ramparts, for nowhere could I see the least trace of a tumulus. Toltecs or Mistecs, the inhabitants of the *Dead City* probably interred their dead beyond the valley, in ground now invaded by the pine forest.

For three days more we wandered among the ruins, killing armadilloes, salamanders, and scorpions. Célestin sometimes tried to decipher the insoluble enigmas engraved on the stones, and his explanations did not fail to enliven us. From time to time we discovered a small figure representing sometimes a monkey, sometimes a bird, and sometimes a warrior. Our most interesting discovery was that of a marble tablet, on which was represented a young woman in a kneeling posture, pressing two children to her bosom. As I was trying to think what goddess in the Mexican theology this might be, Eulalio had pity on my ignorance, and told me that he recognized the Virgin Mary with the infant Jesus, and St. John the Baptist.

The tower possessed an interior staircase, a dozen steps of which we succeeded in clearing. The passage was dark and narrow, and one of us was constantly obliged to light the worker. Above the twelfth step a solid block put a sudden stop to our work. Vignon wanted to try and blow it up by sacrificing some of our cartridges. I had a great deal of trouble in proving the uselessness of such an attempt, the only result of which would have been to deprive us of our gunpowder.

At sunset we liked to climb to the top of the pyramid, a gigantic structure which we never tired of admiring. Vignon could not admit that it had been built by the former inhabitants of the town; it must have taken many centuries to heap up such a considerable mass of materials. According to my companion's rather ingenious hypothesis, we were in a place

which had formerly been consecrated, and where the images of
the divinities of the Toltec mythology were preserved. In what
other way could the foundation of a town in an almost inaccessible valley, fortified with scrupulous care, be explained? The
ruins of the temple, the *débris* of which occupied a third of the
town, undoubtedly covered golden statues enriched with pearls
and diamonds, for the Toltecs were acquainted with precious
stones. Vignon spoke with so much conviction, that Célestin
was constantly prowling round the ruins, and sometimes
seconded the narrator in the vain attempt to displace a block
of stone which twenty men could not have moved.

But the powder was running short, and our health began to
resent the purely animal food to which we had been condemned,
so that we were obliged to think of returning to the boat. Vignon was in despair, and rebelled against this necessity. He
proposed that Célestin and Eulalio should be sent for provisions,
spades, pickaxes, and powder, whilst we continued to study the
ground. My companion wanted, at any price, to make excavations among the ruins of the temple; he was determined not to
confess that months, and an army of workmen, would scarcely
have sufficed to carry out such an enterprise.

My reasonings at last ended in convincing him. Our visit
to the ruins had already been too prolonged. We had been
obliged to use a considerable amount of ammunition, and the
return to the boat became urgent, even imperative for famine
was overtaking us.

Immediately on his return to Cosamaloapam, Vignon proposed to embark for Vera-Cruz, in order to inform the governor
of our discovery, and of the great interest there would be in
undertaking excavations, which would fully compensate for any
expenditure. Alas! it was but a day-dream. Mexico, especially
those parts of it near the famous Isthmus of Tehuantepec, is
strewn with imposing ruins; but its rulers, always engaged in
defending their rights, can have neither the leisure nor the
means of exploring them.

I wished to spend our last day in the valley in visiting the
pine forest situated at the other end of the gorge; there also we
found fine ruins.

In one of the most picturesque glades, we picked up hundreds of agate arrow-heads. The brook, describing a long curve, probably flows into the Obispo. I was tempted for a moment to take it as a guide; but I dared not venture further upon unknown ground when our powder was running short, and prudence required us to cross the inhospitable desert again.

Towards five o'clock, enriched with three fine squirrels, we made up our fire at the same place where we had first discovered the " Dead City." I took a farewell glance of it, for the next day, at the time of our departure, it was still enveloped in a mist, above which the vultures and falcons seemed to like to hover.

Finally, the principal characters of the architecture of the strange town which we were leaving, resembled those of all the ruins of the same kind in Mexico: a simple, solid, severe style. The temple, the pyramid, and the tower, were perfectly situated; that is to say, they faced the four cardinal points. The height of the steps leading to the terrace measured more than two feet; one would have said that it was a staircase intended for giants. If it were absolutely necessary to find a point of comparison, a resemblance with the art of a nation known through the monuments they have left, I should choose the Assyrians, notwithstanding the general opinion which assimilates the nations of the New World to those of ancient Egypt. Palanqué is very certainly more nearly related to Nineveh than to Memphis.

We got back to our boat by a series of forced marches. A storm, or a marauding animal, might have caused irreparable damage to our baggage, which would have been a serious misfortune.

Happily, we found all in good order, and being anxious to leave the pine woods as quickly as possible, we at once set out towards the region of insects, alligators, and suffocating heat, but also to the land of plenty. The next day we camped in a glade on the border of a gay little brook, which fell into the Obispo from the top of a raised slope. From the look of the water we thought we recognized the stream which bathed the ruins of the " Dead City," whither Vignon's thoughts were incessantly turning. We had determined to rest for at least a day in this pleasant place, and I resolved to devote the time to enriching my natural history collection. A band of monkeys with prehensile tails came up as we were breakfasting, and enlivened us with their performances, swinging themselves on trapezes formed by the stout branches of the creepers. For an hour I admired the most marvellous acrobatic tricks that could possibly be imagined. Mad chases from branch to branch, perilous leaps, somersaults, quarrels, fights, the spectacle was as varied as we could have wished; there was nothing wanting but a tumble, as Célestin remarked. To be sure, one cannot but admire the lightness, skilfulness, and spinal flexibility of the monkeys in their large cages at the Zoological Gardens; but, there they only execute their simplest feats. In order to appreciate them according to their merit, they must be seen frolicking in the open forest, swinging, jumping from one tree to another, and enjoying themselves as though in defiance of the laws of equilibrium.

Two days later we camped at the entrance of Lake Vignon.

Whilst wandering on its muddy banks, I discovered a row of pink flamingoes' nests—heaps of earth which the bird makes with its claws, arranging at the top a hollow where it can place its eggs. The long legs of the *phenicopter*—the name given by ornithologists to the pink flamingo—prevent it from sitting on its nest. It stands patiently and seriously close to the mound it has constructed, and covers its eggs with the feathers of its tail. Nothing can be more melancholy than to see these birds, about three feet high, standing motionless, pensive, and silent, until they take their flight, when they utter a peculiarly wild, plaintive cry, which is deeply impressive.

After this we let the boat take its own course down the stream. Banks bordered with flowers passed before our eyes, whilst myriads of ephemera danced fantastic sarabands in the boat's wake. I took pleasure in studying the capricious evolutions of the rapid insects, wondering what signal they obeyed to mount up, descend, whirl round, and mingle together without ever coming into contact with each other. From time to time,

T

a bird darted past like a flash of lightning. Good heavens, what victims! The executioner carried away his beak full; but the shock of his wings dashed a still greater number into the water. The giddy host resumed their frantic sport as though nothing had happened. What an imperious reason for enjoying life have these transparent, fragile beings, whose whole existence is contained between the rising and setting of the sun!

If ever you are desirous of travelling, reader, I can recommend to you the picturesque banks of the Obispo, the source of which still remains to be discovered. For ten years I have been intending to return to see the "Dead City," and have never yet been able to accomplish the journey. Vignon has not been more fortunate than myself. It is true, that for five years he has been wandering among the Oajaca Mountains in search of a lake, at the bottom of which—he was told this secret by an Indian—were buried, on the 8th of July, 1520, at four o'clock in the afternoon, the immense treasures of the great Aztec Emperor Montcuczoma, whom the French will persist in calling *Montézume*.

THE UNICORN.

Nor Rosalino—The *anteburro*—Lying in ambush—An anxious moment—
The unicorn—The tapir.

It was five o'clock in the afternoon, and I was then exploring the uninhabited banks of the Rio San Nicolas, in the tropical parts of Mexico. After a long day spent in looking for insects, I ordered the Indians who had accompanied me to pitch our camp. My tent was instantly raised, and slices of dried meat which were to serve for our dinner put to broil before a clear fire. We were in the heart of the woods, at about two hundred feet from the river, and Enrique, my nominal servant, set out with our guide, *Nor Rosalino*, to fill our gourds with fresh water.

I sat down near the fire, and admired the ancient trees around me. The shades of night were beginning to fall over the forest, and the wild turkeys, perched on the topmost branches of the highest trees, were greeting the last rays of the setting sun with their loud gobbling. All at once a sharp whistle sounded, and I heard a noise of broken branches and hurried footsteps in the underwood to my left. I sprung to my feet, and had hardly time to seize my gun, when Rosalino, pale, breathless, knife in hand, visibly scared, stood before me.

It must have been some extraordinary occurrence which could have frightened Nor Rosalino, the brave tiger-hunter.

" What is the matter?" I asked, going up to him.

He signed me to be quiet, and stooped forward to listen.

" Where is Enrique?" I again asked.

Another noise of broken branches in the underwood. Rosalino

quickly sprang on one side, and at the same time my servant made his appearance. Like his companion, he was pale, and seemed to be a prey to some great fright.

"Will you tell me now what is the matter?" cried I again.

"The matter is that the evil spirit is on our heels, and that we must get away from here as quickly as possible," said the hunter at last.

"The evil spirit!"

"The unicorn, if you like it better."

"Have you seen an unicorn?"

"As clearly as we see you now, and we shall have him upon us before five minutes' time."

"Take your guns," said I to the two Indians, "and now that we have six balls to discharge upon any intruder who may dare to attack us, tell me all that has happened."

"We have seen the *antéburro*, señor," replied Rosalino. "Fortunately, we were to leeward, or we should not be alive now. Let us be off."

"One moment, lads; what is an unicorn? What do you mean by the *antéburro?*"

"No one less than Satan himself," replied Rosalino.

"Did you see a man, then?"

My question betrayed such ignorance, that they looked at me with visible compassion; and instead of answering, they began to take down my tent.

"Stay!" said I; "if it is really the evil one we have to deal with, I have a holy talisman which will cause his evil deeds to fall back upon himself."

This time the two Indians regarded me with distrust. My zeal in collecting insects, reptiles, and plants with an object unknown to them, made them think that I practised sorcery. They gradually recovered their self-possession, and told me that just as they were bending to fill the gourds, their attention had been attracted towards the opposite bank by a movement among the reeds. After waiting a moment, they had seen a grey-coloured quadruped, the size of an ass, with a long horn in the middle of his forehead, slowly climb the bank. My men did

not agree as to the height of the animal, but both of them had
seen its croup, its mane, and above all, the long spike in the
centre of its forehead. They assured me that to meet with an
unicorn, or *antéburro*, was a sign of misfortune, that the animal
was invulnerable, and that those who attempted to hunt it
exposed their souls to serious danger.

I again tried to reassure my companions; but in vain. They
begged and entreated me to camp further off; but I refused.
Having asked for the gourds, I learnt that they had been left
on the river-bank, so for that evening we were obliged to content
ourselves with the muddy water of the pond near us. During
our conversation, night had come on, and I was obliged to give
up the idea of going to look for the gourds, in hope of seeing
the famous unicorn which, according to my guides, was by no
means a fabulous animal.

Enrique and Rosalino ate without any appetite. They were
continually looking in the direction of the river, and refused to
lie down. They shuddered when I told them that at break
of day we would go and look for this quadruped which had
frightened them so terribly. They declared peremptorily that,
notwithstanding their devotion to me, they were, above everything, good Christians, and that they were not going, either
from recklessness or to please me, to run into the claws of the
spirit of darkness, who having lost one of his horns in his
battle with St. Michael, now only possessed one, which he
allowed to grow to a great length. I was told that an old
Indian chief, the possessor of a holy bullet, had one day
struggled with an unicorn and succeeded in killing it; but not
daring to carry away his game, the hunter contented himself
with cutting off a piece of the horn. From that day everything the priest undertook turned out well; as conqueror of the
evil one, he found himself shielded from the thousand and one
troubles with which the enemy of mankind amuses himself by
thwarting the projects of the sons of Eve. Whilst excusing
themselves for not being able to assist me in hunting the
unicorn, my two Indians begged me, if chance or science
rendered me master of the animal, not to forget the valuable

properties of the horn, and to be good enough to gratify them with a small piece of this talisman. In exchange for this gift, they engaged themselves to accompany me without complaining into the virgin forests and neighbouring savannahs.

I had some difficulty in getting to sleep. Without putting any faith in the existence of the unicorn, I believed that I was on the way to making a great discovery in natural history. The imagination flies quickly; I already saw myself in possession of a quadruped unknown to the learned, the sight of which would make all Europe marvel. Thus, long before daybreak I was up, cleaning my gun and preparing my cartridges.

Another conversation with Rosalino informed me that the *antéburro* was generally met with on the banks of rivers. The hunter affirmed with such apparent honesty and conviction that the animal he had seen the evening before was the second of its kind which ill-fortune had thrown across his path, that I believed more than ever in the existence of a new quadruped.

When the sun appeared above the horizon, it found me hidden among the reeds which border the banks of the San Nicolas. I remained on the watch for more than three hours, examining a small prairie in front of me. I was beginning to give up hope, when suddenly the reeds were moved, and I heard the sound of a heavy body plunging into the water. At first I thought it was a crocodile coming up slyly to surprise me; but the water was covered with bubbles, and a great black body crossed the water, just keeping its head under the surface. Soon the rushes on the opposite bank parted, and I saw a croup very much like that of an ass. My two shots were fired together; the animal plunged, regained the bank from which he had started, and my gun was scarcely reloaded before the forest had resumed its peaceful calm.

I had hoped to see my companions run up at the report of my double shot; but nothing stirred in the underwood. Getting into our boat, I carefully explored both sides of the river. After a quarter of an hour of vain searching, I was obliged to acknowledge that I had been very clumsy, and I returned to the encampment very much perplexed.

To what order of the animal kingdom could this quadruped belong, the croup of which I had distinctly seen? Was it a wild horse? I should then have seen its head, for horses do not swim under water any more than deer or bulls. I thought of the hippopotamus, although this animal does not certainly belong to the American fauna. My curiosity was excited to the highest degree; and if the discovery of an unknown insect always delighted me, my feelings may be imagined when I thought I was on the eve of discovering an unknown quadruped.

I found my companions crouching near the tent, and told them the negative result of my excursion. They looked at each other with consternation when I said that directly after breakfast I should go and lay in watch again, and that I would not leave the banks of the Rio San Nicolas until I had secured the skin of one of the fantastic animals, a description of which I was again obliged to listen to. Dazzling as my offers were, I could not persuade either of my Indians to assist me. They even entreated me to let them remove the tent five hundred feet further off, into a glade where they could see the enemy coming, if from being pursued it became the pursuer. I allowed them to do as they wished, and making a hasty breakfast, I set off with my gun to the river-bank.

After having carefully examined the ground, I resolved to go on to the other bank and to lie in ambush near the small prairie where the animal was going to land when I frightened it. I crossed the river, then, after having hidden my boat so that the sight of it would not scare the game, I explored the prairie. I noticed several marks of cloven feet on the bank; but far from concluding that they were the footprints of an evil spirit, I thought I had to deal with a ruminant. I taxed my memory for a long time to try and think what animal of this species could be rare enough in those regions to be unknown to the Indians, and which swam under water like the afore-mentioned amphibious quadrupeds. I made a thousand and one suppositions, and could not in the least explain the enigma.

I remained for a long time motionless, watching the river, and if the animal I was waiting for took the same route as on the preceding evening, it must come out just in front of me. I saw some dozens of alligators pass by, and a flock of pink flamingoes silently perched on the bushes near me. Around me, owing to the proximity of the water, was a luxuriant entanglement of creepers, a floral network which prevented any access to the virgin forests, but beyond which almost all herbaceous vegetation ceases. A band of monkeys at one moment filled the forest with their cries. I resisted the temptation of chasing them, in order not to abandon my post.

The day was lowering; I was annoyed and fatigued with my long watch. Nevertheless, the wild inhabitants of tropical forests generally come to drink at a water-course at sunrise and sunset; wild boars, for instance, always come at that time to water their young ones. Thus I made up my mind to remain till night closed in, although somewhat uneasy as to the way in which I should get back to the tent if I stayed too long.

There is scarcely any twilight in the tropics, where dense darkness almost immediately follows the disappearance of the sun. The flamingoes had taken flight again, the alligators no longer skimmed their grim muzzles over the sleeping water; all day sounds died away, and the silence grew deeper, calmer, and more solemn. Already the trees seemed to grow confused and assume fantastic forms. Had it not been for the pangs of hunger, I should have borne my ill-luck with patience, and persisted in my watch. Unfortunately, not thinking of such a long stay, I had neglected to provide myself with any food. I was getting up to return to the tent, when a dull noise attracted my attention. I heard the reeds crushed as before, and the sound of a heavy body plunging into the water.

A slight tremor ran through my whole frame; I had a cold chill down my back, and my hair showed a certain tendency to stand on end. I was frightened, and my heart beat violently. I knew not what enemy I was about to deal with, and the unknown is always a cause of terror for man. By a violent effort of will I resisted the inclination to fly which seized me, and sheltering myself behind the trunk of a tree, armed with my

gun, and Enrique's revolver within reach, I listened anxiously. There was a long silence, and then I heard the crackle of the dry reeds being crushed on the bank where I was. I saw a black form slowly ascend the bank, and then, as though undecided which way to take, it turned towards me. I fired. A strange hoarse cry, which I had never before heard, told me that the animal had been hit. I stood ready to fire again. There was a great noise in the thicket, and then I saw and heard nothing more.

What had become of it? That I could not tell; I was only certain that I had hit the body at which I fired. To set out in search of my game seemed a dangerous proceeding. I exposed myself to falling into the marshes and to coming face to face with some wild beast which, although wounded, might be quite equal to attack me. With endless precautions, holding my breath, and walking on tiptoe, I had the good fortune to find the boat without difficulty. It was an immense relief to find myself on the other bank, and I went back to the tent, calling to Enrique and Rosalino with repeated shouts.

I rejoined the Indians near an immense fire; they came and shook my hands, and overwhelmed me with questions. When I told them that I had fired at and hit the animal which I could scarcely see through the darkness, and declared besides that we should find its dead body on the morrow, my companions smiled incredulously.

I made up for my long fast, and then, whilst I smoked, I was again favoured with new accounts of the unicorn. In reality, I believed I had fired at a bear. Soon following the example of the Indians, I fell asleep.

I was awakened by the screeching of a hundred paroquets perched in the branches of the palm-trees. With great repugnance, but led by curiosity, the two Indians agreed to accompany me to the other side of the river, and to help me look for the game which I believed I had killed. A trace of blood showed that my conjectures were not without foundation, and soon I heard Rosalino's voice shouting out to me—

"The unicorn!"

I ran up to the sportsman, and saw lying before me a magnificent tapir, shot right through by one of my bullets.

"Well," said I to my companions, "I do not see either an evil spirit, an unicorn, or an *antéburro*, but a simple herbivorous animal, which I scarcely expected to meet with in these parts."

"It is an unicorn," said Rosalino.

"It is an *antéburro*," said Enrique.

"Where is its horn or its ears?" I asked, smiling.

"Do not joke, señor," continued the sportsman. "You have killed the wife of the evil beast instead of killing the brute itself; that is why it has no horn."

"The tapir," said I to Rosalino, "is the largest quadruped of America; it is harmless, gentle, and timid. Naturalists, after confounding it with the hippopotamus, then considering it as a diminutive elephant, have at last allowed that it is a simple herbivorous animal. The abundance of herbaceous food which it requires, draws it to water-courses, but it does not eat fish. A good runner, and a good swimmer, it is a difficult animal to catch. Finally, it does not live exclusively in South America, as is still affirmed; the body we have before our eyes peremptorily proves this fact."

When I proposed to cut a slice out of the thigh of the tapir for our breakfast, the two Indians manifested such horror that I thought it better not to risk their prejudices. Nevertheless, they begged me to cut off the animal's paws and make them a present of its hoofs. These talismans had not, like the horn of the male tapir, the property of drawing on its possessor a succession of fortunate events, but they have the virtue to ward off misfortune. I keep a tapir's hoof in my collection; it has never protected me from the sting of gnats, nor from the venom of slander; from which I conclude that Rosalino and Enrique are deceived in their estimation, and that the Mexican tapir, although smaller than that of India, is nevertheless, like it, a pachydermatous animal, which has nothing whatever in common with the evil spirit.

THE GROTTO OF THE TOLTECS.

CHAPTER I.

Guatemala—The Toltecs—The grotto—Necessary precautions—A general panic.

On the 26th of June, 186—, about five o'clock in the morning, I left the little village of Santa Maria, situated on the boundary line which separates the Mexican province of Chiapas from the republic of Guatemala. My travelling companion was a priest of the diocese of Oajaca, Don Silvester Alarcon, who had the well-earned reputation of being the most learned man in the country with regard to the ancient history of his native land, and he took me to the grotto of the Toltecs, celebrated for sixty miles round. The Indians all spoke of the riches it contained, although no one had as yet dared to penetrate into its depths.

The air was cold, and yet we were in midsummer, and near the equator. Well wrapped up in warm clothes, we at first advanced silently, letting our mules choose their own ground. Bautista took the lead, and following him, we had soon to climb a bare rocky mountain-side, the stones of which, of volcanic origin, rolled away at each step our steeds made. We took no less than an hour ascending this hill. When we had reached the top, a band of purple along the horizon announced the near approach of dawn. Almost at the same time the sun rose above a broken mountain ridge, looking like a great red ball. It quickly left the bed of mist hovering over the Cordilleras, and we were dazzled by the bright light suddenly shed over us.

I quickly took off the blanket which served as a cloak, and my example was soon followed by my companions. We were in a violent perspiration on descending the mountain, rather different from the shivering state in which we had climbed it. On our way I admired the valley which opened before us—a verdant glade bordered by virgin forests. Beautiful birds, with red, blue, or green plumage, fluttered around us, and I listened with delight to their sweet, varied notes.

"What a magnificent country yours is!" I cried, turning to the priest. "I have travelled over it from north to south, from east to west, and its nature is so varied that I am continually finding something to admire."

"We are no longer in Mexico," replied the priest, "and your eulogies are now addressed to the republic of Guatemala, on which ground we have been treading ever since we passed the woods lying to our right. Guatemala, as you must know, formerly held the power of the emperors of Mexico in check. In 1821 it formed an alliance with the provinces of Honduras, San Salvador, Nicaragua, and Costa-Rica, which enabled it to shake off the Spanish yoke."

"Did not these five provinces then take the title of the United States of Central America?" I asked of my guide.

"Exactly so; but since then a spirit of anarchy, which is the plague of the old Spanish colonies, broke out among the five provinces, each of them disputing for the supremacy, and at last ended in constituting them independent states."

We entered a wood, where the path through the trees became so narrow, that we were obliged to pass in single file until we came to a glade, where I again took my place beside the curé.

"Although we have barely space to let our horses walk abreast, we are nevertheless on the high-road followed by the mysterious nation of the Toltecs in their emigration across Northern America," said my companion to me.

"Why do you call the Toltecs a mysterious nation?" I asked.

"Because everything is ambiguous in their history. They preceded the Aztecs on Mexican soil; but whence did they come?

From the north, every one allows that; but from what point? Their first settlements are to be found far below California. Their course can be traced from the Colorado River to Mexico, from Mexico to Yucatan, from Yucatan and Guatemala, and lastly, from Guatemala to Peru, across the Isthmus of Panama. The Toltecs were not ravagers like the barbarians who overran the Roman empire. Their name signifies *skilful workmen*; and they well merit this title, for wherever they settled they have left monuments, the ruins of which are as wonderful for their imposing bulk as for the intellectual culture they reveal."

We were again obliged to ride in single file, climbing hills, and at last reaching the bottom of a deep ravine where flowed a brook, the water of which, impregnated with iron, had an unbearable inky flavour. We alighted to camp and get our breakfast, after which, having fettered our horses so that they could graze, we each of us provided ourselves with torches. We followed the right bank of the stream for more than a quarter of an hour, being often obliged to cut a passage through the creepers.

The curé had taken the lead, but he often hesitated as to which path to follow. Ten years previously one of his parishioners had taken him to see the grotto of the Toltecs. Hardly had they entered a dark passage, when the two explorers heard strange noises, and prudently beat a retreat. Since then, notwithstanding his great desire to visit the grotto, the good priest had never been able to make up his mind to undertake another excursion, and I had much difficulty in persuading him to accompany me.

My guide's only beacon was, he said, a gigantic mahogany-tree, the thick foliage of which entirely shaded the entrance to the grotto. Unfortunately, there was no lack of ancient mahogany-trees around us, and we made a series of marches and counter-marches, going uphill and downhill, and making reconnoitres which lasted no less than two long hours.

"It is there," cried the curé at last.

And in fact, a quarter of an hour later we set down our burdens before an opening situated half-way down the ravine, and shaded by the dark foliage of a mahogany-tree laden with fruit.

I examined the spot. Here and there were rocks bearing beautiful fossil impressions. The mouth of the grotto, two yards wide and three high, seemed to have been roughly hewn by human hands. Nowhere was there the faintest indication of a path; nothing showed that this place had been formerly frequented, and it was only attainable by a somewhat perilous climb.

I walked down an incline and found myself in front of a corridor, which turned off abruptly to the right. There was no trace of vegetation on the soil, but along the sides of the passage were enormous tufts of pale green wall-wort.

"How far did you penetrate?" I asked the curé, on returning to prepare the torches.

"I took twenty steps down the corridor which you have seen, and then I turned back, as I have already told you. I seemed to hear some one walking in the black darkness, as though coming towards me. The Indian who was with me had been filling my mind with such wonderful stories, that I expected every moment to see a dragon or some other fabulous animal start up. In fact, after having ridden a whole day with the express intention of thoroughly examining the cave, I came away as I went, and I have never since tried the experiment.

"Ah, well," said I gaily, "we shall know how much is to be believed of the marvellous traditions before an hour is over. I warn you beforehand that a great deal will have to be curtailed. This is not the age of apparitions; our century has replaced everything by plain matter of fact, and the noise which you heard was undoubtedly produced by an echo."

"That is possible," said the curé, watching me as I arranged the torches. "But are you going to penetrate into that den without any preparation?"

"What do you mean?"

"That it would be well to say a few prayers first. No one can ever repent of having asked God's help in a perilous undertaking."

THE GROTTO OF THE TOLTECS. 287

I approved of my friend's words. Followed by Bautista, the curé went towards the entrance of the cave. The Indian held a bottle which until then I thought full of cognac or sugar-cane brandy, but which in reality contained holy water, with which the entrance of the cave was sprinkled. After this ceremony, my two companions declared themselves ready. I advised them to follow me slowly, and never to take a step without trying the solidity of the ground, holes and precipices being much more to be feared in the subterraneous place than demons. At last I passed the vault, and we entered the narrow passage.

I listened, hoping to hear the echo, which I did not doubt had been the cause of the good curé's fright on his first excursion. Profound silence reigned; the echo did not even exist, and my companion's fright had been groundless. I again advanced.

"Listen," said Bautista, suddenly. A dull noise resounded.

I stood still, wondering what was the cause of the noise. Again all was absolute silence.

"Let us turn back," said the curé.

"Turn back!" I cried; "what for?"

"We are tempting the evil spirit, and it is no business that for good Christians."

"The devil tempts us so often," replied I, laughing, "that really I do not see the harm of giving him tit for tat once in a way. Besides, señor, I have already told you that I have never entered a cave without hearing strange, inexplicable, sometimes even terrifying noises. Upon examination, we have found that these noises were caused by the wind, or by water slowly trickling into natural basins, or even by the buzzing of an insect."

"Insects, in this darkness?" said my companion with a look of incredulity.

"Yes, insects; and what is more, insects whose visual organs have become withered and useless by long habitation in darkness. The Darwinists, who do not exactly pretend that men are descended from monkeys, but who consider this transformation as possible, see a decisive argument in favour of the slow transformation of human beings in the absence of eyes in coleoptera, and fish found in caves."

" Those are but mere conjectures, señor. If nature is intelligent, if it transform itself, it owes its impetus to the Creator, and not to its unconscious power."

" Listen," said Bautista again.

This time, a dull vibration certainly agitated the heated air around us.

" A stone must have fallen from the top of the vault," I said; " that is one of the dangers we have to fear."

My companions drew closer to me. For several minutes we were perfectly silent, and could hear ourselves breathe. I again went forward. The passage we were following made another bend, and grew wider so rapidly, that we could no longer see the wall on the left side; at the same time a hot breath fanned our faces: we had just entered a room which we must explore. Suddenly a bright speck of light appeared before us. The curé seized my arm.

" It is the light of one of our torches reflected by a stalactite . . . ."

I ceased speaking; the light flickered, and we stood motionless.

" *Vade retro! vade retro!*" cried the curé.

The light disappeared, and a plaintive voice seemed to repeat, " *Vade retro!* "

My two companions let their torches fall, and jostled against each other in their attempt to fly. Frightened out of their senses, they knocked against the walls and implored God to help them. They went back, and gradually disappeared, notwithstanding my repeated calls to them. I remained firm, to all appearance; but fear is almost always contagious. My heart beat violently, and I felt my hair bristle. I tried to reason, when another noise was heard. Then, losing the little self-possession I had retained, I rushed in my turn towards the entrance of the cave, believing myself pursued by I know not what phantom, which repeated, in a sepulchral voice, " *Vade retro! vade retro!* "

CHAPTER II.

Discouragement—Useless entreaties—New excursions—An unexpected meeting—Discoveries—Departure.

DIRECTLY I was out of the grotto, I saw my two companions rolling rather than running down the side of the ravine, in their desperate haste to get away. I called to them, and the first result of the sound of my voice was to make them fly quicker than ever. They stopped at last and made frantic signs for me to join them; but the sight of the trees and the daylight had put an end to my panic. I was already ashamed of having yielded to a groundless fear.

We had evidently been duped by a reflection and an echo, and, like the hare in the fable, we had just been trembling at our own shadows. I at last succeeded, with some difficulty, in bringing back the curé and Bautista to the entrance of the grotto.

"Well, we have had an adventure that I shall never forget, even if I live to twice the age of Methuselah. Let us take our belongings and get back to our horses. I do not feel at all comfortable here."

"What, go away? No, thank you. We must see into the cause of this incredible panic of which we have just been the heroes—or the victims, so that we may know at least what frightened us."

"What do you mean?" asked the curé, with a scared look.

"That we have come to see the grotto, and that it would be very unreasonable to go away without having explored it."

"Are you in your right senses, señor?"

"Yes," I replied. "I have recovered my reason, which I confess I lost a few minutes ago."

"Then let us be off without delay, and be thankful that we are safe."

"I shall not be satisfied until I have seen the grotto."

U

The curé and Bautista exchanged glances; they thought I had gone mad. I talked to them for a long while, and tried to bring them round; but it was trouble for nothing. They refused to listen to me with such persistence, that at last I saw the futility of my persuasions, and determined to make another attempt alone.

After having looked to see that the primings of my revolver were in good condition, I lit a torch and prepared myself for a second exploration, quite determined this time that no noise should frighten me, however strange it might seem. I would not listen to the good curé's entreaties, and once more I entered the dark passage.

Having reached the spot from which I had fled, I advanced very cautiously. An acrid, resinous odour, like that produced by the burning of storax branches, almost suffocated me. The idea at once occurred to me that visitors, having entered the cave before us, were lighting themselves by aid of these natural torches, and that our presence must have caused them quite as much fright as we had experienced. Convinced that I was right in my supposition, I gave a loud shout. My voice died away without an echo; but I thought I heard quiet footsteps and a rustling against the side of the rock. I raised my torch above my head, in order to see more clearly, and I caught a glimpse of a shadow gliding before me.

"Who is there?" I cried.

No one answered.

"Speak," I continued, "if you value your life."

"Mercy!" cried a faltering voice; "mercy!"

I hurried towards the spot whence the voice came, and I found myself beside an Indian lying flat on the ground, his head covered with his arms, and trembling violently all over. For a moment I stood dumb with surprise.

"Holloa, José!" said I at last. "Get up; don't be alarmed. I am a Christian."

The poor wretch dared not stir.

"Mercy!" said he again. "Oh! good genius, I did not want to offend thee; I came to beg thy assistance. Do not harm me, I pray thee."

"I am neither genius nor devil, but a traveller exploring the cave. Who are you?"

"Néotli, from the village of Santa Maria."

"And what are you looking for in this dark place?"

The Indian was silent; terror paralyzed him.

"I am not going to do you any harm," said I to him. "Come; be sensible."

Néotli at last ventured to raise his head, but he scarcely dared to look at me.

"Come!" said I to him.

He followed me mechanically. When I reached the entrance of the grotto, the curé and Bautista drew back.

"Alive!" cried the curé.

"Alive," I replied, laughing.

"Did I dream it, or were you speaking to some one?"

"You have not been dreaming at all, señor."

"Then did you see the spirit of darkness, and have you been speaking to him?"

"No; I simply spoke to Néotli, one of your countrymen."

The Indian appeared. The curé and Bautista could scarcely believe their eyes, and went up to their friend, who looked as though he scarcely recognized them. I gave him something to drink, and his tongue became loose at last. From the curé's cross-examination it appeared that Néotli, tired of being poor, had resolved to get possession of some of the riches which, according to the elders of his tribe, lay buried and useless in the grotto of the Toltecs. The Indian had had this plan in his head for a long time, and by a singular coincidence he had chosen the evening before to put it into execution. Having started from Santa Maria in the evening, he had been wandering since morning in the grotto. Our appearance had convinced the poor man that the spirits of darkness, disturbed from their rest, had come to punish him. His fright had been so great at the sight of our light, that he had fainted. On recovering consciousness, he had wandered about in the darkness trying to find the opening by which he had entered. Finally he thought his last hour was come on seeing me, and hearing me call him.

The poor wretch still looked terribly frightened, and the least noise made him tremble.

"If I had listened to you," said I to the curé, " we should be far from here now, and one more superstition would have barred the entrance to the grotto."

"True. Nevertheless, I think it is much better to leave these mysterious places in peace; and if you will take my advice, we will go quietly home."

"No, indeed," I cried. "Though I am to go back again by myself, the grotto shall reveal its secrets this time!"

I questioned Néotli. He told me that the chamber in which I had met him communicated with another much larger, in the middle of which was a sheet of water; this large room, full of stalactites, more than a hundred feet long, and as wide in proportion, was so high that he could not see the vault. Néotli's experience was valuable; but when I asked him to follow me into the cave, he drew back and shook his head.

By dint of arguments, reasonings, and entreaties, strengthened by several glasses of grog, I persuaded my companions to accompany me, and for the third time I entered the mysterious cavern.

The first room was explored without difficulty. I rummaged in every recess in the hope of finding fossils; but there was nothing but hard, smooth ground. A heap of fallen rocks blocked up the entrance to the second room, and it was no easy matter climbing over the wet, slippery stones. Having passed this awkward barrier, our torches illumed an immense gallery bordered with stalactites, in the middle of which, as Néotli had told us, was a long basin filled with limpid, icy water. We made up a large fire here.

The spectacle was magnificent, and alone well worth the trouble of our excursion. Néotli had spoken the truth; the top of the vault was lost to sight, and the light of our torches could not banish the darkness which covered it. On the other hand, our fire illumined the motionless surface of the lake.

"One would think that it was a lake of molten gold," cried Bautista, pointing to the luminous sheet of water.

"THIS ROOM-FULL OF STALACTITES......"

"A lake of gold set with diamonds," said the curé, looking at the stalactites, which were reflecting all the colours of the rainbow.

My companions were right, and the magical effect, produced by the play of the light on the water and the limestone concretions which are often to be found in caves, must have contributed in establishing legends of the unheard-of riches buried in their depths.

I proceeded to examine the gallery, and soon found some *débris* of earthenware statuettes. The head of a warrior, his brow crowned with feathers, perfectly represented the Toltec type, which is to be found on all the Palenqué monuments, and which singularly reminds one of the type of the Bourbon family.

Ten steps further on, I made another discovery. This time it was the head of a serpent roughly hewn from a piece of lava. I regretted that we could not dig through the crust of chalk which covered the ground; unfortunately, the necessary implements were wanting. Having reached the other end of the gallery, a heap of rock barred our passage, and we were obliged to turn back and examine the right side of the immense gallery. There again I picked up broken pieces of statuettes, but so damaged that I did not trouble to keep them. The heads of a warrior and a serpent were the only riches I brought away with me from the grotto of the Toltecs.

My companions were more disappointed than I was. The curé in his inmost soul had reckoned on discovering treasure enough to rebuild his church; this he confessed to us.

"We shall still have to continue our service under a roof of palm-leaves," said he to Bautista.

"The Child Jesus and his Divine Mother could change it into a roof of diamonds if they liked," replied the Indian, uncovering his head.

"Well spoken, Bautista," said the good curé. "Let us be content with what God does, and get out of this place."

Before going away, I looked for insects under the stones and along the sides of the rocks, also for shells on the border of the little lake; but my trouble was in vain. To my great surprise, three or four small fish came to the space lighted by my torch; it was a valuable discovery. Alas!—and here all naturalists will heave a sigh with me—scarcely had I stirred the water, when these singular inhabitants of the darkness disappeared. For an hour I watched for them to return, but in vain. My torches were burning out, and I then determined, very much against my inclination, to return to my companions, who had been sitting for some time under the mahogany-tree.

Just as I was re-entering the first chamber I gave a last glance at the immense gallery with its glittering pillars, now again left to the silence of the night. An hour later, I bid a long farewell to the grotto of the Toltecs. Accompanied by Bautista and Néotli, I took the road to Old Guatemala, that ancient capital which, destroyed in 1774 by an earthquake, is constantly threatened by two volcanoes, one of which throws up flames, the other water.

AZTEC EDUCATION.

True Aztecs—A father to his son—A mother to her daughter.

SOME years ago a showman exhibited in London, and then in Paris, two deformed dwarfs, of a copper-coloured complexion and woolly hair, whom he called Aztecs. "A dauntless traveller," so said the newspapers, "crossing the deserts, as far as the town of Acayucan, has brought back, through many perils, these two specimens of a race which is every day dying out, and seems as though it must soon disappear." I had now just arrived at Acayucan, a village of five or six hundred souls, situated to the south of Vera-Cruz. As these parts are inhabited, not by Aztecs, but by admirably constituted Totanacs, I was highly amused at the explanations of the manners and customs of the Indians given by our intrepid traveller. The two poor deformed creatures, whose keeper he had made himself, would have been phenomena at Acayucan quite as much as in London or Paris. Nevertheless, the public took the thing seriously. Learned men—professedly learned men if you please—wrote long dissertations, which tended to do nothing less than ratify the daring traveller's imposture. Upon the statement of learned men the crowd admired, and all Europe, with the exception of a small number of disbelievers, still represents the Aztecs under the deformed figure of the two dwarfs, whom I have since found at New York in the famous Barnum Museum.

Let us say a word now about the true Aztecs, that powerful,

civilized nation, whose last emperors were Montézuma and Guatimozin.

Towards the thirteenth century the Aztecs, or Mexicans—these two names designate the same people—appeared on the extensive table-land where the town of Mexico stands at the present day. They came from the north. The etymology of the word Aztec is not known; as to that of *Mexicatl*, or Mexican, it comes from *Mexitli*, warlike divinity. In less than a century the Mexicans conquered all the surrounding nations. Like the Romans, with whom they offer more than one analogy, they borrowed their civilization and divinities from the conquered people. Without laying aside their warlike character, they cultivated the arts and sciences. The arrival of Fernando Cortez and his companions, in 1519, surprised them at the height of their prosperity. Notwithstanding the wisdom of the laws which the Aztecs had established, several of their conquests were too recent for the natives not to profit by the first favourable occasion to revolt. Cortez did not fail to call these enemies, still quivering under their defeat, to his standard, when they became his auxiliaries. People like to talk of the great Spanish adventurer taking possession of Mexico with three hundred of his countrymen. It may be remarked, however, that he had as allies the Totanacs and the republicans of Tlascala, that is, more than two hundred thousand fighting men.

The Aztecs—the Indians, as they are called at the present day, for the name Mexican applies particularly to men of mixed blood—are gifted with healthy, robust constitutions. They are of middle height, tall rather than short, with olive complexions, retreating foreheads, slightly flattened noses, large mouths, and coarse black hair. Their lower jaw is prominent, and their beard scanty. The general expression of their features betokens little intelligence, but much gentleness; their eyes are not expressive, whilst their humble and awkward manners give them the appearance of overgrown children.

The respect due to parents and old people seems innate in the Aztec race. A young Indian is never heard to contradict any one older than himself. The parents on their side evince blind tenderness for their children, and the families are so united that more than one European nation might draw many a useful lesson from a New World cabin.

Domestic education occupied a great place in Aztec life. The queens themselves nursed their children, who were accustomed from their earliest infancy to bear hunger, heat, and cold. In his fifth year the son of a noble entered a seminary, to be instructed by the priests with plebeian scholars, who were only received as day pupils. The pupils were inspired with horror of vice, respect due to old age, and love of work. Accustomed to sleep on the bare ground, they only received sufficient food to maintain health. As they grew up they were taught to handle weapons. The soldier took his sons to war in order that he might accustom them to brave danger. The mother taught her daughters to spin and weave; when they were too fond of walking about, their feet were tied. The rule was that young people should be always occupied.

Whenever a child was convicted of telling a falsehood, its tongue was pricked with thorns. The veneration inspired towards parents was so deeply rooted, that a man, although married, scarcely dared to speak before his father or mother.

Clavigero learnt from Sahagun the exhortation of a Mexican to his son, and that of a Mexican mother to a daughter. These two admirable discourses will give an excellent idea of Aztec morals about the year 1400.

THE FATHER TO HIS SON.

"My son," said the father, "thou art now a man, and art preparing to run thy race in the world, without it being permitted us to know how long we may keep the precious jewel which Heaven has given us in thee. Come what may, walk uprightly, and pray God to aid thee. He hath created thee, thou belongest unto Him. He is thy father, and loves thee yet more than I do. Think of Him day and night. Never stand silent before an unhappy or poor person; on the contrary, do all you can to comfort them with good words. Honour thy father and thy mother, to whom thou owest obedience, fear, and service.

Do not imitate children who, like brutes, know not how to profit by good advice: do what they may, such will at last fall into the bottomless pit.

"Never ridicule old people, nor those whose bodies are deformed. Do not jeer at those who have committed a fault, for fear lest the same thing happen to thee. Abstain from going where thou art not wanted, and never scrutinize the actions of others. Let thy speech be always polite; and when thou conversest with any one, use not many words, taking care not to interrupt thy companion, nor to force him to listen to thee.

"Listen to those who are speaking to thee without moving thy feet, twisting thy cloak, or sitting down impatiently. When thou sittest at table, eat slowly, and do not let it be seen if the food is not to thy liking. If a stranger happens to come in, share with him; do not watch him eating, for fear of intimidating him.

"Walk circumspectly, so that thou annoy no one. Never pass before an old man, unless he tells thee to do so. If thou eatest in company with an elder, do not drink before him, and wait upon him in order that he may be pleased with thee.

"In receiving a present, show thy gratitude. If the gift is valuable, do not be vain of it; if it is of little value, do not disdain it—it was offered thee to give thee pleasure. If thou shouldst become rich, beware of being presumptuous—the gods, the authors of thy prosperity, may be angered with thy haughtiness, and pour thy riches into more worthy hands. Live by the work of thy hands, thou wilt only be the happier for it. Son, I have nourished thee with the fruit of my labours, I have given thee all that thou needest, without depriving others; I have fulfilled my duties, do thou the same.

"Never tell a falsehood. Weigh thy words in repeating what thou hast heard. Slander no one. Avoid sowing discord; and when thou art entrusted with a commission, if the person to whom thou art sent is wroth with thy sender, soften the language of his anger, so that thy indiscretion may not separate two friends.

"Oh, my son! may these counsels strengthen thy heart.

Beware of forgetting or despising them, for thy existence and thy happiness depend upon them."

These are not like the counsels of Lord Chesterfield, who is anxious above all that his heir should make a distinguished figure in the world. The exhortations of the mother seem no less wise and touching.

THE MOTHER TO HER DAUGHTER.

"'Child of my heart, dove born of my anguish," said she, "I have fed thee; I have tried to polish thee as an emerald, so that thou mayest be a jewel of virtue in the eyes of men. Be good, or who would wish thee for a wife? Life is full of trouble, and we should do well to make the most of the benefits showered upon us. Be diligent and laborious; let order reign in thy house. Bring thy husband water, and prepare the bread for thy family with thy own hands. Walk slowly and be modest in thy demeanour. Do not laugh at those whom thou mayest meet; look not to the right or to the left when thou art walking if thou valuest thy reputation. Answer politely those who greet thee or ask thee anything.

"Be active when thou art spinning, weaving, sewing, or embroidering, so that thou mayest merit esteem, and provide thyself with necessary things. Never be idle; idleness harbours vice. In working, think only of the gods or of thy parents. Obey at once. Never reply with arrogance or bad humour; and if thou findest thyself unable to execute thy father's order, excuse thyself humbly. Never offer to perform a task which thou art not sure of fulfilling. Deceive no one, for the gods see everything. Live in peace with the world; love thy fellow-creatures, in order that they may love thee.

"Never yield to the evil dictates of thy heart, which will soil thy soul as mud soils water. Do not associate with bad women —their example is pernicious; never forget that vice is a venomous herb, which will cause death sooner or later.

"When thou art married, respect thy husband. Be not proud nor disdainful toward him; love him if he is poor, however rich thou mayest have been. If he grieve thee, speak to him gently and without taking another confidant. Take care of thy possessions and thy family, rendering to each their dues.

"I am old, I have had experience of the world; I am thy mother, and I speak to thee in thy own interest. May the gods aid thee if thou follow my counsels!"

It must be confessed that a nation who taught young people such maxims and made them practise them, were in more than one respect superior to the rough soldiers commanded by Cortez.

Brave, even to heroism, the Aztecs struggled energetically to defend their liberty against these invaders, whose fire-arms and cavalry gave them the victory. With profound policy, the Spanish general warily made use of the dissensions which weakened his enemies, and conquered one by the aid of another. What has become of that civilization which surprised even him? Where are the forty millions of men whom he found settled in Mexico?

Oppressed, trodden down by their conquerors, who refused to recognize them as being gifted with reason, the Aztecs at the present day, reduced to barely five millions, still refuse to learn the language or adopt the customs of their oppressors. Serious and silent, accustomed to obedience, they allow themselves to be ruled by six hundred thousand half-bred offsprings of themselves and the Spaniards.

Such are the Aztecs; a very different people from the two poor idiots exhibited in Europe as specimens of their race—the descendants of that Guatimozin who, placed by the Spanish conquerors on a burning pile, calmly answered his fellow-sufferers' complaints, saying, "And am I on a bed of roses?"

THE END.

LONDON: PRINTED BY WILLIAM CLOWES AND SONS, STAMFORD STREET
AND CHARING CROSS.

A Catalogue of American and Foreign Books Published or Imported by MESSRS. SAMPSON LOW & CO. *can be had on application.*

Crown Buildings, 188, *Fleet Street, London,*
April, 1877.

A List of Books

PUBLISHED BY

SAMPSON LOW, MARSTON, SEARLE, & RIVINGTON.

A CLASSIFIED *Educational Catalogue of Works* published in Great Britain. Demy 8vo, cloth extra. Second Edition, revised to the year 1877, 5*s*.

Ablett (H.) Reminiscences of an Old Draper. 1 vol. small post 8vo, 2*s*. 6*d*.

Abney (Captain W. de W., R.E., F.R.S.) Thebes, and its Five Greater Temples. Forty large permanent photographs, with descriptive letter-press. Super-royal 4to, cloth extra, 63*s*.

Adventures of Captain Mago. A Phœnician's Explorations 1000 years B.C. By LEON CAHUN. Numerous Illustrations. Crown 8vo, cloth extra, gilt, 10*s*. 6*d*.

Adventures of a Young Naturalist. By LUCIEN BIART, with 117 beautiful Illustrations on Wood. Edited and adapted by PARKER GILLMORE. Post 8vo, cloth extra, gilt edges, New Edition, 7*s*. 6*d*.

Adventures in New Guinea. The Narrative of the Captivity of a French Sailor, Louis Trégance, for Nine Years among the Savages in the Interior. Small post 8vo, with Illustrations and Map, cloth gilt, 6*s*.

"Captain Lawson's wonderful stories about New Guinea are totally eclipsed by this Narrative of a French sailor."—*Athenæum.*

Africa, and the Brussels Geographical Conference. Translated from the French of EMILE BANNING, by R. H. MAJOR, F.S.A. With Map, crown 8vo, 7*s*. 6*d*.

Alcott (Louisa M.) Aunt Jo's Scrap-Bag. Square 16mo, 2*s*. 6*d*. (Rose Library, 1*s*.)

—— *Cupid and Chow-Chow.* Small post 8vo, 3*s*. 6*d*.

—— *Little Men: Life at Plumfield with Jo's Boys.* By the Author of "Little Women." Small post 8vo, cloth, gilt edges, 2*s*. 6*d*. (Rose Library, 1*s*.)

—— *Little Women.* 2 vols., 2*s*. 6*d*. each. (Rose Library. 2 vols., 1*s*. each.)

—— *Old-Fashioned Girl.* Best Edition, small post 8vo, cloth extra, gilt edges, 2*s*. 6*d*. (Rose Library, 2*s*.)

A

Alcott (Louisa M.) Work and Beginning Again. A Story of Experience. 1 vol., small post 8vo, cloth extra, 6s. Several Illustrations. (Rose Library, 2 vols., 1s. each.)
—— *Beginning Again.* A Sequel to "Work." 1s.
—— *Shawl Straps.* Small post 8vo, cloth extra, gilt, 3s. 6d.
—— *Eight Cousins; or, the Aunt Hill.* Small post 8vo with Illustrations, 3s. 6d.
—— *The Rose in Bloom.* Small post 8vo, cloth extra, 3s. 6d.
—— *Silver Pitchers.* Small post 8vo, cloth extra, 3s. 6d.
"Miss Alcott's stories are thoroughly healthy, full of racy fun and humour . . . exceedingly entertaining . . . . We can recommend the 'Eight Cousins.'"— *Athenæum.*

Andersen (Hans Christian) Fairy Tales. With Illustrations in Colours by E. V. B. Royal 4to, cloth, 25s.

Andrews (Dr.) Latin-English Lexicon. 14th Edition. Royal 8vo, pp. 1670, cloth extra, price 18s.
"The best Latin Dictionary, whether for the scholar or advanced student."— *Spectator.*
"Every page bears the impress of industry and care."— *Athenæum.*

Anecdotes of the Queen and Royal Family. Collected and Edited by J. G. HODGINS, with Illustrations. New Edition, revised by JOHN TIMBS, 5s.

Animals Painted by Themselves. Adapted from the French of Balzac, Louis Baude, G. Droz, Jules Janin, E. Lemoine, A. de Musset, Georges Sand, &c., with 200 Illustrations by GRANDVILLE. 8vo, cloth extra, gilt, 10s. 6d.

Atmosphere (The). See FLAMMARION.

THE BAYARD SERIES.

Comprising Pleasure Books of Literature produced in the Choicest Style as Companionable Volumes at Home and Abroad.
"We can hardly imagine better books for boys to read or for men to ponder over."—*Times.*
Price 2s. 6d. each Volume, complete in itself, flexible cloth extra, gilt edges, with silk Headbands and Registers.

The Story of the Chevalier Bayard. By M. DE BERVILLE.
De Joinville's St. Louis, King of France.
The Essays of Abraham Cowley, including all his Prose Works.
Abdallah; or the Four Leaves. By EDOUARD LABOULLAYE.
Table-Talk and Opinions of Napoleon Buonaparte.
Vathek: An Oriental Romance. By WILLIAM BECKFORD.
The King and the Commons. A Selection of Cavalier and Puritan Song. Edited by Prof. MORLEY.
Words of Wellington: Maxims and Opinions of the Great Duke.
Dr. Johnson's Rasselas, Prince of Abyssinia. With Notes.
Hazlitt's Round Table. With Biographical Introduction.

The Bayard Series, continued:—
The Religio Medici, Hydriotaphia, and the Letter to a Friend.
By Sir THOMAS BROWNE, Knt.
Ballad Poetry of the Affections. By ROBERT BUCHANAN.
Coleridge's Christabel, and other Imaginative Poems. With Preface by ALGERNON C. SWINBURNE.
Lord Chesterfield's Letters, Sentences, and Maxims. With Introduction by the Editor, and Essay on Chesterfield by M. DE STE.-BEUVE, of the French Academy.
Essays in Mosaic. By THOS. BALLANTYNE.
My Uncle Toby; his Story and his Friends. Edited by P. FITZGERALD.
Reflections; or, Moral Sentences and Maxims of the Duke de la Rochefoucauld.
Socrates, Memoirs for English Readers from Xenophon's Memorabilia. By EDW. LEVIEN.
Prince Albert's Golden Precepts.
A suitable Case containing 12 Volumes, price 31s. 6d.; or the Case separately, price 3s. 6d.

BEAUTY and the Beast. An Old Tale told, with Pictures by E. V. B. Demy 4to, cloth extra, novel binding. 10 Illustrations in Colours (in same style as those in the First Edition of "Story without an End"). 12s. 6d.

Beumer's German Copybooks. In six gradations at 4d. each.

Bickersteth's Hymnal Companion to Book of Common Prayer.
A new Edition, with 160 Additional Hymns and numerous new tunes has has been issued; the Original Editions are kept in print.
An 8pp. prospectus and price lists will be sent post free on application.
*** *A liberal allowance is made to Clergymen.*

The Church Mission Hymn Book has been recently issued: it contains 120 Hymns for Special Mission and Schoolroom Services, selected, with a few additions, from the Hymnal Companion. Price 8s. 4d. per 100. or 1½d. each.

The Hymnal Companion is also sold, strongly bound with a Sunday-School Liturgy, in two sizes, price 4d. and 8d.

Bickersteth (Rev. E. H., M.A.) The Reef and other Parables.
1 vol., square 8vo, with numerous very beautiful Engravings, uniform in character with the Illustrated Edition of Heber's Hymns, &c., 7s. 6d.

—— *The Master's Home-Call; or, Brief Memorials of* Alice Frances Bickersteth. 20th Thousand. 32mo, cloth gilt, 1s.
"They recall in a touching manner a character of which the religious beauty has a warmth and grace almost too tender to be definite."—*The Guardian.*

—— *The Shadow of the Rock.* A Selection of Religious Poetry. 18mo, cloth extra, 2s. 6d.

—— *The Clergyman in his Home.* Small post 8vo, 1s.

Bickersteth (Rev. E. H., M.A.) The Shadowed Home and the Light Beyond. 6th Edition, crown 8vo, cloth extra, 5s.

Bida. The Authorized Version of the Four Gospels, with the whole of the magnificent Etchings on Steel, after drawings by M. BIDA, in 4 vols., appropriately bound in cloth extra, price 3l. 3s. each.

Also the four volumes in two, bound in the best morocco, by Suttaby, extra gilt edges, 18l. 18s., half-morocco, 12l. 12s.

Bidwell (C. T.) The Balearic Islands. Illustrations and a Map. Crown 8vo, cloth, 10s. 6d.

——— *The Cost of Living Abroad.* Crown 8vo, 6s.

Black (Wm.) Three Feathers. Small post 8vo, cloth extra, 6s.

——— *Lady Silverdale's Sweetheart, and other Stories.* 1 vol., crown 8vo, 10s. 6d.

——— *Kilmeny: a Novel.* Small post 8vo, cloth, 6s.

——— *In Silk Attire.* 3rd edition, small post 8vo, 6s.

"A work which deserves a hearty welcome for its skill and power in delineation of character."—*Saturday Review.*

——— *A Daughter of Heth.* 11th Edition, crown 8vo, cloth extra, 6s. With Frontispiece by F. Walker, A.R.A.

"If humour, sweetness, and pathos, and a story told with simplicity and vigour, ought to insure success, 'A Daughter of Heth' is of the kind to deserve it."—*Saturday Review.*

Blackmore (R. D.) Lorna Doone. 10th Edition, cr. 8vo, 6s.

"The reader at times holds his breath, so graphically yet so simply does John Ridd tell his tale."—*Saturday Review.*

——— *Alice Lorraine.* 1 vol., small post 8vo, 6s., 6th Edition.

——— *Clara Vaughan.* Revised Edition, 6s.

——— *Cradock Nowell.* New Edition, 6s.

——— *Cripps the Carrier.* 3rd Edition, small post 8vo, cloth extra, 6s.

——— *Georgics of Virgil.* Small 4to, 4s. 6d.

Blue Banner. Translated from the French of LEON CAHUN. With very numerous Illustrations. Crown 8vo, cloth extra, gilt, 10s. 6d.

Book of the Play. By DUTTON COOK. 2 vols., crown 8vo, 24s.

Bowles (T. G.) The Defence of Paris, narrated as it was seen. 8vo, 14s.

Bradford (Wm.) The Arctic Regions. Illustrated with Photographs, taken on an Art Expedition to Greenland. With Descriptive Narrative by the Artist. In One Volume, royal broadside, 25 inches by 20, beautifully bound in morocco extra, price Twenty-Five Guineas.

Brett (E.) Notes on Yachts. Fcp., 6s.

Bryant (W. C., assisted by S. H. Gay.) A Popular History of the United States. About 4 vols., to be profusely Illustrated with Engravings on Steel and Wood, after Designs by the best Artists. Vol. I., super-royal 8vo, cloth extra, gilt, 42s., is ready.

Burton (Captain R. F.) Two Trips to Gorilla Land and the Cataracts of the Congo. By Captain R. F. BURTON. 2 vols, demy 8vo, with numerous Illustrations and Map, cloth extra, 28s.

Butler (W. F.) The Great Lone Land; an Account of the Red River Expedition, 1869-70, and Subsequent Travels and Adventures in the Manitoba Country, and a Winter Journey across the Saskatchewan Valley to the Rocky Mountains. With Illustrations and Map. Fifth and Cheaper Edition, crown 8vo, cloth extra, 7s. 6d. (The first Three Editions were in 8vo, cloth, 16s.)

——— *The Wild North Land; the Story of a Winter Journey* with Dogs across Northern North America. Demy 8vo, cloth, with numerous Woodcuts and a Map, 4th Edition, 18s. Crown 8vo, 7s. 6d.

——— *Akim-foo: the History of a Failure.* Demy 8vo, cloth, 16s., 2nd Edition. Also, in crown 8vo, 7s. 6d.

CADOGAN (Lady A.) Illustrated Games of Patience. Twenty-four Diagrams in Colours, with Descriptive Text. Foolscap 4to, cloth extra, gilt edges, 12s. 6d. 3rd Edition.

Cahun (Leon) Adventures of Captain Mago. See "Adventures."

——— *Blue Banner*, which see.

California. See NORDHOFF.

Ceramic Art. See JACQUEMART.

Changed Cross (The), and other Religious Poems. 2s. 6d.

Child's Play, with 16 Coloured Drawings by E. V. B. Printed on thick paper, with tints, 7s. 6d.

——— *New*, which see.

Choice Editions of Choice Books. 2s. 6d. each, Illustrated by C. W. COPE, R.A., T. CRESWICK, R.A., E. DUNCAN, BIRKET FOSTER, J. C. HORSLEY, A.R.A., G. HICKS, R. REDGRAVE, R.A., C. STONEHOUSE, F. TAYLER, G. THOMAS, H. J. TOWNSHEND, E. H. WEHNERT, HARRISON WEIR, &c.

Bloomfield's Farmer's Boy.	Milton's L'Allegro.
Campbell's Pleasures of Hope.	Poetry of Nature. Harrison Weir.
Coleridge's Ancient Mariner.	Rogers' (Sam.) Pleasures of Memory.
Goldsmith's Deserted Village.	Shakespeare's Songs and Sonnets.
Goldsmith's Vicar of Wakefield.	Tennyson's May Queen.
Gray's Elegy in a Churchyard.	Elizabethan Poets.
Keat's Eve of St. Agnes.	Wordsworth's Pastoral Poems.

"Such works are a glorious beatification for a poet."—*Athenæum.*

Clara Vaughan. Revised Edition, 6s. See BLACKMORE.

Cook (D.) Young Mr. Nightingale. A Novel. 3 vols, 31s. 6d.

——— *The Banns of Marriage.* 2 vols., crown 8vo, 21s.

——— *Book of the Play.* 2 vols., crown 8vo, 24s.

Cradock Nowell. New Edition, 6s. See BLACKMORE.

Cripps the Carrier. 3rd Edition, 6s. See BLACKMORE.

Cruise of H.M.S. "Challenger" (The). By W. J. J. SPRY, R.N. With Route Map and many Illustrations. 4th Edition. In 1 vol., demy 8vo, cloth extra, price 18s.
"The book before us supplies the former information in a manner that leaves little to be desired. 'The Cruise of H M.S. *Challenger*' is an exceedingly well-written, entertaining, and instructive book."—*United Service Gazette*.
"Agreeably written, full of information, and copiously illustrated."—*Broad Arrow*.

Cumming (Miss C. F. G.) From the Hebrides to the Himalayas; Eighteen Months' Wanderings in Western Isles and Eastern Highlands. By Miss CONSTANCE F. GORDON CUMMING, with very numerous Full-page and other Woodcut Illustrations, from the Author's own Drawings. 2 vols., medium 8vo, cloth extra, 42s.

DANA (R. H.) Two Years before the Mast and Twenty-four years After. Revised Edition with Notes, 12mo, 6s.

Dana (Jas. D.) Corals and Coral Islands. Numerous Illustrations, charts, &c. New and Cheaper Edition, with numerous important Additions and Corrections. Crown 8vo, cloth extra, 8s. 6d.
"Professed geologists and zoologists, as well as general readers, will find Professor Dana's book in every way worthy of their attention."—*The Athenæum*.

Daughter (A) of Heth. By WILLIAM BLACK. 13th and cheaper Edition. 1 vol., crown 8vo, 6s.

Day of my Life (A) ; or, Every Day Experiences at Eton. By an ETON BOY. Super-royal 16mo, cloth extra, 2s. 6d. Second Edition.

Discoveries of Prince Henry the Navigator, and their Results; being the Narrative of the Discovery by Sea, within One Century, of more than Half the World. By RICHARD HENRY MAJOR, F.S.A. Demy 8vo, with several Woodcuts, 4 Maps, and a Portrait of Prince Henry in Colours. Cloth extra, 15s.
"Mr. R. H. Major has supplied a serious gap in our biographical literature. . . . One of the most interesting volumes of biography we have yet had under review."—*Daily Telegraph*.

Dodge (Mrs. M.) Hans Brinker; or, the Silver Skates. An entirely New Edition, with 59 Full-page and other Woodcuts. Square crown 8vo, cloth extra, 7s. 6d. ; Text only, paper, 1s.

——— *Theophilus and Others*. 1 vol., small post 8vo, cloth extra, gilt, 3s. 6d.

ECHOES of the Heart. See MOODY.
——— *English Catalogue of Books (The)*. Published during 1863 to 1871 inclusive, comprising also the Important American Publications.
This Volume, occupying over 450 Pages, shows the Titles of 32,000 New Books and New Editions issued during Nine Years, with the Size, Price, and Publisher's Name, the Lists of Learned Societies, Printing Clubs, and other Literary Associations, and the Books issued by them ; as also the Publisher's Series and Collections— altogether forming an indispensable adjunct to the Bookseller's

Establishment, as well as to every Learned and Literary Club and Association, 30s. half-bound.

⁎ The previous Volume, 1835 to 1862, of which very few remain on sale, price 2*l*. 5*s*. ; as also the Index Volume, 1837 to 1857, price 1*l*. 6*s*.

English Catalogue of Books (The). Supplements, 1863, 1864, 1865, 3*s*. 6*d*. each ; 1866, 1867 to 1876, 5*s*. each.

Eight Cousins. See ALCOTT.

English Painters of the Georgian Era. Hogarth to Turner. Biographical Notices. Illustrated with 48 permanent Photographs, after the most celebrated Works. Demy 4to, cloth extra, 18*s*.

Erckmann-Chatrian. Forest House and Catherine's Lovers. Crown 8vo, 3*s*. 6*d*.

——— *The Brothers Rantzau : a Story of the Vosges.* 2 vols., crown 8vo, cloth, 21*s*. New Edition, 1 vol., profusely Illustrated, cloth extra, 5*s*.

Evans (C.) Over the Hills and Far Away. By C. EVANS, Author of " A Strange Friendship." One Volume, crown 8vo, cloth extra, 10*s*. 6*d*.

——— *A Strange Friendship.* Crown 8vo, cloth, 5*s*.

FAITH GARTNEY'S Girlhood. By the Author of " The Gayworthys." Fcap. with Coloured Frontispiece, 3*s*. 6*d*.

Familiar Letters on some Mysteries of Nature. See PHIPSON.

Few (A) Hints on Proving Wills. Enlarged Edition, 1*s*.

Fish and Fishing. By J. J. MANLEY, M.A. Crown 8vo, with Illustrations, 10*s*. 6*d*.

Five Weeks in Greece. By J. F. YOUNG. Crown 8vo, 10*s*. 6*d*.

Flammarion (C.) The Atmosphere. Translated from the French of CAMILLE FLAMMARION. Edited by JAMES GLAISHER, F.R.S., Superintendent of the Magnetical and Meteorological Department of the Royal Observatory at Greenwich. With 10 Chromo-Lithographs and 81 Woodcuts. Royal 8vo, cloth extra, 30*s*.

Footsteps of the Master, 6*s*. See STOWE (MRS. BEECHER).

Forrest (John) Explorations in Australia; being MR. JOHN FORREST's Personal Account of his Journeys. 1 vol., demy 8vo, cloth, with several Illustrations from the Author's Sketches, drawn on wood by G. F. Angas, and 3 Maps, 16*s*.

Forrest's (R. W.) Gleanings from the Pastures of Tekoa. By the Rev. R. W. FORREST, M.A., Vicar of St. Jude's, South Kensington. 1 vol, small post 8vo, 260 pp., cloth extra, 6*s*.

Fowler (R. Nicholas, M.A.). See Visit to Japan, China, &c.

Franc (Maude Jeane) Emily's Choice, an Australian Tale. 1 vol., small post 8vo. With a Frontispiece by G. F. ANGAS, 5*s*.

——— *Hall's Vineyard.* Small post 8vo, cloth, 4*s*.

Franc (Maude Jeane) John's Wife: a Story of Life in South Australia. Small post 8vo, cloth extra, 4s.
—— *Marian; or, the Light of Some One's Home.* Fcap. 8vo, 3rd Edition, with Frontispiece, 5s.
—— *Silken Cords and Iron Fetters.* 4s.
—— *Vermont Vale.* Small post 8vo., with Frontispiece, 5s.
—— *Minnie's Mission.* Small post 8vo, with Frontispiece, 4s.

GAMES of Patience. See CADOGAN.
   Garvagh (Lord) The Pilgrim of Scandinavia. By LORD GARVAGH, B.A., Christ Church, Oxford, and Member of the Alpine Club. 8vo, cloth extra, with Illustrations, 10s. 6d.
Gayworthys (The): a Story of New England Life. Small post 8vo, 3s. 6d.
Gentle Life (Queen Edition). 2 vols. in 1, small 4to, 10s. 6d.

THE GENTLE LIFE SERIES

Printed in Elzevir, on Toned Paper, handsomely bound, forming suitable Volumes for Presents. Price 6s. each ; or in calf extra, price 10s. 6d.

The Gentle Life. Essays in aid of the Formation of Character of Gentlemen and Gentlewomen. 21st Edition.
  " Deserves to be printed in letters of gold, and circulated in every house."—*Chambers' Journal.*

About in the World. Essays by the Author of "The Gentle Life."
  " It is not easy to open it at any page without finding some handy idea."—*Morning Post.*

Like unto Christ. A New Translation of Thomas à Kempis' "De Imitatione Christi." With a Vignette from an Original Drawing by Sir THOMAS LAWRENCE. 2nd Edition.
  " Could not be presented in a more exquisite form, for a more sightly volume was never seen."—*Illustrated London News.*

Familiar Words. An Index Verborum, or Quotation Handbook. Affording an immediate Reference to Phrases and Sentences that have become embedded in the English language. 3rd and enlarged Edition.
  " The most extensive dictionary of quotation we have met with."—*Notes and Queries.*

Essays by Montaigne. Edited, Compared, Revised, and Annotated by the Author of "The Gentle Life." With Vignette Portrait. 2nd Edition.
  " We should be glad if any words of ours could help to bespeak a large circulation for this handsome attractive book."—*Illustrated Times.*

The Countess of Pembroke's Arcadia. Written by Sir PHILIP SIDNEY. Edited, with Notes, by the Author of "The Gentle Life." Dedicated, by permission, to the Earl of Derby. 7s. 6d.
  " All the best things in the Arcadia are retained intact in Mr. Friswell's edition." *Examiner.*

The Gentle Life Series, continued :—
The Gentle Life. 2nd Series, 8th Edition.
"There is not a single thought in the volume that does not contribute in some measure to the formation of a true gentleman."—*Daily News.*

Varia: Readings from Rare Books. Reprinted, by permission, from the *Saturday Review, Spectator,* &c.
"The books discussed in this volume are no less valuable than they are rare, and the compiler is entitled to the gratitude of the public."—*Observer.*

The Silent Hour: Essays, Original and Selected. By the Author of "The Gentle Life." 3rd Edition.
"All who possess 'The Gentle Life' should own this volume."—*Standard.*

Half-Length Portraits. Short Studies of Notable Persons. By GIBSON CRAIG. Small post 8vo, cloth extra, 6s.

Essays on English Writers, for the Self-improvement of Students in English Literature.
"To all (both men and women) who have neglected to read and study their native literature we would certainly suggest the volume before us as a fitting introduction."—*Examiner.*

Other People's Windows. By J. HAIN FRISWELL. 3rd Edition.
"The chapters are so lively in themselves, so mingled with shrewd views of human nature, so full of illustrative anecdotes, that the reader cannot fail to be amused."—*Morning Post.*

A Man's Thoughts. By J. HAIN FRISWELL.

German Primer; being an Introduction to First Steps in German. By M. T. PREU. 2s. 6d.

Getting On in the World; or, Hints on Success in Life. By WILLIAM MATHEWS, LL.D. Small post 8vo, cloth extra, 2s. 6d.; gilt edges, 3s. 6d.

Gleams through the Mists; Literary and Domestic. By C. BICKERSTETH WHEELER, Author of "John Lang Bickersteth," "Memorials of a Beloved Mother," "Taking the Consequences," &c. 1 vol., post 8vo, cloth extra, 3s. 6d.

Gouffé. The Royal Cookery Book. By JULES GOUFFÉ; translated and adapted for English use by ALPHONSE GOUFFÉ, Head Pastrycook to Her Majesty the Queen. Illustrated with large plates printed in colours. 161 Woodcuts, 8vo, cloth extra, gilt edges, 2l. 2s.

——— Domestic Edition, half-bound, 10s. 6d.
"By far the ablest and most complete work on cookery that has ever been submitted to the gastronomical world."—*Pall Mall Gazette.*

——— *The Book of Preserves; or,* Receipts for Preparing and Preserving Meat, Fish salt and smoked, Terrines, Gelatines, Vegetables, Fruit, Confitures, Syrups, Liqueurs de Famille, Petits Fours, Bonbons, &c., &c. 1 vol., royal 8vo, containing upwards of 500 Receipts and 34 Illustrations, 10s. 6d.

——— *Royal Book of Pastry and Confectionery.* By JULES GOUFFÉ, Chef-de Cuisine of the Paris Jockey Club. Royal 8vo, Illustrated with 10 Chromo-lithographs and 137 Woodcuts, from Drawings by E. MONJAT. Cloth extra, gilt edges, 35s.

Gouraud (*Mdlle.*) *Four Gold Pieces.* Numerous Illustrations.
Small post 8vo, cloth, 2s. 6d.   *See also* Rose Library.

Gower (*Lord Ronald*) *Handbook to the Art Galleries, Public and Private*, of Belgium and Holland.   18mo, cloth, 5s.

―――― *The Castle Howard Portraits.*   2 vols., folio, cl. extra, 6l. 6s.

Greek Grammar.   See WALLER.

Greek Testament.   See Novum Testamentum.

Guizot's History of France.   Translated by ROBERT BLACK. Super-royal 8vo, very numerous Full-page and other Illustrations.   In 5 vols., cloth extra, gilt, each 24s.

"It supplies a want which has long been felt, and ought to be in the hands of all students of history "—*Times.*

"Three-fourths of M. Guizot's great work are now completed, and the 'History of France,' which was so nobly planned, has been hitherto no less admirably executed."—*From long Review of Vol. III. in the Times.*

" M. Guizot's main merit is this, that, in a style at once clear and vigorous, he sketches the essential and most characteristic features of the times and personages described, and seizes upon every salient point which can best illustrate and bring out to view what is most significant and instructive in the spirit of the age described."—*Evening Standard,* Sept 23, 1874.

"We must, in conclusion, say a word as to Mr. Black's translation, which is at once idiomatic and spirited."—*Echo.*

―――― *History of England.*   In 3 vols. of about 500 pp. each, containing 60 to 70 full-page and other Illustrations, cloth extra, gilt, 24s. each.

"For luxury of typography, plainness of print, and beauty of illustration, these volumes, of which but one has as yet appeared in English, will hold their own against any production of an age so luxurious as our own in everything, typography not excepted."—*Times.*

Guillemin.   See World of Comets.

Guyot (*A.*) *Physical Geography.*   By ARNOLD GUYOT, Author of "Earth and Man."   In 1 volume, large 4to, 128 pp., numerous coloured Diagrams, Maps, and Woodcuts, price 10s. 6d.

HACKLANDER (*F. W.*) *Bombardier H. and Corporal Dose;* or, Military Life in Prussia. Translated from the German of F. W. HACKLANDER.   Crown 8vo, cloth extra, 5s.

Handbook to the Charities of London.   See Low's.

―――――――― *Principal Schools of England.*   See Practical.

Half-Length Portraits.   Short Studies of Notable Persons. By GIBSON CRAIG.   Small post 8vo, cloth extra, 6s.

Hall (*S. P.*) *Sketches from an Artist's Portfolio.*   See Sketches.

Hall (*W. W.*) *How to Live Long;* or, 1408 *Health Maxims,* Physical, Mental, and Moral.   By W. W. HALL, A.M., M.D. Small post 8vo, cloth, 2s.   Second Edition.

"We can cordially commend it to all who wish to possess the *mens sana in corpore sano.*"—*Standard.*

Hans Brinker; or, *the Silver Skates.*   See DODGE.

Hazard (*S.*) *Santo Domingo, Past and Present ; with a Glance at Hayti.*   With upwards of 150 beautiful Woodcuts and Maps, demy 8vo, cloth extra, 18s.

List of Publications.

Hazard (S.) Cuba with Pen and Pencil. Over 300 Fine Woodcut Engravings. New Edition, 8vo, cloth extra, 15*s.*
Hazlitt (William) The Round Table. BAYARD SERIES, 2*s.* 6*d.*
Healy (M.) Lakeville. 3 vols., 1*l.* 11*s.* 6*d.*
——— *A Summer's Romance.* Crown 8vo, cloth, 10*s.* 6*d.*
——— *The Home Theatre.* Small post 8vo, 3*s.* 6*d.*
——— *Out of the World.* A Novel. 3 vols., 31*s.* 6*d.*
——— *Storm Driven.* 3 vols., crown 8vo, 31*s.* 6*d.*
"We are glad to recommend 'Storm-Driven' as one of the books to be read."—*Vanity Fair.*
Heber's (Bishop) Illustrated Edition of Hymns. With upwards of 100 beautiful Engravings. Small 4to, handsomely bound, 7*s.* 6*d.* Morocco, 18*s.* 6*d.* and 21*s.*
Hector Servadac. See VERNE.
Henderson (A.) Latin Proverbs and Quotations; with Translations and Parallel Passages, and a copious English Index. By ALFRED HENDERSON. Fcap. 4to, 530 pp., 10*s.* 6*d.*
Hitherto. By the Author of "The Gayworthys." New Edition, cloth extra, 3*s.* 6*d.* Also in Rose Library, 2 vols., 2*s.*
Hofmann (Carl) A Practical Treatise on the Manufacture of Paper in all its Branches. Illustrated by 110 Wood Engravings, and 5 large Folding Plates. In 1 vol., 4to, cloth; about 400 pages, 3*l.* 13*s.* 6*d.*
How to Live Long. See HALL.
Hugo (Victor) "Ninety-Three." Translated by FRANK LEE BENEDICT and J. HAIN FRISWELL. New Edition. Illustrated. One vol, crown 8vo, 6*s.*
——— *Toilers of the Sea.* Crown 8vo. Illustrated, 6*s.*; fancy boards, 2*s.*; cloth, 2*s.* 6*d.*; On large paper with all the original Illustrations, 10*s.* 6*d.*
Hymnal Companion to Book of Common Prayer. See Bickersteth.

ILLUSTRATIONS of China and its People. By J. THOMSON, F.R.G.S. Being Photographs from the Author's Negatives, printed in permanent Pigments by the Autotype Process, and Notes from Personal Observation.
*** The complete work embraces 200 Photographs, with Letterpress Descriptions of the Places and People represented. Four Volumes imperial 4to, each £3 3*s.*
Is that All? By a well-known American Author. Small post 8vo, cloth extra, 3*s.* 6*d.*
Jacquemart (A.) History of the Ceramic Art: Descriptive and Analytical Study of the Potteries of all Times and of all Nations. By ALBERT JACQUEMART. 200 Woodcuts by H. Catenacci and J. Jacquemart. 12 Steel-plate Engravings, and 1000 Marks and Mono-

grams. Translated by Mrs. BURY PALLISER. In 1 vol., super-royal 8vo, of about 700 pp., cloth extra, gilt edges, 42s.
"This is one of those few gift-books which, while they can certainly lie on a tab't and look beautiful, can also be read through with real pleasure and profit."—*Times.*

Johnson (R. B.) Very Far West Indeed. A few rough Experiences on the North-West Pacific Coast. Crown 8vo, cloth, 10s. 6d. New Edition—the 4th, fancy boards, 2s.

KENNEDY'S (Capt. W. R.) Sporting Adventures in the Pacific. With Illustrations, demy 8vo, 18s.

King (Clarence) Mountaineering in the Sierra Nevada. Crown 8vo. 3rd and Cheaper Edition, cloth extra, 6s.

Kingston (W. H. G.). See SNOW-SHOES.

Koldewey (Capt.) The Second North German Polar Expedition in the Year 1869-70, of the Ships "Germania" and "Hansa," under command of Captain Koldewey. Edited and condensed by H. W. BATES, Esq. Numerous Woodcuts, Maps, and Chromo-lithographs. Royal 8vo, cloth extra, 1l. 15s.

LEARED (A.) Morocco and the Moors. Being an Account of Travels, with a Description of the Country and its People. By ARTHUR LEARED, M.D., Member of the Royal Irish Academy, and of the Icelandic Literary Society. With Illustrations, 8vo, cloth extra, 18s.

Le Duc (V.) How to build a House. By VIOLLET-LE-DUC, Author of "The Dictionary of Architecture," &c. Numerous Illustrations, Plans, &c. 1 vol., medium 8vo, cloth, gilt edges. 2nd Edition, 12s.

—— *Annals of a Fortress.* Numerous Illustrations and Diagrams. Demy 8vo, cloth extra, 15s.

—— *The Habitations of Man in all Ages.* By E. VIOLLET-LE-DUC. Illustrated by 103 Woodcuts. Translated by BENJAMIN BUCKNALL, Architect. 8vo, cloth extra, 16s.

—— *Lectures on Architecture.* By VIOLLET-LE-DUC. Translated from the French by BENJAMIN BUCKNALL, Architect. In 2 vols., royal 8vo, 3l. 3s. Also in Parts 10s. 6d. each.

—— *On Restoration.* By VIOLLET-LE-DUC, with a Notice of his Works in connexion with the Historical Monuments of France. By CHARLES WETHERED. Crown 8vo, with a Portrait on Steel of VIOLLET-LE-DUC, cloth extra, 2s. 6d.

Lindsay (W. S.) History of Merchant Shipping and Ancient Commerce. Over 150 Illustrations, Maps and Charts. In 4 vols., demy 8vo, cloth extra. Vols. 1 and 2, 21s. each; vols. 3 and 4, 24s. each; 4 vols., 4l. 10s.
"Another standard work."—*Times.*

Lion Jack: a Story of Perilous Adventures amongst Wild Men and Beasts. Showing how Menageries are made. By P. T. BARNUM. With Illustrations. Crown 8vo, cloth extra, price 6s.

Little King: or, the Taming of a Young Russian Count. By S. BLANDY. Translated from the French. 64 Illustrations. Crown 8vo, cloth extra, gilt, 7s. 6d.

"There is a great deal worth reading in this book."—*Pall Mall Gazette.*
"A very pleasant and interesting volume, which we would recommend to our readers."—*Spectator.*

Locker (A.) The Village Surgeon. A Fragment of Autobiography. By ARTHUR LOCKER, Author of "Sweet Seventeen." Crown 8vo, cloth. New Edition, 3s. 6d.

Long (Col. C. Chaillé) Central Africa. Naked Truths of Naked People : an Account of Expeditions to Lake Victoria Nyanza and the Mabraka Niam-Niam, West of the White Nile. Demy 8vo, numerous Illustrations, 18s.

Low's German Series.

The attention of the Heads of Colleges and Schools is directed to this New Series of German School Books, which has been projected with a view to supply a long-felt want, viz., thoroughly reliable Text-Books, edited by German scholars of the highest reputation, at a price which will bring them within the reach of all. The Series comprises :—

1. **The Illustrated German Primer.** Being the easiest introduction to the study of German for all beginners. 1s.
2. **The Children's own German Book.** A Selection of Amusing and Instructive Stories in Prose. Edited by Dr. A. L. MEISSNER, Professor of Modern Languages in the Queen's University in Ireland. Small post 8vo, cloth, 1s. 6d.
3. **The First German Reader, for Children from Ten to Fourteen.** Edited by Dr. A. L. MEISSNER. Small post 8vo, cloth, 1s. 6d.
4. **The Second German Reader.** Edited by Dr. A. L. MEISSNER, Small post 8vo, cloth, 1s. 6d.

Buchheim's Deutsche Prosa. Two Volumes, sold separately :—

5. **Schiller's Prosa.** Containing Selections from the Prose Works of Schiller, with Notes for English Students. By Dr. BUCHHEIM, Professor of the German Language and Literature, King's College, London. Small post 8vo, 2s. 6d.
6. **Goethe's Prosa.** Containing Selections from the Prose Works of Goethe, with Notes for English Students. By Dr. BUCHHEIM. Small post 8vo, 3s. 6d.

Low's Standard Library of Travel and Adventure. Crown 8vo, bound uniformly in cloth extra, price 7s. 6d.

1. **The Great Lone Land.** By W. F. BUTLER, C.B.
2. **The Wild North Land.** By W. F. BUTLER, C.B.
3. **How I found Livingstone.** By H. M. STANLEY.
4. **The Threshold of the Unknown Region.** By C. R. MARKHAM. (4th Edition, with Additional Chapters, 10s. 6d.)
5. **A Whaling Cruise to Baffin's Bay and the Gulf of Boothia.** By A. H. MARKHAM.
6. **Campaigning on the Oxus.** By J. A. MACGAHAN.
7. **Akim-foo: the History of a Failure.** By MAJOR W. F. BUTLER, C.B.

Low's Standard Novels. Crown 8vo, 6s. each, cloth extra.

Three Feathers. By WILLIAM BLACK.
A Daughter of Heth. 13th Edition. By W. BLACK. With Frontispiece by F. WALKER, A.R.A.
Kilmeny. A Novel. By W. BLACK.
In Silk Attire. By W. BLACK.
Alice Lorraine. By R. D. BLACKMORE.
Lorna Doone. By R. D. BLACKMORE. 8th Edition.
Cradock Nowell. By R. D. BLACKMORE.
Clara Vaughan. By R. D. BLACKMORE.
Cripps the Carrier. By R. D. BLACKMORE.
Innocent. By Mrs. OLIPHANT. Eight Illustrations.
Work. A Story of Experience. By LOUISA M. ALCOTT. Illustrations. *See also* " Rose Library."
Mistress Judith. A Cambridgeshire Story. By C. C. FRAZER-TYTLER.
Never Again. By Dr. MAYO, Author of "Kaloolah."
Ninety-Three. By VICTOR HUGO. Numerous Illustrations.
My Wife and I. By Mrs. BEECHER STOWE.

Low's Handbook to the Charities of London for 1877. Edited and revised to February, 1877, by C. MACKESON, F.S.S., Editor of " A Guide to the Churches of London and its Suburbs," &c. 1s.

MACGAHAN (J. A.) Campaigning on the Oxus, and the Fall of Khiva. With Map and numerous Illustrations, 4th Edition, small post 8vo, cloth extra, 7s. 6d.

—— *Under the Northern Lights; or, the Cruise of the* " Pandora" to Peel's Straits, in Search of Sir John Franklin's Papers. With Illustrations by Mr. DE WYLDE, who accompanied the Expedition. Demy 8vo, cloth extra, 18s.

Macgregor (John) "Rob Roy" on the Baltic. 3rd Edition, small post 8vo, 2s. 6d.

—— *A Thousand Miles in the "Rob Roy" Canoe.* 11th Edition, small post 8vo, 2s. 6d.

—— *Description of the " Rob Roy" Canoe*, with Plans, &c., 1s.

—— *The Voyage Alone in the Yawl " Rob Roy."* 2nd Edition, small post 8vo, 5s.

Markham (A. H.) The Cruise of the " Rosario." By A. H. MARKHAM, Commander, R.N.) 8vo, cloth extra, with Map and Illustrations.

—— *A Whaling Cruise to Baffin's Bay and the Gulf of* Boothia. With an Account of the Rescue, by his Ship, of the Survivors of the Crew of the "Polaris;" and a Description of Modern Whale Fishing. 3rd and Cheaper Edition, crown 8vo, 2 Maps and several Illustrations, cloth extra, 7s. 6d.

Markham (C. R.) The Threshold of the Unknown Region.
Crown 8vo, with Four Maps, 4th Edition, with Additional Chapters, giving the History of our present Expedition as far as known, and an Account of the Cruise of the "Pandora." Cloth extra, 10*s*. 6*d*.

Maury (Commander) Physical Geography of the Sea, and its Meteorology. Being a Reconstruction and Enlargement of his former Work, with Charts and Diagrams. New Edition, crown 8vo, 6*s*.

Price 1s. 6d., a New Monthly Periodical,

Men of Mark: a Gallery of Contemporary Portraits of the most Eminent Men of the Day taken from Life.

Michael Strogoff. 10s. 6d. *See* VERNE.

Mistress Judith. A Cambridgeshire Story. By C. C. FRASER-TYTLER, Author of "Jasmine Leigh." A New and Cheaper Edition in 1 vol., small post 8vo, cloth extra, 6*s*.

Mohr (E.) To the Victoria Falls of the Zambesi. By EDWARD MOHR. Translated by N. D'ANVERS. Numerous Full-page and other Woodcut Illustrations, four beautiful Chromo-lithographs and a Map. 1 vol., demy 8vo, cloth extra, 24*s*.

Mongolia, Travels in. See PREJAVALSKY.

Montaigne's Essays. See GENTLE LIFE SERIES.

Moody (Emma) Echoes of the Heart. A Collection of upwards of 200 Sacred Poems. 16mo, cloth, gilt edges, price 3*s*. 6*d*.

Morocco, Adventures in. See ROHLF.

—— *and the Moors. See* LEARED.

NAPOLEON I., Recollections of. By MRS. ABELL. 3rd Edition. Revised, with additional matter by her daughter, Mrs. CHARLES JOHNSTONE. Demy 8vo, with Steel Portrait and Woodcuts, cloth extra, gilt edges, 10*s*. 6*d*.

Napoleon III. in Exile. The Posthumous Works and Unpublished Autographs. Collected and arranged by COUNT DE LA CHAPELLE. 8vo, cloth extra, 14*s*.

New Testament. The Authorized English Version; with the various readings from the most celebrated Manuscripts, including the Sinaitic, the Vatican, and the Alexandrian MSS., in English. With Notes by the Editor, Dr. TISCHENDORF. Revised and carefully collected for the Thousandth Volume of Baron Tauchnitz's Collection. Cloth flexible, gilt edges, 2*s*. 6*d*.; cheaper style, 2*s*.; or sewed, 1*s*. 6*d*.

Notes and Sketches of an Architect taken during a Journey in the North-West of Europe. Translated from the French of FELIX NARJOUX. 214 Full-page and other Illustrations. Demy 8vo, cloth extra, 16*s*.

"His book is vivacious and sometimes brilliant. It is admirably printed and illustrated."—*British Quarterly Review.*

Nothing to Wear, and Two Millions. By WILLIAM ALLEN BUTLER. 1*s*.

Novum Testamentum Græce. Edidit OSCAR DE GEBHARDT. 18mo, cloth, 3*s*. 6*d*.

OLD-Fashioned Girl. See ALCOTT.

Old Masters. Da Vinci, Bartolomeo, Michael Angelo, Romagna, Carlo Dolci, &c., &c. Reproduced in Photography from the Celebrated Engravings by Longhi, Anderloni, Garavaglia, Toschi, and Raimondi, in the Collection of Prints and Drawings in the British Museum, with Biographical Notices, by STEPHEN THOMPSON. Imperial folio, cloth extra, 3*l.* 13*s.* 6*d.*

Oleographs. Catalogue and price lists post free on application.

Oliphant (Mrs.) Innocent. A Tale of Modern Life. By Mrs. OLIPHANT, Author of "The Chronicles of Carlingford," &c., &c. With Eight full-page Illustrations, small post 8vo, cloth extra, 6*s.*

Our Little Ones in Heaven. Edited by the Rev. H. ROBBINS. With Frontispiece after Sir JOSHUA REYNOLDS. Fcap. cloth extra, New Edition, the 3rd, with Illustrations, 5*s.*

PAINTERS of All Schools. By LOUIS VIARDOT, and other Writers. 500 pp., super-royal 8vo, 20 Full-page and 70 smaller Engravings, cloth extra, 25*s.*
"A handsome volume, full of information and sound criticism."—*Times.*
"Almost an encyclopædia of painting. . . . . It may be recommended as a handy and elegant guide to beginners in the study of the history of art."—*Saturday Review.*

Palliser (Mrs.) A History of Lace, from the Earliest Period. A New and Revised Edition, with additional cuts and text, upwards of 100 Illustrations and coloured Designs. 1 vol. 8vo, 1*l.* 1*s.* 3rd Edition.
"One of the most readable books of the season; permanently valuable, always interesting, often amusing, and not inferior in all the essentials of a gift book."—*Times.*

———— *Historic Devices, Badges, and War Cries.* 8vo, 1*l.* 1*s.*

———— *The China Collector's Pocket Companion.* With upwards of 1000 Illustrations of Marks and Monograms. 2nd Edition, with Additions. Small post 8vo, limp cloth, 5*s.*
"We scarcely need add that a more trustworthy and convenient handbook does not exist, and that others besides ourselves will feel grateful to Mrs. Palliser for the care and skill she has bestowed upon it."—*Academy.*

Parisian Family. From the French of Madame GUIZOT DE WITT. Fcap., 5*s.*

Phelps (Miss) Gates Ajar. 32mo, 6*d.*

———— *Men, Women, and Ghosts.* 12mo, sewed, 1*s.* 6*d.*; cl., 2*s.*

———— *Hedged In.* 12mo, sewed, 1*s.* 6*d.*; cloth, 2*s.*

———— *Silent Partner.* 5*s.*

———— *Trotty's Wedding Tour.* Small post 8vo, 3*s.* 6*d.*

———— *What to Wear.* Fcap. 8vo, fancy boards, 1*s.*

Phillips (L.) Dictionary of Biographical Reference. 8vo, 1*l.* 11*s.* 6*d.*

Phipson (Dr. T. L.) Familiar Letters on some Mysteries of Nature and Discoveries in Science. Crown 8vo, cloth extra, 7*s.* 6*d.*

Photography (*History and Handbook of*). See TISSANDIER.

Picture Gallery of British Art (*The*). 38 Beautiful and Permanent Photographs after the most celebrated English Painters. With Descriptive Letterpress. Vols. 1 to 5, cloth extra, 18s. each. Each separate and complete in itself.
*** *For particulars of the Monthly Parts, see page* 46.

Pike (*N.*) *Sub-Tropical Rambles in the Land of the Aphanapteryx.* In 1 vol., demy 8vo, 18s. Profusely Illustrated from the Author's own Sketches. Also with Maps and Meteorological Charts.

Plutarch's Lives. An Entirely New and Library Edition. Edited by A. H. CLOUGH, Esq. 5 vols., 8vo, 2l. 10s.; half-morocco, gilt top, 3l. Also in 1 vol., royal 8vo, 800 pp., cloth extra, 18s. half-bound, 21s.

—— *Morals.* Uniform with Clough's Edition of "Lives of Plutarch." Edited by Professor GOODWIN. 5 vols., 8vo, 3l. 3s.

Poems of the Inner Life. A New Edition, Revised, with many additional Poems, inserted by permission of the Authors. Small post 8vo, cloth, 5s.

Polar Expeditions. See KOLDEWEY and MARKHAM.

Practical (*A*) *Handbook to the Principal Schools of England.* By C. E. PASCOE. Showing the cost of living at the Great Schools, Scholarships, &c., &c. Crown 8vo, cloth extra, 3s. 6d.
"This is an exceedingly useful work, and one that was much wanted."—*Examiner.*

Preces Veterum. Collegit et edidit Joannes F. France. Crown 8vo, cloth, red edges, 5s.

Prejevalsky (*N. M.*) *Travels in Mongolia.* By N. M. PREJEVALSKY, Lieutenant-Colonel, Russian Staff. Translated by E. DELMAR MORGAN, F.R.G.S., and Annotated by Colonel YULE, C.B. 2 vols., demy 8vo, cloth extra, numerous Illustrations and Maps, 2l. 2s.

Preu (*M. T.*) *German Primer.* Square cloth, 2s. 6d.

Price (*Sir Rose, Bart.*). See The Two Americas.

Publishers' Circular (*The*), *and General Record of British and Foreign Literature.* Giving a transcript of the title-page of every work published in Great Britain, and every work of interest published abroad, with lists of all the publishing-houses.
Published on the 1st and 15th of every Month, and forwarded post free to all parts of the world on payment of 8s. per annum.

Purdy (*W.*) *The City Life, a Review of Finance and Commerce.* Crown 8vo, cloth, 7s. 6d.

RALSTON (*W. R. S.*) *Early Russian History.* Four Lectures delivered at Oxford by W. R. S. RALSTON, M.A. Crown 8vo, cloth extra, 5s.

Read (*S.*) *Leaves from a Sketch Book.* Pencillings of Travel at Home and Abroad. By SAMUEL READ. Royal 4to, containing about 130 Engravings on Wood, cloth extra, 25s.
"We do not think that the season is likely to yield a more artistic, suggestive, and beautiful gift-book than this."—*Nonconformist.*

Retzsch (M.) Outlines to Burger's Ballads. 15 Etchings by MORITZ RETZSCH. With Text, Explanations, and Notes. Oblong 4to, cloth extra, 10s. 6d.

—— *Outlines to Goethe's Faust.* Etchings by MORITZ RETZSCH. 26 Etchings. Oblong 4to, cloth extra, 10s. 6d.

—— *Outlines to Schiller's "Fight with the Dragon,"* and "Fridolin." 26 Etchings by MORITZ RETZSCH. Oblong 4to, cloth extra, 10s. 6d.

—— *Outlines to Schiller's "Lay of the Bell."* Comprising 42 Etchings engraved by MORITZ RETZSCH. With Lord Lytton's Translation. New Edition. Oblong 4to, cloth extra, 10s. 6d.

Rose in Bloom. See ALCOTT.

Rose Library (The). Popular Literature of all countries. Each volume, 1s.; cloth, 2s. 6d. Many of the Volumes are Illustrated. The following is a list:—

1. **Sea-Gull Rock.** By JULES SANDEAU. Illustrated.
2. **Little Women.** By LOUISA M. ALCOTT.
3. **Little Women Wedded.** Forming a Sequel to "Little Women."
4. **The House on Wheels.** By MADAME DE STOLZ. Illustrated.
5. **Little Men.** By LOUISA M. ALCOTT.
6. **The Old-Fashioned Girl.** By LOUISA M. ALCOTT. Double vol., 2s.; cloth, 3s. 6d.
7. **The Mistress of the Manse.** By J. G. HOLLAND.
8. **Timothy Titcomb's Letters to Young People, Single and Married.**
9. **Undine, and the Two Captains.** By Baron DE LA MOTTE FOUQUÉ. A New Translation by F. E. BUNNETT. Illustrated.
10. **Draxy Miller's Dowry, and the Elder's Wife.** By SAXE HOLM.
11. **The Four Gold Pieces.** By Madame GOURAUD. Numerous Illustrations.
12. **Work.** A Story of Experience. First Portion. By LOUISA M. ALCOTT.
13. **Beginning Again.** Being a Continuation of "Work." By LOUISA M. ALCOTT.
14. **Picciola; or, the Prison Flower.** By X. B. SAINTINE. Numerous Graphic Illustrations.
15. **Robert's Holidays.** Illustrated.
16. **The Two Children of St. Domingo.** Numerous Illustrations.
17. **Aunt Jo's Scrap Bag.**
18. **Stowe (Mrs. H. B.) The Pearl of Orr's Island.**
19. —— **The Minister's Wooing.**
20. —— **Betty's Bright Idea.**
21. —— **The Ghost in the Mill.**
22. —— **Captain Kidd's Money.**
23. —— **We and our Neighbours.** Double vol., 2s. Post 8vo, cloth, 3s. 6d.
24. —— **My Wife and I.** Double vol., 2s. Post 8vo, cloth, 3s. 6d.
25. **Hans Brinker; or, the Silver Skates.**

List of Publications. 19

Rose Library (The), continued:—
26. **Lowell's My Study Window.**
27. **Holmes (O. W.) The Guardian Angel.**
28. **Warner (C. D.) My Summer in a Garden.**
29. **Hitherto.** By the Author of "The Gayworthys." 2 vols., 1s. each.
30. ***Helen's Babies.** By their Latest Victim.
31. ***The Barton Experiment.** By the Author of "Helen's Babies."
  * *Notice.*—The only editions of this author's works published in this country with his sanction, and in the profit of which he participates.

Russell (W. H., LL.D.) The Tour of the Prince of Wales in
India, and his Visits to the Courts of Greece, Egypt, Spain, and Portugal. By W. H. RUSSELL, LL.D., who accompanied the Prince throughout his journey; and fully Illustrated by SYDNEY P. HALL, M.A., the Prince's Private Artist, with His Royal Highness's special permission to use the Sketches made during the Tour. Super-royal 8vo, cloth extra, gilt edges, 52s. 6d.; Large Paper Edition, 84s.

SCHWEINFURTH (Dr. G.) The Heart of Africa; or, Three
Years' Travels and Adventures in the Unexplored Regions of the Centre of Africa. By Dr. GEORG SCHWEINFURTH. Translated by ELLEN E. FREWER. 2 vols., 8vo, with 130 Woodcuts from Drawings made by the Author, and 2 Maps, 42s. 2nd Edition.

—— *Artes Africanæ.* Illustrations and Descriptions of Productions of the Natural Arts of Central African Tribes. With 26 Lithographed Plates, imperial 4to, boards, 28s.

Sea-Gull Rock. By JULES SANDEAU, of the French Academy. Translated by ROBERT BLACK, M.A. With 79 very beautiful Woodcuts. Royal 16mo, cloth extra, gilt edges, 7s. 6d. Cheaper Edition, cloth gilt, 2s. 6d. *See also* Rose Library.
"It deserves to please the new nation of boys to whom it is presented."—*Times.*

Seonee: Sporting in the Satpura Range of Central India, and in the Valley of the Nerbudda. By R. A. STERNDALE, F.R.G.S. 8vo, with numerous Illustrations. 21s.

Shakespeare from an American Point of View; including an Inquiry as to his Religious Faith and his Knowledge of Law; with the Baconian Theory considered. By GEORGE WILKES. Demy 8vo, cloth extra, 16s.

Shooting: its Appliances, Practice, and Purpose. By JAMES DALZIEL DOUGALL, F.S.A., F.Z.A. Author of "Scottish Field Sports," &c. Crown 8vo, cloth extra, 10s. 6d.
"The book is admirable in every way. . . . We wish it every success."—*Globe.*
"A very complete treatise. . . . Likely to take high rank as an authority on shooting."—*Daily News.*

Silent Hour (The). See GENTLE LIFE SERIES.

Silver Pitchers. See ALCOTT.

Sketches from an Artist's Portfolio. By SYDNEY P. HALL. About 60 Facsimiles of his Sketches during Travels in various parts of Europe. Folio, cloth extra, 3l. 3s.
"A portfolio which any one might be glad to call their own."—*Times.*

Sketches of Life and Scenery in Australia. By a Twenty-five Years' Resident. 1 vol., demy 8vo, cloth extra, 14s.

Sleepy Sketches; or, How we Live, and How we Do Not Live. From Bombay. 1 vol., small post 8vo, cloth, 6s.
"Well-written and amusing sketches of Indian society."—*Morning Post.*

Smith (G.) Assyrian Explorations and Discoveries. By the late GEORGE SMITH. Illustrated by Photographs and Woodcuts. Demy 8vo, 18s. 6th Edition.

—— *The Chaldean Account of Genesis.* Containing the Description of the Creation, the Fall of Man, the Deluge, the Tower of Babel, the Times of the Patriarchs, and Nimrod; Babylonian Fables, and Legends of the Gods; from the Cuneiform Inscriptions. By the late G. SMITH, of the Department of Oriental Antiquities, British Museum. Author of "History of Assurbanipal," "Assyrian Discoveries," &c., &c. With many Illustrations. Demy 8vo, cloth extra, 16s. 5th Edition.

Snow-Shoes and Canoes; or, the Adventures of a Fur-Hunter in the Hudson's Bay Territory. By W. H. G. KINGSTON. 2nd Edition. With numerous Illustrations. Square crown 8vo, cloth extra, gilt, 7s. 6d.

Spain. Illustrated by GUSTAVE DORÉ. Text by the BARON CH. D'AVILLIER. Containing over 240 Wood Engravings by Doré, half of them being Full-page size. Imperial 4to, elaborately bound in cloth, extra gilt edges, 3l. 3s.

Stanley (H. M.) How I Found Livingstone. Crown 8vo, cloth extra, 7s. 6d. Demy 8vo, 10s. 6d.

—— *"My Kalulu," Prince, King, and Slave.* A Story from Central Africa. Crown 8vo, about 430 pp., with numerous graphic Illustrations, after Original Designs by the Author. Cloth, 7s. 6d.

—— *Coomassie and Magdala.* A Story of Two British Campaigns in Africa. Demy 8vo, with Maps and Illustrations, 16s. 2nd Edition.

Sterndale (R. A.) See Seonee.

Storey's (Justice) Works. See Low's American Catalogue.

Story without an End. From the German of Carové, by the late Mrs. SARAH T. AUSTIN. Crown 4to, with 15 Exquisite Drawings by E. V. B., printed in Colours in Facsimile of the original Water Colours; and numerous other Illustrations. New Edition, 7s. 6d.

—— square 4to, with Illustrations by HARVEY. 2s. 6d.

Stowe (Mrs. Beecher) Dred. Tauchnitz Edition. 12mo, 3s. 6d., also in boards, 1s.

—— *Footsteps of the Master.* With Illustrations and red borders. Small post 8vo, cloth extra, 6s.

—— *Betty's Bright Idea.*

Stowe (Mrs. Beecher) My Wife and I; or, Harry Henderson's History. Small post 8vo, cloth extra, 6s.*
—— *Minister's Wooing*, 5s.; Copyright Series, 1s. 6d.; cl., 2s.*
—— *Old Town Folk.* 6s.; Cheap Edition, 2s. 6d.
—— *Old Town Fireside Stories.* Cloth extra, 3s. 6d.
—— *We and Our Neighbours.* 1 vol., small post 8vo, 6s. Sequel to "My Wife and I." *
—— *Pink and White Tyranny*, Small post 8vo, 3s. 6d.; Cheap Edition, 1s. 6d. and 2s.
—— *Queer Little People.* 1s.; cloth 2s.
—— *Chimney Corner.* 1s.; cloth, 1s. 6d.
—— *The Pearl of Orr's Island.* Crown 8vo, 5s.*
—— *Little Pussey Willow.* Fcap., 2s.
—— *Woman in Sacred History.* Illustrated with 15 Chromolithographs and about 200 pages of Letterpress. Demy 4to, cloth extra, gilt edges, 25s.
* *See also* Rose Library.

Street Life in London. By J. THOMSON, F.R.G.S., and ADOLPHE SMITH. Each Monthly Part, 4to size, in Wrapper, price 1s. 6d., contains Three permanent Photographs, taken from Life expressly for this Periodical.
*** The object of the Work is to present to the reader some account of the present condition of London Street Folk, and to supply a series of faithful pictures of the people themselves.

TAUCHNITZ'S English Editions of German Authors. Each volume, cloth flexible, 2s.; or sewed, 1s. 6d. Catalogues post free on application.
Tauchnitz (B.) German and English Dictionary. Paper, 1s.; cloth, 1s. 6d.; roan, 2s.
—— *French and English.* Paper, 1s. 6d.; cloth, 2s.; roan, 2s. 6d.
—— *Italian and English.* Paper, 1s. 6d.; cloth, 2s.; roan, 2s. 6d.
—— *Spanish and English.* Paper, 1s. 6d.; cloth, 2s.; roan, 2s. 6d.
—— *New Testament.* Cloth, 2s.; gilt, 2s. 6d.

Textbook (A) of Harmony. For the Use of Schools and Students. By the late CHARLES EDWARD HORSLEY. Revised for the Press by WESTLEY RICHARDS and W. H. CALCOTT. Small post 8vo, cloth extra, 3s. 6d.

Thebes, and its Five Greater Temples. See ABNEY.

Thomson (J.) The Straits of Malacca, Indo-China, and China; or, Ten Years' Travels, Adventures, and Residence Abroad. By J. THOMSON, F.R.G.S., Author of "Illustrations of China and its People." Upwards of 60 Woodcuts, from the Author's own Photographs and Sketches. Demy 8vo, cloth extra, 21s.

Thorne (E.) The Queen of the Colonies; or, Queensland as I saw it. 1 vol., with Map, 6s.

Tissandier (Gaston) A History and Handbook of Photography. Translated from the French of GASTON TISSANDIER; edited by J. THOMPSON, F.R.G.S. Imperial 16mo, over 300 pages, and 75 Wood Engravings and a Frontispiece, cloth extra, 6s.

"This work should find a place on the shelves of every photographer's library."—*The British Journal of Photography.*

"This capital handbook will tend to raise photography once more to its true position as a science, and to a high place among the fine arts."—*The Spectator.*

Tour of the Prince of Wales in India. *See* RUSSELL.

Trollope (A.) Harry Heathcote of Gangoil. A Story of Bush Life in Australia. With graphic Illustrations. In 1 vol., small post, cloth extra, 5s. 2nd Edition.

Turkistan. Notes of a Journey in the Russian Provinces of Central Asia and the Khanates of Bokhara and Kokand. By EUGENE SCHUYLER, Secretary to the American Legation, St. Petersburg. Numerous Illustrations. 2 vols, demy 8vo, cl. extra, 2l. 2s. 5th Edition.

Two Americas; being an Account of Sport and Travel. With Notes of Men and Manners in North and South America. By Sir ROSE PRICE, Bart. 1 vol., demy 8vo, with Illustrations, cloth extra, 18s. 2nd Edition.

"We have seldom come across a book which has given us so much pleasure."—*Land and Water.*

VERNE'S (Jules) Works. Translated from the French, with from 50 to 100 Illustrations. Each cloth extra, gilt edges.

Large post 8vo, price 10s. 6d. each.
1. Fur Country.
2. Twenty Thousand Leagues under the Sea.
3. From the Earth to the Moon, and a Trip round It.
4. Michael Strogoff, the Courier of the Czar.
5. Hector Servadac. [*In the press.*

Imperial 16mo, price 7s. 6d. each.
1. Five Weeks in a Balloon.
2. Adventures of Three Englishmen and Three Russians in South Africa.
3. Around the World in Eighty Days.
4. A Floating City, and the Blockade Runners.
5. Dr. Ox's Experiment, Master Zacharius, A Drama in the Air, A Winter amid the Ice, &c.
6. The Survivors of the "Chancellor."
7. Dropped from the Clouds. }
8. Abandoned.   } The Mysterious Island. 3 vols
9. Secret of the Island.   }   . 22s. 6d.

List of Publications. 23

The following Cheaper Editions are issued with a few of the Illustrations, in handsome paper wrapper, price 1s. *; cloth, gilt,* 2s. *each.*

1. Adventures of Three Englishmen and Three Russians in South Africa.
2. Five Weeks in a Balloon.
3. A Floating City.
4. The Blockade Runners.
5. From the Earth to the Moon.
6. Around the Moon.
7. Twenty Thousand Leagues under the Sea. Vol. I.
8. ——— Vol. II. The two parts in one, cloth, gilt, 3s. 6d.
9. Around the World in Eighty Days.
10. Dr. Ox's Experiment, and Master Zacharius.
11. Martin Paz, the Indian Patriot.
12. A Winter amid the Ice.

The public must kindly be careful to order LOW'S AUTHOR'S EDITIONS.

Visit to Japan, China, and India. By R. N. FOWLER, M.A., F.R.G.S. 1 vol., crown 8vo, 10s. 6d.

WALLER *(Rev. C. H.) The Names on the Gates of Pearl,* and other Studies. By the Rev. C. H. WALLER, M.A. Crown 8vo, cloth extra, 6s.

——— *A Grammar and Analytical Vocabulary of the Words in* the Greek Testament. Compiled from Brüder's Concordance. For the use of Divinity Students and Greek Testament Classes. By the Rev. C. H. WALLER, M.A., late Scholar of University College, Oxford. Tutor of the London College of Divinity, St. John's Hall, Highbury. Part I., The Grammar. Small post 8vo, cloth, 2s. 6d.

Warburton's (Col. Egerton) Journey across Australia. An Account of the Exploring Expedition sent out under the command of Colonel E. Warburton. With Illustrations and a Map. Edited, with an Introductory Chapter, by H. W. BATES, Esq., F.R.G.S. Demy 8vo, cloth, 16s.

Warner (C. D.) My Summer in a Garden. Boards, 1s. 6d. ; cloth, 2s. (Low's Copyright Series.)

——— *Back-log Studies.* Boards, 1s. 6d.; cloth, 2s. (Low's Copyright Series).

——— *Mummies and Moslems.* 8vo, cloth, 12s.

Weppner (M.) The Northern Star and Southern Cross. Being the Personal Experiences, Impressions, and Observations of M. Weppner, in a Voyage round the World. 2 vols., cr. 8vo, cloth, 24s.

Werner (Carl) Nile Sketches, Painted from Nature during his Travels through Egypt. Imperial Folio, in Cardboard Wrapper. Complete in 5 Parts. The 4 first at 3l. 10s. each ; Part V., 2l. 5s.

Westropp (*H. M.*) *A Manual of Precious Stones and Antique Gems.* By HODDER M. WESTROPP, Author of "The Traveller's Art Companion," "Pre-Historic Phases," &c. Numerous Illustrations. Small post 8vo, cloth extra, 6s.

White (*J.*) *Te Rou ; or, the Maori at Home.* Exhibiting the Social Life, Manners, Habits, and Customs of the Maori Race in New Zealand prior to the Introduction of Civilization amongst them. Crown 8vo, cloth extra, 10s. 6d.

Whitney (*Mrs. A. D. T.*) *The Gayworthys.* Small post 8vo, 3s. 6d.

——— *Faith Gartney.* Small post 8vo, 3s. 6d. And in Low's Cheap Series, 1s. 6d. and 2s.

Whitney (*Mrs. A. T. D.*) *Real Folks.* 12mo, crown, 3s. 6d.

——— *Hitherto.* Small post 8vo, 3s. 6d. and 2s. 6d.

——— *Sights and Insights.* 3 vols., crown 8vo, 31s. 6d.

——— *Summer in Leslie Goldthwaite's Life.* Small post 8vo, 3s. 6d.

——— *The Other Girls.* Small post 8vo, cloth extra, 3s. 6d.

——— *We Girls.* Small post 8vo, 3s. 6d.; Cheap Edition, 1s. 6d. and 2s.

Woolsey (*C. D., LL.D.*) *Introduction to the Study of International Law* ; designed as an Aid in Teaching and in Historical Studies. Reprinted from the last American Edition, and at a much lower price. Crown 8vo, cloth extra, 8s. 6d.

Worcester's (*Dr.*) *New and Greatly Enlarged Dictionary of the English Language.* Adapted for Library or College Reference, comprising 40,000 Words more than Johnson's Dictionary. 4to, cloth, 1834 pp., price 31s. 6d. well bound ; ditto, half-morocco, 2l. 2s.
"The volume before us shows a vast amount of diligence ; but with Webster it is diligence in combination with fancifulness,—with Worcester in combination with good sense and judgment. Worcester is the soberer and safer book, and may be pronounced the best existing English Lexicon."—*Athenæum*.

World of Comets. By A. GUILLEMIN, Author of "The Heavens." Translated and edited by JAMES GLAISHER, F.R.S. 1 vol., super-royal 8vo, with numerous Woodcut Illustrations, and 3 Chromo-lithographs, cloth extra, 31s. 6d.

XENOPHON'S Anabasis ; or, Expedition of Cyrus. A Literal Translation, chiefly from the Text of Dindorff, by GEORGE B. WHEELER. Books I to III. Crown 8vo, boards, 2s.

——— *Books I. to VII.* Boards, 3s. 6d.

London:
SAMPSON LOW, MARSTON, SEARLE, & RIVINGTON,
CROWN BUILDINGS, 188, FLEET STREET.

www.ingramcontent.com/pod-product-compliance
Lightning Source LLC
Chambersburg PA
CBHW032022220426

43664CB00006B/338